THE

INTERNATIONAL

CHOCOLATE

COOKBOOK

To Ken,
Here are
Sweets for
the Sweet,
you! always
Liz

NANCY BAGGETT

T H E

INTERNATIONAL

CHOCOLATE

COOKBOOK

Photographs by
MARTIN JACOBS

STEWART, TABORI & CHANG
NEW YORK

Frontispiece: White Chocolate Butter Layer Cake with
White Chocolate-Sour Cream Frosting

Text copyright © 1991 Nancy Baggett
Photographs copyright © 1991 Martin Jacobs

Published by Stewart, Tabori & Chang, Inc.
575 Broadway, New York, New York 10012

Distributed in Canada by General Publishing Co.
Ltd., 30 Lesmill Road, Don Mills, Ontario,
Canada M3B 2T6

Distributed in the English language elsewhere in
the world (except Central and South America)
by Melia Publishing Services, P.O. Box 1639,
Maidenhead, Berkshire SL6 6YZ England.
Central and South American accounts should
contact Sales Manager, Stewart, Tabori & Chang.

Library of Congress Cataloging-in-Publication
Data

Baggett, Nancy, 1943—
The international chocolate cookbook/
by Nancy Baggett: photographs
by Martin Jacobs
ISBN 1-55670-178-0 (hardcover)
ISBN 1-55670-363-5 (paperback)
1. Cookery (Chocolate) I. Title.
TX767-C5B24 1991
641.6'374—DC20   91-3124
                                  CIP

Printed in Japan
10 9 8 7 6 5 4 3 2 1

ACKNOWLEDGMENTS

The assistance and caring of many people were key ingredients in creating *The International Chocolate Cookbook*. I am especially indebted to the following:

To my editor, Leslie Stoker, for her enthusiasm, guidance, and vision, and for assembling such an extraordinary group of people to work with me on this book.

To photographer Marty Jacobs, whose images never cease to enchant me, and whose creativity, caring, and desire for excellence show in every photograph.

To designer Rita Marshall, for giving *The International Chocolate Cookbook* such an elegant and distinctive look.

To food stylist Deborah Mintcheff, for her good cheer, great professionalism, and unparalleled ability to make food look both beautiful *and* appetizing.

To prop stylist Linda Johnson, for her unerring sense of style, and her dedication to finding just the right props for each picture.

To copyeditor Melanie Falick and to the Stewart, Tabori & Chang staff, for their support, hard work, and friendliness.

To those who helped with the recipes: Selvin Martinez, who cheerfully assisted in my kitchen throughout the project; Denise Donahue, who home-tested many of the recipes, and Mary Jane McCraven and Trish Trahan, who also served as testers. Also, to the TIS group for faithfully tasting, rating, and offering helpful comments and suggestions.

To the Berko Gallery in New York City, for giving me the use of Fernand Toussaint's painting *Lady in Pink*.

To Erika Lieben, Swiss National Tourist Board; Elizabeth Karba, Austrian National Tourist Office; Robert Kurtz, Confiserie Sprüngli Am Paradeplatz, Zurich; and Hans Geller, Lindt & Sprüngli Chocolate Factory, Kilchberg, Switzerland, for assisting me with my research of chocolate and chocolate specialties in their countries.

To those who generously shared their recipes and recipe ideas: Dietmar Fercher, Elizabeth Esterling, Marianne Kaltenbach, Cathy Williams, Marilyn Wankum, Miriam Baggett, Sally Churgai, and especially Roland Mesnier, whose artistry, pursuit of perfection, and mastery of technique have inspired me.

To my agent Linda Hayes, for her generous and thoughtful support and steadying presence throughout this and every project.

To Roc and David, for always being there when I need them.

To my mother, Elizabeth Reinoehl Adams, whose love and support were always unwavering, and in whose fond memory this book is dedicated.

A SHORT, SWEET HISTORY OF CHOCOLATE

Among the most singular and serendipitous events in modern culinary history was the appearance of chocolate on the world scene. The occurrence forever altered our notion of the word "ambrosial" and ultimately revolutionized the dessert maker's trade. Before chocolate, cooks had to rely on honey-spice cookies, a fruit or nut loaf, or perhaps a blancmange pudding to satisfy a sweet tooth. Since chocolate, they can turn to truffles, brownies, Devil's food cake, chocolate mousse, and a host of other truly ethereal creations.

Discovered by Central American and Mexican Indians, introduced into Europe by Spanish conquistadors, carried back to America by the Dutch and the British, and finally improved dramatically by the Dutch and the Swiss, chocolate may represent the most complex and sustained international culinary collaboration ever. It is as if the mystical food of the cocoa plant (whose Greek botanical name, *theobroma*, means food of the gods) was *meant* to be a gift to the entire world.

Probably the most critical moment in chocolate history took place in Montezuma's court at the height of the Mexican Aztec civilization: In 1519, the emperor greeted the Spanish explorer Cortez with a goblet of dark, frothy brew called *chocolatl* (or "fruit water" in the Nahuatl language). Sweetened with only a little honey and made pungent with spices, the ground cocoa bean beverage was bitter (and probably grainy), but the Aztecs revered it as a love elixir, stimulant, and tonic, and Cortez, too, gradually succumbed to its powers and charms.

When Cortez returned to Spain nine years later he carried with him some precious *cacahuatl* beans (the Spaniards shortened the word to cacao), as well as knowledge of how to ferment, roast, hull, and crush them into a usable paste. The exotic spiced chocolate drink, which King Charles V improved with a bit of cane sugar, became the rage of the Spanish court and ultimately of all other citizens who could afford it.

By the mid-1600s much of the rest of Western Europe had adopted the habit of drinking chocolate. Early on, Italian visitors to Spain took the custom back to their country. The daughter of Spanish King Phillip III introduced it into France when she married French King Louis XIII in 1615. Chocolate traveled across to Britain in 1657 when an enterprising Parisian merchant opened the first of what would become a host of popular chocolate taverns, or chocolate houses, in London.

In the same period, chocolate traversed an ocean yet again. The Dutch, who were already in the chocolate trade, sent cocoa beans to the New Amsterdam colony in America. English merchants soon followed suit with shipments to Massachusetts Bay, and by the early 1700s Boston apothecaries were selling chocolate beverages as restoratives. The Bay Colony's first—and now America's oldest—chocolate company was co-founded in 1765 by a physician, Dr. James Baker. (In the comparatively straight-laced American colonies, marketers shrewdly promoted chocolate's medicinal properties, and not its tastiness or presumed effect on sexual performance!)

Through a series of improvements and innovations, the world took several giant chocolate steps forward in the 18th and 19th centuries. During the 1700s, the Austrians discovered that chocolate paste could be used when baking cakes. (They have been busy creating extraordinary chocolate cakes ever since.) The Dutch added an important piece to the puzzle in the 1820s when, in an aim to improve drinking chocolate, they learned to extract the cocoa butter from chocolate by using presses (the substance that remains after pressing is cocoa powder). The availability of cocoa butter led to another innovation by the the English in the 1840s—simple chocolate candy. It was not the mellow, refined product we enjoy today, but was the most divine-tasting sweet created up to that point.

The last, and still preeminent, figures on the European chocolate scene were the Swiss and the Belgians. Near the end of the 19th century, several manufacturers devised techniques and products that would usher in the modern chocolate era. First, Daniel Peter and Henri Nestlé came up with milk chocolate. Then, Rodolphe Lindt found a way to give chocolate melt-in-the-mouth texture. His innovation involved adding extra cocoa butter to the chocolate paste and slowly kneading the mixture by machine for a number of hours. Called conching, this revolutionary (and still vital) process spreads the cocoa butter evenly over the ground chocolate particles, so they seem to glide over the tongue. Finally, Swiss and Belgian chocolatiers created some of our

ONE

most popular confectionery items, including filled chocolates, chocolate-covered candies, and elegant boxed assortments.

In the same period, a continent away, successful Pennsylvania caramel manufacturer Milton Hershey clearly saw the modern age of chocolate dawning. "Caramels are only a fad," he asserted. "Chocolate is a permanent thing." In 1893, he bought new chocolate-making equipment from Germany, and the rest of the Hershey story, as they say, is history.

Chocolate has indeed turned out to be more than a fad. In many countries, including our own, it is undoubtedly the most popular foodstuff and has insinuated itself into cultural and culinary life. Chocolate chip cookies, chocolate milk, cocoa with marshmallows, and Hershey kisses are a treasured part of American childhood. Adults have come to expect to give or receive boxed chocolates for Valentine's Day and regularly turn to chocolate cakes, tortes, cheesecakes, or ice creams at the end of fine meals. We even have a magazine devoted to the subject.

Chocolate is equally adored in many European nations. In France, a beloved after-school snack is a warm *pain au chocolat,* a croissant-like pastry enfolding a thin chocolate bar. For more sophisticated, adult palates there are dozens of chocolate *gâteaux,* tarts, and mousses. The French take their chocolate confections so seriously that members of an elite Parisian club called *Les Croqueurs de Chocolat* (the Chocolate Nibblers) carefully sample, assess, and catalog the efforts of chocolatiers in a hundred French cities and towns.

Throughout Switzerland and Austria life sometimes appears to revolve around chocolate. Most towns have not one but several fine chocolatiers, all of whom turn out fresh, exquisitely made truffles, bonbons, and other chocolate confections on a daily basis. Customers jam the sweet shops, tea houses, and cafés at all hours for a cup of hot chocolate or a succulent chocolate pastry, cookie, or cake.

In the lands where the benevolent Aztec god Quetsalcoatl is said to have first bestowed his mystical gift of chocolate, he continues to hold sway. Though Mexican and Central American cooks have never taken much to baking with chocolate (they do use it in cooking), chocolate beverages are still an integral part of Latin American life. In fact, the tale of chocolate ends where it began. As in the distant past, cocoa beans are still ground to a simple paste, sweetened, combined with water, and then whisked into a frothy drink with a carved wooden beater called a *molinet,* or *molinillo.* Chocolate, the divine gift, changes and becomes ever more lush and luxurious, yet it also remains the same.

Chocolate Mousse Cake with Ruffles

WORKING WITH CHOCOLATE

Chocolate is the undisputed diva of the dessert world. Nothing else has so many devoted fans or such drawing power. Nothing can match it for drama, dazzle, and deep-down allure.

However, like most superstars, chocolate is complex and must be handled carefully. To ensure its satiny texture and appearance and its matchless aroma and taste, there are some important do's and don'ts to follow. Ignore them, and chocolate can become dull, crumbly, or—incredible as it may seem—unpleasant to eat.

Despite chocolate's temperamental nature, be reassured that you do not need expertise to work with it. The recipes in this book provide all the necessary information, including techniques, safeguards—and even shortcuts and tricks used by professional chocolatiers. If you follow the recipe directions carefully, you can expect satisfying results.

Nevertheless, understanding the basics presented in this chapter will provide insight into why certain procedures are important. The information will also enable you to buy, store, chop, melt, and incorporate chocolate into recipes with greater confidence.

MELTING AND MIXING CHOCOLATE

Anyone who has ever had a chocolate candy melt in the hand knows something important about this foodstuff—it is very heat-sensitive and *melts readily when merely warmed*. When chocolate must be melted, high heat is not only unnecessary, it can drastically alter chocolate's texture, appearance, and taste. Even a temperature of 125°F. (which feels just slightly hot to the hand) can cause chocolate to scorch and develop an unpleasant flavor. In the case of milk chocolate and white chocolate (both of which contain milk proteins that burn and clump easily), too much heat can also cause graininess and lumping.

The basic rule is always the same when melting chocolate: *Keep the heat gentle and the chocolate dry*. Chocolate is also very sensitive to moisture, so be careful not to splash water into it during melting. Even a drop of moisture can cause chocolate to suddenly stiffen (confectioners call this seizing) and become unworkable. (The mixture can sometimes be rescued by adding about a tablespoon of water for each 1 to 1½ ounces of chocolate, but this yields a thick, sometimes grainy chocolate paste rather than pure, silky-smooth melted chocolate.)

One of the most convenient, quick, and reliable ways to melt chocolate is over indirect heat—specifically, in a double boiler top or metal bowl set over about an inch of *hot but not quite simmering* water. However, this method does take some care. If using a bowl, choose one large enough not to slip down into the water bath, but small enough not to overhang excessively and expose the chocolate around its sides to flames. Also, make sure the water doesn't touch the bottom of the double boiler inset. And don't allow it to simmer rapidly or boil. (Besides overheating the chocolate, this creates steam droplets that can cause seizing.) To easily control the temperature of the water, place the double boiler bottom on the stove top and bring the water just to a simmer; then turn the burner to its lowest setting and place the double boiler top or bowl of chocolate over the double boiler bottom. Usually, the residual heat will be sufficient to melt the chocolate, and it can simply be stirred occasionally until melted. (Of course, the water can be reheated slightly if need be.) Never cover the chocolate, as dreaded water droplets may condense on the lid and lead to seizing.

Patience is the watchword when melting chocolate, but if you must hurry, do so by chopping the chocolate more finely before placing it in the pan, not by increasing the heat. Cutting the chocolate into smaller pieces exposes more of the surface area to heat, effectively reducing melting time without increasing the risk of burning the chocolate.

The quickest way to melt a large quantity of chocolate is in a microwave oven. In this method, bombarding electromagnetic waves excite molecules and generate heat throughout the chocolate. Keep in mind that the *interior of the chocolate often melts before its surface even appears warm,* and that due to the continuing molecular agitation, *melting continues for some time after microwaving ceases.* To minimize chances of overheating, remember these guidelines: microwave only on 50-percent, or medium, power (use low power for white chocolate and milk chocolate); stir the chocolate and rotate the bowl frequently; stop microwaving before melting is complete, and then stir to finish the job.

TWO

Care must also be taken when melting chocolate along with other ingredients. It can be readily melted with oil or solid shortening over hot water, or—if the quantity of fat is large enough to bathe and insulate the chocolate, and the mixture is stirred continuously—over low direct heat. Melting chocolate with butter is a bit trickier because butter contains moisture as well as fat. Often, this moisture reacts with the natural starch in the chocolate, which causes the mixture to thicken rather than thin out as you might expect. When the chocolate *must* be kept fluid, recipes will require that you clarify the butter, a simple process that removes the moisture.

Chocolate does not mix readily with large quantities of liquids (milk, cream, water, or coffee, for example). To avoid difficulties, *warm the liquid first and then incorporate it into the chocolate very gradually or in stages,* stirring vigorously. The hot liquid heats the chocolate (without burning it) and is then smoothly incorporated as the chocolate melts from its warmth. To facilitate this melting/mixing process, be sure to chop the chocolate finely and stir well after each addition of liquid. The exact amount of warm liquid that can be smoothly incorporated all at once depends on the type and brand of chocolate and fluidity of the liquid, but as a general rule, whenever there are more than 1½ teaspoons of liquid per ounce of chocolate, add the liquid gradually or the chocolate may break, or separate into small particles.

TEMPERING CHOCOLATE

Tempering is the special process of cooling and mixing melted chocolate to ensure it will set up shiny and hard. This process controls the natural fat—called cocoa butter—that is found in all chocolate. Because cocoa butter is an unstable fat, it must be coaxed, through tempering, into a particular crystalline state. Once the cocoa butter reaches the correct state, the chocolate, which is still fluid, must then set (start to firm up) before the cocoa butter separates out or changes structure again. It is properly handled cocoa butter that makes chocolate crisp and glossy and gives it a rich, smooth taste. When cocoa butter is improperly handled, it can cause chocolate to be dull and crumbly and have surface streaks, or blotches, called bloom.

You need to temper only when real chocolate or white chocolate is melted alone or with a pure fat, such as solid shortening, vegetable oil, or clarified butter *and* only if you are letting it set again. This situation occurs when you dip candy centers, form molded chocolates, glaze a cake or cookies with pure chocolate, or turn melted chocolate into decorative items like the "woven" baskets and edible chocolate boxes presented in this book. Tempering is necessary in these instances because it ensures that the melted chocolate will set up shiny and hard.

Tempering is never required when chocolate is mixed with a liquid (including not only milk and water, but eggs, corn syrup, and honey, too). This means that you can prepare most chocolate recipes—sauces, puddings, pies, cakes, frostings, and glazes containing liquids—without tempering.

Tempering was once considered a task best left to professionals, but nowadays there are some "quick" tempering methods that require neither advanced skills nor special equipment. (You can even temper without understanding the technical details, if you carefully follow the Master Recipe for Quick-Tempering on page 220). Just remember to work on a cool, dry day or in a cool work area; heat and humidity make tempering very difficult.

While classic tempering involves working melted chocolate back and forth with a scraper on a marble slab, the quick method in this book requires only stirring a bowl of chocolate with a spoon. I have designed the method to be as easy, convenient, and reliable as possible. First, you completely melt most of the chocolate over a water bath, then gradually stir in some hard, shiny, never-melted chocolate. This addition serves two important purposes: It helps lower the temperature toward the setting point and, as it melts, it introduces the right kind of cocoa butter crystals into the mixture, or seeds the batch. These "seed" crystals provide the desired pattern for the rest of the cocoa butter to follow as it cools. To be sure the right kind of cocoa butter crystals are introduced, use only chocolate that is in a hard, lustrous tempered state (its original purchased condition) for seeding.

My quick-tempering method also calls for adding a little solid white vegetable shortening to the chocolate. This coats and helps stabilize the cocoa butter molecules, making them a little less likely to separate out and cause bloom even if the chocolate doesn't set as rapidly as it should. (The advantage of solid shortening over other fats is that it is hard at room temperature and thus does not soften the chocolate and reduce its crispness significantly.) The solid shortening is also added to make the tempered, cooling chocolate more fluid and easier to use.

The only difficult aspects of this quick-tempering method are determining when the chocolate has neared the setting point and not letting it cool and stiffen too much to dip, pour, or spread. Professionals often avoid guesswork by finding out the exact setting temperature of the chocolate they are using (this varies depending on the type and brand), but there is a good, fuss-free alternative method that yields satisfactory results in the home kitchen. When the chocolate feels cool (when touched to the upper lip), simply dip the tip of a knife into the mixture, then withdraw it and time whether the chocolate sets (hardens and dulls) on the knife within 1½ minutes. When this occurs, you can assume that the rest of the batch is also very near the setting point and is ready to be used. (If it takes longer than 1½ minutes to set, the cocoa butter will have time to separate, an occurrence you are trying to avoid.) To further ensure prompt setting of the chocolate, many of the recipes call for *lightly* chilling the items to be prepared before and/or after the chocolate is added. (Avoid the temptation to over-chill, however, as this can cause the setting chocolate to contract excessively and become too brittle.)

To eliminate the need for tempering entirely, manufacturers sometimes deliberately remove cocoa butter from chocolate, which yields a more stable, chocolate-like product called compound coating or summer coating. Although it isn't likely to bloom, this kind of coating doesn't have the full-bodied flavor of fine chocolate. An alternative way to avoid tempering real melted chocolate without sacrificing flavor is to chill it as soon as it is used and to keep it chilled until serving time. (The cool temperature firms the chocolate and prevents the cocoa butter from separating.)

SELECTING AND STORING CHOCOLATE

The flavor, texture, and aroma of each kind of chocolate depends on a complex set of factors, including the type and original condition of the cocoa beans; the length of fermentation and drying; the roasting time and temperature; the amount of sugar and other ingredients added; and the amount of conching, or kneading, of the chocolate mixture. In particular, brands from different countries are often distinctly different from one another because of wide variations in manufacturing practices and approaches.

Despite these differences, there is no need to worry about selecting just the "right" brand. All the recipes in this book specify the general chocolate type required (such as unsweetened, semisweet, or milk), and as long as you choose a chocolate of that type, you can be assured of good results. Of course, by using your favorite brands, you can tailor desserts to your own tastes.

The starting point for selecting chocolate is a label description such as "semisweet" or "unsweetened," but much more information is needed. Is a chocolate creamy or grainy, smooth or waxy, mellow or sharp, flavorful or bland, crisp or crumbly? Answering such questions requires sacrifice: You must smell, touch, and, yes, even sample chocolates to decide which ones you like.

Though chocolate preferences are highly individual, I find that people usually prefer the higher-quality brands. Price is one indicator of quality, but there are other, more reliable signs. A good sweetened dark chocolate looks glossy, is crisp enough to break apart with a snap (due to the abundance of that precious ingredient, cocoa butter), and has an appetizing chocolatey smell (whether pungent, fudgy, nutty, or mellow). It melts quickly on the tongue without either waxiness or grittiness. It is flavorful and full-bodied and leaves a clean, appealing (never cloying or unpleasant) aftertaste in the mouth.

Following are descriptions of the types of chocolate and chocolate products called for in this book. They are unique and cannot be substituted for one another unless indicated in a recipe. Note the differences, especially between unsweetened (or bitter) chocolate and bittersweet chocolate, which are often confused because of the similarity of their names. Unsweetened chocolate is very bitter and cannot be eaten plain, while bittersweet is a tasty sweetened chocolate with a pronounced chocolate flavor and a slightly bitter edge.

Unsweetened Chocolate—Also called baking chocolate or bitter (*not* bittersweet) chocolate, this is pure chocolate liquor, or the meat of the cocoa bean with no sugar added. It has an intense chocolate flavor, partially because of the concentration of chocolate solids (42 to 50 percent).

The rest of the flavor and the fluidity come from cocoa butter, which, by U.S. standards, must make up at least 50 to 58 percent of the total. Since unsweetened chocolate has a much higher percentage of chocolate solids and fat (the cocoa butter) than most sweetened chocolate, you cannot simply add sugar and substitute it for sweetened chocolate; the final product may be too oily and taste too strong.

Semisweet, Bittersweet, and Dark Chocolate—Most sweetened dark (not milk) chocolates fall into this category. They range from very dark and slightly bitter (in which case they are *usually* called bittersweet) through moderately dark and fairly sweet (*usually* called semisweet). All chocolates in this group are blends of chocolate solids, cocoa butter, sugar, lecithin (an emulsifier), and flavorings. Proportions of sugar and added cocoa butter vary from brand to brand, but all must contain at least 35 percent chocolate liquor and many of the darker, less sweet chocolates contain more than 50 percent. The proportion of chocolate solids and cocoa butter is usually about equal.

Due to differing nomenclature and standards of composition in various countries, choosing among dark sweetened chocolates can be confusing. If you are selecting among European brands, you will come across chocolates labeled simply "dark chocolate," with no information on the degree of sweetness. As a rule, dark chocolates are comparable to American bittersweet brands, although a few are nearly as sweet as typical American semisweets.

Even among American brands there are no absolute indicators of sweetness, because there are no legal definitions of the terms bittersweet and semisweet. What one company calls semisweet may be judged bittersweet by another. Moreover, it is the blend of ingredients and smoothness of the final product, not just the quantity of sugar, that makes a chocolate taste bold and slightly bitter or fairly mild and sweet. (The recipes in this book have been designed so that, in most instances, the various dark sweetened chocolates can be used interchangeably. In a few cases where one chocolate yields far superior results, it is specified in the ingredients list.)

Several of the more readily available brands that I especially like are Callebaut bittersweet and semisweet, Lindt Excellence, and Ghiradelli bittersweet.

Milk Chocolate—As the name suggests, milk chocolate must contain milk, specifically about 12 percent milk solids and about 3.5 percent butterfat. Generally considered an eating rather than cooking chocolate, it must also contain at least 10 percent chocolate liquor. The relatively small quantity of chocolate liquor makes milk chocolate too mild and delicate to be substituted for dark chocolate in most baked goods, although in some recipes for sauces and frosting it adds an appealing mellow, creamy taste all its own. Because of the milk solids, this chocolate must be heated very slowly or it will scorch.

White Chocolate—In the United States white chocolate cannot be labeled as such, because it contains only cocoa butter and no chocolate solids (and by law every product labeled chocolate must contain both). This leads to consumer confusion as manufacturers must describe their white chocolate—a blend of cocoa butter, milk solids, butterfat, sugar, lecithin, and flavorings—without using the word chocolate. Some typical names are white confectionery bar or morsels, white confectionery coating, or white baking bar. To compound the confusion, some manufacturers sell a different product that also goes by the name white confectionery bar or coating. Unlike "real" white chocolate, this white, chocolatey-looking product contains no cocoa butter and is not the least bit chocolatey. It is merely a white-colored coating mixture of shortening, sugar, milk solids, and flavorings.

Since the product names don't tell you which is real white chocolate, you must check label ingredients to be sure. The best white chocolates, most of which are European, will include cocoa butter and no other fats. (The most readily available high-quality white chocolate is Lindt Blancor, also called Lindt Swiss Confectionery Bar.) Real white chocolates are ivory-colored (as cocoa butter is) and have a delicate, faintly chocolatey aroma and taste. In contrast, the imitation white confectionery coatings are often whitish and have a cloying, overly sweet taste and smell.

White chocolates are very sensitive to heat and must be melted slowly or they will lump or scorch.

Couverture Chocolate—Couverture chocolate, or covering chocolate, is any high-quality semisweet, bittersweet, milk, or white chocolate that is specially formulated for dipping and coating. Most fine couvertures contain at least 35 percent cocoa butter (some contain much more), which makes them flow easily and form exceptionally thin, crisp, mellow-tasting coatings. Usually these chocolates are clearly labeled "couverture."

Chocolate and White Chocolate Morsels or Chips—These products are specifically designed to hold their shape when heated, so are not as fluid as most chocolates and do not melt as well. Don't substitute them for other chocolates or melt them unless instructed to do so in a recipe.

Cocoa Powder—Cocoa is the substance left when chocolate liquor is pressed and most of its cocoa butter is removed. The concentrated, unsweetened cocoa left behind has a distinctive chocolate taste, but since it retains only 10 to 22 percent of its cocoa butter it usually lacks some of the full, rounded flavor of good-quality chocolate. (Don't confuse cocoa with instant cocoa drink mix, which is a mixture of milk powder, sugar, cocoa, and flavorings.)

There are two popular and quite different styles of cocoa powder, American non-alkalized and Dutch-process (also called European-style). In American-style cocoa powders (such as Hershey's), the chocolate's natural acid is left untreated, giving the finished product a robust, slightly sharp taste. In Dutch-process, or European-style, cocoas (such as Droste), this acid is neutralized with an alkali, giving the cocoa powder a milder taste but darker, noticeably reddish color.

In recipes with large quantities of cocoa and in those containing significant amounts of baking soda (which depends on acid for activation), one style of cocoa is often clearly preferred and is called for. In cases where the amount of cocoa is small and it is incorporated mainly to boost the flavor of a chocolate, either style can be used.

Most of the chocolate products called for in this book can be purchased in small quantity, but for couverture and a good selection of the better dark, semisweet, or bittersweet chocolates, you must buy in bulk. (See page 278 for a list of suppliers.) Bulk sizes range from approximately one- to five-pound slabs for some brands to 10- or 11-pound blocks for others. These may at first seem impractical for home use, but projects like dipping, molding, or chocolate-crafting require surprisingly large amounts of chocolate. Also, good-quality chocolates are often much more economically priced when sold in bulk. And keep in mind that when wrapped airtight and stored in a cool dry place, unsweetened and dark sweetened chocolates keep well for at least a year. Because of their milk content, white chocolates and milk chocolates keep for only about six months.

If you do buy in bulk, you will need a small kitchen scale for measuring quantities and a tool for breaking the hard blocks into pieces. Don't try to use an ordinary knife for this; even a heavy chef's knife may snap. The best tool I've found is a wood chisel with a one- to two-inch-wide wedge-shaped metal blade (sold with woodworking supplies in hardware stores). Used along with a kitchen mallet, it can chisel off shavings, small pieces, or large chunks easily. If handled carefully, an ice pick can also be used to break large slabs of chocolate into chunks.

CAKES

Tivoli Torte

CHAPTER

Mocha Marjolaine

THREE

Named in honor of Copenhagen's fanciful amusement park, Tivoli Gardens, this buttercream-and-almond meringue torte is similar to the classic French meringue desserts known as dacquoises.

TIVOLI TORTE

Tivoli Tærte

Position two racks in center of oven and preheat oven to 325°F. Line two 12-by-16-inch or larger baking sheets with baking parchment. Marking with a dark pencil line, draw guidelines on each sheet for two 8-inch circles, separating circles as much as possible. Turn over sheets so meringue will be on unmarked surface. (Do not substitute wax paper as meringue will stick to it.)

To prepare meringue layers: Spread almonds in a roasting pan and toast, stirring occasionally, for six to eight minutes, or until tinged with brown but not burned. Measure out ⅔ cup attractive almond slices and reserve for garnishing torte top. Set pan aside until remaining almonds are cooled. Transfer cooled almonds and ¾ cup granulated sugar to food processor fitted with steel blade. Grind mixture until *very fine* but not oily. Add cornstarch to almond mixture, stirring until thoroughly and evenly incorporated.

In a completely grease-free large mixer bowl with mixer set on low speed, beat egg whites for about 30 seconds. Gradually raise speed to high, beating whites until frothy and opaque. Add cream of tartar and continue beating until whites just begin to stand in soft peaks. Immediately begin adding remaining sugar a bit at a time. Add vanilla and almond extract. Continue beating until whites stand in firm but not dry peaks. Using a rubber spatula, fold about a third of ground almond mixture into whites, until blended. Add remainder to whites and continue folding until ingredients are thoroughly blended but not overmixed. Immediately spoon ¼ of batter onto center of one circle marked on parchment and spread evenly almost to circle's perimeter, using a long-bladed spatula or table knife. Repeat process to form remaining circles.

Immediately place pans in oven, staggered and on separate racks. Bake at

Meringue Torte Layers

2½ cups (about 8 ounces) blanched almond slices

1½ cups granulated sugar, divided

¼ cup cornstarch

1 cup (about 8 large) egg whites, completely free of yolk

½ teaspoon cream of tartar

½ teaspoon vanilla extract

Generous ¼ teaspoon almond extract

Chocolate-Almond Buttercream and Garnish

5 ounces bittersweet (not unsweetened) chocolate, coarsely broken or chopped

2 large eggs

½ cup granulated sugar

¼ cup light corn syrup

⅓ cup unsweetened cocoa powder, preferably Dutch-process (European-style)

½ teaspoon vanilla extract

½ teaspoon almond extract

1¼ cups (2½ sticks) cool, just slightly firm unsalted butter

⅔ cup lightly toasted blanched almond slices (reserved from preparing meringue layers), for garnish

325°F. for 25 minutes. Lower heat to 300°F. and bake 25 to 30 minutes, until layers are pale tan and firm at edges, but still slightly soft in center, switching pans on racks and reversing halfway through baking, to ensure even baking. Carefully transfer parchment with meringues still attached to flat surface and let stand until thoroughly cooled. Gently peel off parchment. (Rounds are underdone if they stick a lot or seem gummy in center of underside; return rounds and parchment to oven and bake 10 minutes longer.) Don't worry if there are cracks in meringues as filling will help hold finished layers together. If desired, store airtight for up to 24 hours before assembling torte (or freeze, wrapped airtight, for up to a week; thaw before using).

To prepare buttercream: Melt chocolate in top of double boiler over about 1 inch hot but not simmering water, stirring occasionally. Remove double boiler top and set aside, until chocolate is warm to touch.

Break eggs into large mixer bowl. Set bowl in larger bowl of hot tap water; let stand for 10 minutes until eggs are very warm. Beat on high speed for three or four minutes, until light, foamy, and greatly increased in volume. Meanwhile, combine sugar, corn syrup, and 1 teaspoon hot tap water in a small, heavy saucepan over medium-high heat, stirring until sugar begins to dissolve and mixture comes to a simmer. Wipe sugar from pan sides with a damp paper towel. Cover pan and boil for exactly 1 minute. Immediately remove pan from heat. With mixer on high speed, immediately pour syrup in a thin but steady stream down bowl side (avoid beaters or whip as syrup will stick), adjusting flow so that all syrup is incorporated in about 10 seconds. Beat several minutes longer, until mixture cools to *barely warm to the touch*. Reduce speed to low and beat in cocoa powder, vanilla, and almond extract. Scrape down bowl sides with rubber spatula. Two or 3 tablespoons at a time, beat in cool butter, raising speed to high and beating until completely smooth after each addition. (Mixture will thin out at first, then begin to thicken and fluff up.) Beat in barely warm chocolate until smooth and evenly incorporated, scraping down bowl sides.

Assemble torte as follows: Place a generous dab of buttercream in center of serving plate to anchor meringue. Lay a meringue layer, smooth side down, on plate, fitting together cracked pieces, if necessary. Spread a fourth of buttercream over meringue layer. Press down lightly so filling just squeezes to meringue edge. Repeat layering procedure, covering each meringue with a layer of buttercream, until top meringue layer is added.

To decorate, sift powdered sugar over surface and pipe a decorative border of shells around top edge. Then sprinkle ring of reserved toasted almonds inside piped border. Chill at least 1 hour and up to 6 hours before serving. (If chilled longer than 1 hour allow to warm up slightly before serving.) *Makes 8 to 10 servings*

The inspiration for the following recipe was an outstanding chocolate torte that I sampled at Demels, Vienna's most acclaimed café and pastry shop.

To prepare torte: Position a rack in center of oven and preheat to 350°F. Very generously grease bottom and sides of an 8-inch-by-2½-inch springform pan. Insert wax-paper round cut to fit. Grease paper generously. Dust paper and pan sides with cocoa powder, tapping out excess.

In the top of a double boiler over about 1 inch of hot but not simmering water, heat chocolate, stirring occasionally, until completely melted and smooth. Remove double boiler from heat. Set aside with top still over bottom to keep chocolate warm.

In a large mixer bowl with mixer set on medium speed, beat butter and generous two thirds of sugar, until very light and fluffy. Beat in cocoa until smoothly incorporated. One at a time, beat in egg yolks. Beat until lightened and smooth. Whisk chocolate, then flour and vanilla into egg yolk mixture, until well blended.

In a large, completely grease-free mixer bowl with mixer on medium speed, beat egg whites until frothy and opaque. Raise speed to high and beat until soft peaks just form. A bit at a time, beat in remaining third of sugar. Continue beating until whites just stand in firm but not dry peaks. Using a rubber spatula, fold about 1 cup egg white mixture into batter until evenly incorporated. Then gently but quickly fold remaining whites into yolk mixture, turning bowl and scraping to bottom to incorporate evenly. Immediately turn out batter into prepared pan, spreading to edges.

Quickly transfer pan to oven and bake for 50 minutes. Lower heat to 325°F. and continue baking 15 to 20 minutes longer, or until torte springs back when lightly pressed in center and a toothpick inserted in thickest part comes out clean. Transfer pan to a wire rack and let stand

Torte
6 ounces bittersweet (not unsweetened) chocolate, coarsely chopped or broken into pieces

¾ cup (1½ sticks) unsalted butter, slightly softened

1 cup granulated sugar, divided

⅓ cup unsweetened cocoa powder, preferably Dutch-process

6 large eggs, separated (whites completely free of yolk)

1½ teaspoons vanilla extract

1 cup plus 2 tablespoons all-purpose flour

Rolled Hazelnut Fondant
1¼ cups (about 6 ounces) hazelnuts

1 tablespoon flavorless vegetable oil

½ teaspoon unflavored gelatin

2½ tablespoons light corn syrup

¾ teaspoon vanilla extract

3 tablespoons unsweetened cocoa powder, preferably Dutch-process

2 to 3 cups powdered sugar

Ganache and Garnish
1 cup heavy (whipping) cream

9 ounces bittersweet (not unsweetened) chocolate, chopped moderately fine

VIENNESE CHOCOLATE TORTE WITH ROLLED CHOCOLATE-HAZELNUT FONDANT

Schokoladentorte mit Haselnußfondant, nach Demels Art

until thoroughly cooled. Release cake from springform pan sides. Invert and peel off pan bottom, then paper, working carefully. Cake can be made ahead and stored, well wrapped, for 12 hours (or frozen, airtight, for up to a week; thaw before using).

To prepare chocolate-hazelnut rolled fondant: Position a rack in center of oven and preheat to 350°F. Spread hazelnuts in baking pan. Toast hazelnuts, stirring occasionally, for 12 to 16 minutes, or until hulls loosen and nuts are tinged with brown. Set aside until cooled.

Remove hazelnut hulls by vigorously rubbing nuts between fingers or in a clean kitchen towel, discarding bits of hull as you work. (Nuts do not have to be completely free of hull, but should be relatively clean.) Coarsely chop hazelnuts. In a food processor fitted with a steel blade, process hazelnuts and oil for 3 to 4 minutes, until very smooth and liquified. Strain mixture through a very fine sieve, discarding any bits of hazelnuts that remain. Return strained mixture to processor.

In a heat-proof small bowl or measuring cup, sprinkle gelatin over 3 tablespoons cold water. Let stand about 5 minutes, until gelatin softens. Place bowl in microwave oven and microwave on 100-percent power for a few seconds, until water is hot and gelatin completely dissolves. (Alternatively, place mixture in small saucepan over medium-high heat, stirring until mixture is hot and gelatin is completely dissolved.) Add gelatin mixture, corn syrup, and vanilla to processor. Process a few seconds, until mixture is completely smooth. Add cocoa and process until smoothly incorporated. Add 1 cup powdered sugar, processing until blended. Turn out mixture into a large bowl. Knead in 1 cup more powdered sugar. If necessary, knead in just enough more to yield a slightly firm but smooth and malleable mixture; for the most tender fondant do not oversugar. Wrap airtight in plastic wrap. Let stand at room temperature for at least 1 hour and up to 8 hours before using.

To prepare ganache: Bring cream just to a simmer over medium heat in a medium-sized, heavy saucepan. Remove from heat. Immediately stir in chocolate, until it is completely melted and smooth. Cover and refrigerate ganache for about 1 hour or until slightly stiff but not cold or hard. Transfer to a mixer and beat until light and fluffy.

To assemble torte: Slice cake crosswise into three equal layers. Brush off all loose crumbs. Reserving smooth bottom layer for top of torte, center a layer on serving plate. Spread about a third of ganache over layer. Top with second layer; cover with another third of ganache. Top with reserved layer, placing it smooth side up. Thinly but evenly spread remaining ganache over torte top and sides.

With well-oiled hands, knead fondant until flexible. Lightly oil two squares of wax paper (do not substitute nonstick vegetable cooking spray). Place a third of fondant between two sheets of wax paper and roll out into a round slightly larger than cake top; turn over wax paper and smooth out any creases in underside, as necessary. Peel off one layer of paper and replace it. Turn over fondant; peel off and discard second sheet of wax paper. Using a dessert plate or pattern as a guide, cut out a fondant circle *exactly* the same size as cake top; reserve scraps. With circle still attached to wax paper, center over cake top. Pat into place. Gently peel off paper. Smooth fondant further, if necessary.

Oil a sheet of wax paper long enough to encircle torte and overlap at ends just slightly. Oil your hands and shape remaining fondant (including any scraps from preparing circle) into an 18-inch log. Lay log on the prepared sheet of wax paper. Cover with second sheet of oiled wax paper. Roll fondant out into a band long enough to encircle torte (and overlap slightly) and extend above top edge of torte by about ¼ inch. Peel off top sheet of wax paper. Neatly cut away uneven edges using a large, sharp, well-oiled knife. (Trimmed size of band will need to be about 26 by 3 inches but measure torte to be sure.) Lifting up remaining sheet of wax paper with fondant still attached and holding it on the wax-paper side, match up bottom edge of fondant with bottom edge of cake and then wrap fondant around cake; adjust so fondant is snug. Smooth fondant into place, allowing excess to extend above top rim of cake. At point where ends overlap, trim away excess fondant to form a smooth seam; press ends together. Gently peel away wax paper. Gently shape and re-adjust fondant until surface is completely smooth. Brush top edge of fondant very lightly with vegetable oil; this will prevent it from drying out as it is ruffled. Immediately begin shaping and pinching edge to create a softly ruffled look. Garnish with crystalized roses, if desired (see Note).

Torte may be served immediately, but is best if covered and allowed to stand at room temperature for several hours. Refrigerate, tightly covered for up to 3 or 4 days longer, but allow to return to room temperature before serving. *Makes 12 to 15 servings*

Note: To crystalize roses, carefully and evenly brush petals of fresh, perfect roses with egg white using an artist's brush or small basting brush. Immediately sprinkle petals lightly with granulated or superfine sugar (superfine coats most evenly), shaking off excess. Let roses stand, separated, on wax paper, for at least an hour (and preferably longer), until egg white dries. Roses may be made ahead and stored, tightly covered and in a cool place, for several months.

The following recipe was inspired by the truffle torte I enjoyed at the Café Central in Vienna. The original recipe, featuring alternating layers of mellow hazelnut cake and rum-scented ganache, was created by Dietmar Fercher, one of the city's most esteemed pastry chefs. His truffle torte is topped with small chocolate curls and shavings, and my version may be decorated the same way. Alternatively, finish the torte with chocolate truffles and large, irregular chocolate curls and furled strips, as shown in the photograph.

To prepare cake: Position a rack in center of oven and preheat to 350°F. Very generously grease bottom and sides of an 8-inch-by-at least 2½-inch springform pan. Insert a wax-paper round cut to fit. Grease paper generously. Dust paper and pan sides with flour, tapping out excess.

In the top of a double boiler, over about 1 inch of hot but not simmering water, heat chocolate, stirring occasionally, until completely melted and smooth. Set aside with boiler top still over bottom to keep chocolate warm. Spread hazelnuts in a large roasting pan. Toast in oven, stirring occasionally, for 12 to 15 minutes or until skins loosen and nuts are tinged with brown. In a separate pan, toast almonds for 6 to 8 minutes, stirring occasionally, until tinged with brown. Set nuts aside until cooled. Remove loose hulls from cooled hazelnuts by rubbing a handful at a time between palms or in a kitchen towel. Coarsely chop hazelnuts. Stir together chopped hazelnuts, almonds, and flour.

In two batches, combine flour-nut mixture in a food processor fitted with a steel blade (if using extra-large processor bowl, the entire mixture can be processed at once). Process for several minutes until nuts are *very finely ground* but not oily. Set aside.

In a large bowl with mixer set on medium speed, beat together butter and half of sugar for 3 to 4 minutes until very light and fluffy. One at a time, beat in egg, then yolks, then salt, until very well blended and smooth. Beat in vanilla. On low speed, gradually beat in melted chocolate just until evenly incorporated.

In a large, completely grease-free mixer bowl with mixer on medium

Torte

6½ ounces bittersweet (not unsweetened) or semisweet chocolate, coarsely chopped

1⅓ cups (about 6½ ounces) hazelnuts

½ cup (about 2 ounces) blanched slivered almonds

½ cup all-purpose flour

¾ cup (1½ sticks) unsalted butter, slightly softened

Generous ¾ cup granulated sugar, divided

1 large egg, plus 5 large egg yolks

Pinch of salt

2 teaspoons vanilla extract

5 large egg whites, completely free of yolk

Ganache and Decoration

1⅔ cups heavy (whipping) cream

14 ounces bittersweet chocolate, coarsely chopped (see Note)

1½ to 2 tablespoons light or dark rum

½ teaspoon vanilla extract

3 to 4 ounces small chocolate curls (or shavings), or chocolate truffles and a few large curls and furled strips

VIENNESE TRUFFLE TORTE

Trüffeltorte

Viennese Truffle Torte, Sacher Torte, Linzer Cookies and Mocha-Filled Butter Cookies

speed, beat egg whites until frothy and opaque. Raise speed to high and beat until soft peaks just form. A bit at a time, beat in remaining sugar. Continue beating until whites just stand in firm but not dry peaks. Using a rubber spatula, fold about ½ cup chocolate mixture into whites. Then gently but quickly fold whites and flour-nut mixture into batter, turning bowl and scraping to the bottom to incorporate evenly. Immediately turn out batter into prepared pan, lightly spreading to edges.

Quickly transfer to oven and bake for 45 minutes. Lower temperature to

325°F. and continue baking 15 to 20 minutes longer, until torte springs back when lightly pressed in center and a toothpick inserted in the thickest part comes out clean. Transfer pan to a wire rack and let stand until thoroughly cooled. Release cake from springform pan sides. Invert and peel off pan bottom, then paper, working carefully as cake is tender. Cake can be made ahead, wrapped airtight, and stored (refrigerated for 24 hours and frozen for up to a week), or used immediately if necessary. (It slices better after 24 hours.)

To prepare ganache: In a 2-quart or larger saucepan bring cream just to a boil over high heat. Immediately remove from heat. Pour 1 cup cream over chopped chocolate, stirring until chocolate partially melts and mixture is very well blended. Pour ½ cup more cream over chocolate, stirring until chocolate *completely melts* and mixture is smooth. Stir remaining cream, 1½ tablespoons rum, and vanilla into chocolate until well blended and smooth. Cover and refrigerate mixture about 2 hours, until ganache is cool and thick enough to spread, but not at all hard. (If it is too cold, allow to warm up just a few minutes.) Gently stir to remix. If it is still too stiff to spread, stir in a little more rum or tap water to thin just slightly.

To assemble torte: Slice cake in thirds horizontally using a large serrated knife; if desired, add cutting guides around cake by measuring and marking sides into thirds with toothpicks. Set aside smooth bottom layer for torte top. Center one layer on serving plate. Spread a ⅜-inch layer of ganache over surface. Add second cake layer, patting down slightly, and cover with layer of ganache. Top with reserved third layer, smooth side up, patting down lightly. Transfer remaining ganache to a heavy saucepan and heat over medium-low heat, stirring constantly, until mixture thins to a pourable but not runny consistency. Pour about three fourths of glaze over torte top, quickly spreading out to edges using a long-bladed spatula or large table knife and working with just a few quick strokes. Spread over edges until sides are lightly covered. Touch up sides with remaining glaze. Immediately sprinkle torte top with chocolate shavings or curls until completely covered (or decorate with truffles and large irregular curls). Refrigerate torte at least 2 hours before serving.

Torte may be stored, refrigerated, for 2 or 3 days. Allow to warm up almost to room temperature before serving. *Makes 10 to 12 servings*

Note: If bittersweet chocolate is unavailable, recipe can be prepared using semisweet chocolate, but 2 modifications are necessary to yield a ganache with the proper consistency. Use 16 ounces semisweet chocolate instead of 14 ounces bittersweet. Also, reduce rum to 1 tablespoon.

The famed Sacher Torte was created in the 1830s by Prince Metternich's chef, Franz Sacher. ❖ *Since preparing and applying the traditional chocolate-sugar syrup glaze can be challenging for a home cook, I've provided directions for a simpler, easier-to-handle version. It goes on smoothly and has a nice sheen, but is milder and softer than the traditional glaze. However, if you insist on authenticity, refer to the recipe for Viennese Chocolate-Sugar Glaze on page 230.*

SACHER TORTE

Sachertorte

To prepare cake: Position a rack in center of oven and preheat to 350°F. Very generously grease bottom and sides of an 8½- or 9-inch-by-2½-inch springform pan. Insert wax-paper round cut to fit. Grease paper generously. Dust paper and pan sides with flour, tapping out excess.

In the top of a double boiler over about 1 inch of hot but not simmering water, heat chocolate, stirring occasionally, until completely melted and smooth. Remove double boiler from heat and set aside with top still over bottom to keep chocolate warm. In a large mixer bowl with mixer set on medium speed, beat butter and about two thirds of sugar, until very light and fluffy. One at a time, beat in egg yolks, then salt. Continue beating until very light and smooth. Whisk chocolate, then vanilla into egg yolk mixture, until well blended and smooth.

In a large, grease-free mixer bowl with mixer on medium speed, beat egg whites until frothy and opaque. Raise speed to high and beat until soft peaks just form. A bit at a time, beat in remaining third of sugar. Continue beating until whites just stand in firm but not dry peaks. Using a rubber spatula, fold about 1 cup egg white mixture into chocolate mixture, until evenly incorporated. Then gently but quickly fold remaining whites and flour into chocolate mixture, turning bowl and scraping to bottom to incorporate evenly. Continue folding until whites are evenly incorporated and no white streaks remain. Immediately turn out batter into prepared pan, spreading to edges.

Transfer pan to oven and bake for 40 to 50 minutes, or until torte springs

Torte and Apricot Glaze

6½ ounces bittersweet (not unsweetened) chocolate, coarsely chopped or broken into pieces

¾ cup (1½ sticks) unsalted butter, slightly softened

Scant 1 cup granulated sugar, divided

6 large eggs, separated (whites completely free of yolk)

Pinch of salt

2 teaspoons vanilla extract

1⅓ cups all-purpose flour

1 cup apricot preserves

⅛ teaspoon very finely grated orange zest (orange part of skin), optional

Easy Chocolate Glaze and Garnish

7 ounces bittersweet (not unsweetened) chocolate

6½ tablespoons unsalted butter

⅓ cup light corn syrup

1½ cups heavy (whipping) cream, lightly sweetened (if desired) and whipped, for serving

back when lightly pressed in center and a toothpick inserted in thickest part comes out clean but moist. (Test for doneness frequently as underbaked cake may sink in center as it cools and an overbaked cake may be dry.) Transfer pan to a wire rack and let stand until thoroughly cooled. Release cake from springform pan sides. Invert and peel off pan bottom, then paper, working carefully. Cake can be used immediately or stored, wrapped airtight, in the refrigerator for 24 hours and or in the freezer for up to a week.

Prepare cake for glazing by placing it, bottom side up, on a springform pan bottom, tart pan bottom, or sturdy cardboard round that is the same size or just slightly smaller than cake. Brush off all loose crumbs from cake; trim uneven side if needed for cake to rest flat. Place cake and supporting round on a wire rack set over a baking pan.

To prepare apricot preserves: In a small saucepan, bring apricot preserves to a simmer over medium heat. Simmer, stirring, for one minute. Immediately remove from heat. Strain preserves through a sieve into a small bowl. Stir in grated orange zest, if desired. When preserves are cooled and thickened just slightly, pour generous three fourths over cake top, quickly spreading out to edges and over sides using a wide-bladed spatula or palette knife. Quickly add a little more preserves to sides and smooth to even coating, if necessary. Let stand until set, at least 15 minutes and up to an hour, if preferred.

To prepare chocolate glaze: In a small, heavy saucepan over lowest heat, heat chocolate, butter, and corn syrup, stirring frequently, until mixture is completely melted and smooth. Immediately remove pan from heat. If glaze seems too runny to coat cake thoroughly, let cool for a few minutes, until it thickens just enough to flow smoothly but not run when poured over cake. Pour three fourths of glaze over cake top. Immediately spread and smooth glaze out to edges using a palette knife or long-bladed spatula, sweeping over surface in a few quick strokes. Quickly smooth glaze over sides, touching up with more glaze if needed to cover them evenly. If desired, reserve remaining glaze for writing on cake top. Let cake stand for 10 minutes. If writing on cake top, thin reserved glaze by heating it until slightly more fluid. Decorate by piping the word Sacher in large flowing letters using a piping cone. (If you are not experienced at writing with a piping cone, practice lettering on a sheet of wax paper.) Let cake stand at room temperature for at least 45 minutes, or refrigerate for about 10 minutes, until firmed up slightly. Transfer cake and supporting round to serving plate. (Do not try to remove cake from round as glaze may develop wrinkles.) Glazed torte may be stored, at room temperature, for up to 24 hours. Pass a large bowl of whipped cream with cake, or if serving plated slices, pipe a line of whipped cream alongside each slice.

Makes about 10 to 12 servings

FRANCE

MOCHA MARJOLAINE

Gâteau Marjolaine Moka-Chocolat

Position a rack in center of oven and preheat to 350°F. Line two 10-by-15-inch (or similar) jelly roll pans or baking sheets with baking parchment. Grease parchment or spray with nonstick vegetable cooking spray.

Spread hazelnuts in a roasting pan. Transfer to oven and toast, stirring occasionally, for 13 to 17 minutes or until hulls loosen and nuts are well browned. Spread almonds in a separate pan and toast, stirring occasionally, for 6 to 8 minutes, or until nicely browned. Remove nuts from oven; let cool. Position two racks in center third of oven and *reset oven temperature to 325°F.*

When hazelnuts are cool enough to handle, remove hulls as follows: Working with a handful of nuts at a time, vigorously rub them between your fingers or in a clean kitchen towel, discarding bits of skin as you work. (It's all right if some bits of skin don't come off completely.) Combine hazelnuts and about ⅓ cup sugar in a food processor fitted with a steel blade, and grind until powder fine but *not oily.* Transfer to a medium bowl. Process almonds and about ⅓ cup more sugar until almonds are powder fine but not oily. Add to hazelnuts. Stir flour and salt into nuts until evenly incorporated.

In a completely grease-free, large mixer bowl, with mixer set on medium speed, beat egg whites until frothy. Gradually raise speed to high, beating until soft peaks just form. Immediately begin adding remaining sugar, then vanilla and almond extracts, continuing to beat until incorporated and whites stand in stiff,

Meringue layers
1⅓ cups (about 6½ ounces) hazelnuts
1⅓ cups (about 4½ ounces) blanched almond slices
1¼ cups granulated sugar
2 tablespoons all-purpose flour
⅛ teaspoon salt
1 cup (7 to 8 large) egg whites, completely free of yolk
1½ teaspoons vanilla extract
⅛ teaspoon almond extract
Ganache
1¼ cups heavy (whipping) cream
13 ounces bittersweet (not unsweetened) or semisweet chocolate, coarsely grated or chopped moderately fine
Coffee Buttercream and Garnish
2¾ teaspoons instant coffee powder or granules
1 large egg, plus 2 large egg yolks
½ cup granulated sugar
¼ cup light corn syrup
1 teaspoon vanilla extract
1 cup (2 sticks) unsalted butter, cool and just slightly firm
About 1½ cups lightly toasted blanched almond slices

glossy peaks. Using a rubber spatula, lightly but thoroughly fold nut mixture into whites. Immediately divide batter between parchment-lined pans. Using a wide-bladed spatula, spread mixture to within 1 inch of ends and to edges on 15-inch sides; work carefully so each layer is of even thickness.

Place pans, staggered and on separate racks, in center of oven. Bake for 25 to 30 minutes or until just barely tinged with brown, reversing pans halfway through baking to ensure even baking. Turn oven off. Remove one pan from oven (leave other one in oven) and immediately cut meringue *in half lengthwise,* using a large, sharp knife. Then measure and trim through edges of each half to form a 12-inch-by- about 4½-inch rectangle; exact size is not important but all four rectangles must be the same size. Repeat cutting procedure with second meringue. (If meringue becomes too brittle to cut without breaking, return it to oven for a few minutes to reheat.) With parchment still in place, place meringue rectangles on flat surface to cool. Repeat procedure with second pan.

When rectangles are cool, carefully peel off parchment, discarding cut-away edges. (If parchment sticks and meringues are soft in center bottom, place in a preheated 275°F. oven for about 10 minutes longer, being careful not to crisp them too much. Cool again, then remove parchment.) Work carefully but don't worry too much about any breaks as they can be pieced back together as the gâteau is assembled. The cooled rectangles may be wrapped airtight and stored in a cool place for 2 days or frozen for up to 3 weeks.

To prepare ganache: In a medium saucepan, bring cream just to boiling. Remove pan from heat. Add chocolate, stirring. Continue stirring until chocolate is incorporated and melts completely. Strain through a very fine sieve. Refrigerate mixture for about 1½ hours, or until completely cooled and slightly stiffened.

To prepare coffee buttercream: In a small cup, stir coffee powder into 1 tablespoon hot water, until dissolved; set aside. Put egg and yolks in large mixer bowl set in a larger bowl of hot tap water. Let stand for 10 minutes until eggs are very warm. Beat on high speed for 3 to 4 minutes, or until light, thickened, and greatly increased in volume. Meanwhile, combine sugar, corn syrup, and 1½ teaspoons hot tap water in a small heavy saucepan over medium-high heat, stirring until sugar begins to dissolve and mixture comes to a simmer. Wipe sugar from pan sides using a damp paper towel. Cover pan and boil for exactly one minute. Immediately remove pan from heat. With mixer on high speed, immediately pour syrup in a thin but steady stream down bowl side (avoid beaters or whip as syrup will stick), adjusting flow so that all syrup is incorporated in about 15 seconds. Beat several minutes longer, until mixture cools to *barely warm to the touch.* (Mixture must not be warmer or it will melt butter when added.) Reduce speed to low and beat in coffee mixture and vanilla. Scrape down bowl sides with rubber spatula. Two or three tablespoons at a time, beat in cool butter, raising speed to high and beating buttercream until completely smooth after each addition. (Mixture will thin out at first, then begin to thicken and fluff up.)

To assemble gâteau: In a large mixer bowl, beat chilled ganache on high speed, until lightened and fluffy, about 2 minutes. Remove ¾ cup ganache from bowl; cover and set aside for piping final shell borders. Select the smoothest, most even meringue rectangle to use as top; set aside. Anchor gâteau to a tray or serving platter by placing several generous dabs of ganache along length of tray, then centering a rectangle, smooth side down, on tray. Press down gently. Using a metal spatula or knife, cover meringue surface with scant ¼-inch-thick layer of ganache. Place another meringue rectangle over ganache, gently pressing down until chocolate is just squeezed out to edges. Spread meringue surface with scant ¼-inch-thick layer of coffee buttercream. Place third meringue rectangle over coffee filling, pressing down gently. Whisk together remaining ganache and coffee buttercream, until well blended. Spread a scant ¼-inch-thick layer of mocha mixture over meringue rectangle, pressing down layer. Place remaining rectangle, smooth side up, over mocha filling, pressing down slightly. Spread thin layer of mocha mixture smoothly over gâteau top and sides; do not cover ends. Garnish long sides of gâteau by scooping almonds into palm and pressing against mocha mixture, until evenly coated. Using a pastry bag fitted with a ⅓-inch diameter open-star tip, and reserved chocolate ganache, pipe line of shells down length of torte along bottom and top edges, as shown on page 23. (Leave ends plain.) Let gâteau stand at room temperature for a few minutes to allow meringue layers to soften just slightly.

Freeze gâteau until firm enough that filling will not be squeezed out during cutting, about one hour. Using an electric knife or a large, sharp knife, trim off and discard a thin slice at each end to even surface. (If planning to serve marjolaine buffet-style, cut into individual slices at this point.) Return to freezer, covered airtight, for up to 48 hours, if desired. Before serving, transfer to refrigerator and store until completely thawed. Let refrigerated gâteau warm up slightly before serving.   *Makes 12 to 14 servings*

To prepare cherries: Very thoroughly drain cherries, reserving juice in a 4-quart saucepan. Add cranberry juice concentrate, sugar, and kirsch (if used) to saucepan. Bring mixture to a rolling boil over very high heat. Boil syrup for 3 to 5 minutes until slightly thicker and reduced to a scant ½ cup; as mixture boils down, watch carefully to avoid scorching. Add cherries and immediately remove from heat. Stir in vanilla. Refrigerate, covered, for at least 2 hours and up to 48 hours, if desired.

To prepare cake: Position a rack in center of oven and preheat to 350°F. Grease a 9-inch springform pan. Insert a wax-paper round cut to fit. Grease paper. Place chocolate and butter in a small, heavy saucepan over *lowest* heat. Warm, stirring frequently, until melted and smooth. Set aside.

In a small pan or heat-proof measuring cup, heat kirsch to hot; set aside. In a large mixer bowl with mixer set on medium speed, beat together yolks and about half of sugar until blended and frothy. Raise speed to high and beat in hot kirsch a bit at a time. Beat mixture on high speed for 4 to 5 minutes until very thick and light. Beat in vanilla and salt. Using a rubber spatula, fold in chocolate until evenly incorporated, but not overmixed. Sift flour, cocoa, and baking powder over yolk mixture. Fold several times to partially incorporate dry ingredients; set aside.

In a grease-free mixer bowl with grease-free beaters, beat whites on low speed for about 30 seconds, until foamy and opaque. Raise speed to high and continue beating until soft peaks begin to form. Gradually beat in remaining half of sugar. Continue beating until stiff but not dry peaks form. Using a rubber spatula, add white mixture to chocolate mixture, continuing to fold and scraping to pan

Cherries and Cake

1 can (16 ounces) unsweetened sour (pie) cherries or Hungarian Morello sour cherries, if available (see Note)

⅓ cup frozen cranberry juice concentrate, thawed

⅓ cup granulated sugar

2 tablespoons kirsch, optional

½ teaspoon vanilla extract

4 ounces bittersweet (not unsweetened) or semisweet chocolate, coarsely chopped

3 tablespoons unsalted butter

2 tablespoons kirsch or water

6 large eggs, separated

¾ cup plus 2 tablespoons granulated sugar, divided

1½ teaspoons vanilla extract

¼ teaspoon salt

½ cup all-purpose flour

¼ cup unsweetened cocoa powder, preferably Dutch-process

½ teaspoon baking powder

Stabilized Whipped Cream

¾ teaspoon unflavored gelatin

1 tablespoon plus 1 teaspoon kirsch or water

2½ cups heavy (whipping) cream

½ cup powdered sugar

½ teaspoon vanilla extract

Soaking Syrup and Decorations

Steeping syrup reserved from cherries

1½ ounces bittersweet or semisweet chocolate, coarsely chopped

About 3 to 4 ounces chocolate curls, scrolls, or shavings (see page 255), for garnish

Several red candied cherries for garnish (optional)

Chocolate band (see page 252), for garnish (optional)

Powdered sugar, for dusting

BLACK FOREST CHERRY CAKE

Schwarzwälder Kirschtorte

bottom until ingredients are evenly incorporated but not overmixed. Working quickly and gently, turn out into prepared pan, spreading to edges.

Quickly transfer to oven and bake for 36 to 41 minutes or until center top springs back when lightly pressed and a toothpick inserted in cake center comes out moist but clean. Transfer pan to a wire rack. Let cake stand until completely cooled, at least 1 hour. Run a knife around pan sides and release pan sides. Use cake immediately or wrap airtight for up to 36 hours. (Or wrap and freeze for up to a week. Thaw before using.)

To prepare whipped cream: Sprinkle gelatin over kirsch in a small saucepan. Set aside until gelatin softens, about 5 minutes. Bring mixture to a simmer over medium heat, stirring, until gelatin completely dissolves. Remove from heat and whisk ½ cup cream into gelatin mixture. Immediately stir together gelatin-cream mixture and remaining cream in large mixer bowl. Cover and refrigerate until very well chilled. With mixer on high speed, whip cream *just until very soft peaks form.* Immediately beat in powdered sugar, then vanilla, continuing to beat until slightly firmer peaks form. Return cream to refrigerator for a few minutes while soaking syrup is prepared.

To prepare soaking liquid and assemble torte: *Thoroughly* drain cherries, reserving steeping syrup. Prepare soaking syrup for cake by measuring 2 tablespoons steeping syrup into a small saucepan. Bring syrup just to a boil over high heat; remove from heat. Stir in chopped chocolate until completely melted and smooth. Return pan to burner and stir in kirsch and ¼ cup more steeping syrup until well blended and smooth. Set aside to cool slightly.

Using a large serrated knife, slice cake horizontally into three equal layers. (If desired, add cutting guides around cake by measuring and marking sides into thirds with toothpicks.) Reserve smooth bottom layer to serve as cake top. Center one of remaining layers on serving plate. Using a long-bladed spatula or table knife, spread 2 tablespoons cherry-chocolate syrup over cake surface. Spread generous fourth of whipped cream over layer. If desired, reserve a few of the most attractive cherries for garnishing top of cake; omit this step if candied cherries will be used. Sprinkle half of remaining cherries over whipped cream. Top cherries with second cake layer, pressing down lightly. Spread cake surface with 2 tablespoons cherry-chocolate syrup. Cover with another fourth of whipped cream. Top with remaining cherries. Place reserved cake layer, smooth side up, over cherries. Spread cake surface with 2 tablespoons cherry-chocolate syrup. Brush off loose crumbs from cake top and sides. Very lightly cover top and sides with whipped cream. Smoothly spread remaining whipped cream over cake top and sides; use a palette knife or long-bladed spatula for a very smooth, professional look. (Although it's best to keep cream free of cake crumbs, mistakes can be camouflaged when finished top and sides are sprinkled with chocolate curls and pieces.) Pile some chocolate curls or scrolls in center of cake and out toward edges; for best taste and appearance garnish abundantly. Add reserved cherries or a few candied cherries, tucking attractively among curls.

Using a long-bladed spatula or cupped hand, pat additional small curls and pieces randomly around cake sides, or ready a chocolate band for sides. (Prepare chocolate band and fit around torte sides according to directions on page 252. Band will need to be about 2½ inches high and 27 inches long but measure to be sure. If a chocolate band is added, cake must be cut using a large sharp knife dipped in very hot water and wiped dry between each cut.)

Refrigerate torte, covered, for at least 1 hour and up to 36 hours before serving; longer storage allows flavors to blend. Just before serving dust curls with a little powdered sugar. Let cake warm up for a few minutes before serving. *Makes about 12 servings*

Note: To restore the original flavor and color of canned sour cherries, boil down their juice with a little cranberry-juice concentrate and kirsch; then steep the cherries in this syrup for a few hours.

If imported Hungarian Morello sour cherries can be obtained, use them in place of American sour cherries for most intense flavor and color. Morello cherries are normally packed in light syrup; in this case reduce the ⅓ cup sugar called for in preparing the cherries to 2 tablespoons.

One of the hallmark recipes of American baking is the devil's food layer cake. It is dramatically dark, distinctively flavored (the baking soda alkalizes the cocoa, changing its flavor and deepening its color to reddish black), and tall; this particular devil's food cake rises more than four inches and boasts three large layers! ❖ The cake is particularly appealing frosted with fudge buttercream, which stands out in attractive ribbons against the dark layers of cake. To maintain the soft, creamy texture of the frosting, keep the cake in a cool place, but do not refrigerate.

To prepare cake: Position a rack in center of oven and preheat to 350°F. Very generously grease three 9-inch round cake pans. Line pans with wax-paper rounds cut to fit. Grease paper. Generously dust pans with cocoa powder, tapping out excess.

Place chocolate in top of a double boiler over about 1 inch hot but not simmering water. Warm over medium-low heat, stirring occasionally, until chocolate melts. Remove from heat and set aside with double boiler top still over bottom. Pour ⅔ cup boiling water over cocoa in a medium bowl, stirring until well blended and smooth. Stir in baking soda until well blended; set aside until mixture cools.

Sift together flour, baking powder, and salt; set aside. In a large mixer bowl with mixer set on medium speed, beat butter for 2 minutes until very light and fluffy. Add 2¼ cups sugar and beat about 2 minutes longer, until very light and well blended. One at a time, beat in egg and yolks, then cooled cocoa mixture, until very smooth. Beat in slightly warm chocolate mixture until evenly incorporated. With mixer on low speed, beat in half of dry ingredients, then sour cream and vanilla, then remaining half of dry ingredients just until evenly incorporated and smooth.

In a completely grease-free large mixer bowl, beat egg whites on medium speed until foamy and opaque. Raise speed to high and beat until soft peaks begin to form. Gradually beat in remaining ¼ cup sugar. Continue

Cake

Unsweetened cocoa powder, for dusting

4 ounces unsweetened chocolate, coarsely chopped or broken into small pieces

½ cup plus 2 tablespoons unsweetened, non-alkalized, American-style cocoa powder

1½ teaspoons baking soda

2 cups plus 2 tablespoons unsifted cake flour

½ teaspoon baking powder

Generous ¼ teaspoon salt

1¼ cups (2½ sticks) unsalted butter, slightly softened

2½ cups granulated sugar, divided

1 large egg, plus 5 large egg yolks

1 cup sour cream

1 tablespoon vanilla extract

4 large egg whites

Fudge Buttercream Frosting

1¼ cups heavy (whipping) cream

1⅔ cups granulated sugar

3 tablespoons light corn syrup

5½ ounces unsweetened chocolate, coarsely chopped or broken into small pieces

1½ teaspoons vanilla extract

¾ cup (1½ sticks) unsalted butter, cool and slightly firm

DEVIL'S FOOD LAYER CAKE WITH FUDGE BUTTERCREAM FROSTING

beating until stiff but not dry peaks form. Using a rubber spatula or whisk, fold about 1 cup batter into whites. Then fold whites into chocolate mixture until thoroughly incorporated but not overmixed.

Divide batter among prepared pans, spreading out to edges. Bake for 30 to 35 minutes or until a toothpick inserted in the thickest part comes out clean but still moist and the top springs back slightly when pressed. The layers will be starting to draw away from pan sides. Transfer pans to wire rack and let stand until layers are *completely cooled.*

Working very carefully as cake is quite tender, run a knife around pan edges to loosen cake from bottom. Rap pan sharply and repeatedly against counter until layer is loosened completely. Holding cutting board (or flat plate) against pan, invert cake onto cutting board. Peel off paper. Lay cooling rack on cake bottom. Holding rack and cutting board together, reinvert cake onto rack and lift off board. Repeat with other layers. As needed, carefully transfer layers to serving plate using several wide-bladed spatulas.

To prepare frosting: Using a large wooden spoon, stir together cream, sugar, and corn syrup in a 4-quart or larger heavy saucepan or cast-iron Dutch oven. Bring mixture to a boil over medium-high heat, stirring. Carefully wash all sugar from stirring spoon. Continue to cook, uncovered, stirring *frequently but gently,* for 3 or 4 minutes or until mixture begins to boil down and thicken just slightly.

Lower heat to medium and continue to cook, stirring constantly and watching carefully to prevent scorching, until mixture thickens further and just turns a pale straw color, about 2 minutes longer. Immediately remove pan from heat. Add chocolate, *stirring gently and avoiding scraping pan sides,* until completely melted; do not stir vigorously as this can cause graininess. Immediately set fudge aside, without stirring, until center bottom of fudge is almost cool to the touch, about 1 hour. (To hasten cooling, carefully set pan in a larger pan of cold water, and change water several times as it warms; do not stir fudge.)

Scrape out cooled fudge into a large mixer bowl (it needn't be completely cold, but cool enough not to melt the butter when it is added). Add vanilla and beat until incorporated. Two tablespoons at a time, beat in butter. Continue beating until frosting is lightened and fluffy and butter is completely and evenly incorporated. If mixture is too soft to spread, refrigerate a few minutes, stirring occasionally, but be careful it doesn't firm up too much.

Using a table knife or long-bladed spatula, immediately spread a generous fourth of frosting over thoroughly cooled cake layer. Center a reserved cake layer over frosted layer and add another generous fourth of frosting. Add final cake layer. Cover cake top and sides with remaining frosting, smoothing or swirling it attractively. Let stand a few minutes until frosting firms slightly before serving. Cake is best fresh, but may be stored, covered and in a *cool place* (but not refrigerated), for a day or so. *Makes 12 to 15 servings*

This is a large, regal, three-layer cake, particularly well suited for a birthday, wedding shower, or other special occasion. The taste is rich and buttery; the crumb is fine and tender. It is at its best when very fresh.

❖ *The ivory-colored frosting is exceptionally smooth and spreads and pipes well. Although the white chocolate flavor comes through clearly, the frosting is not overly sweet.*

WHITE CHOCOLATE BUTTER LAYER CAKE WITH WHITE CHOCOLATE-SOUR CREAM FROSTING

Position a rack in center of oven and preheat to 350°F. Grease three 8½- or 9-inch round cake pans. Line pan bottoms with wax-paper rounds cut to fit. Generously grease paper. Dust pans with flour, tapping out excess.

To prepare cake: In the top of a double boiler, over about 1 inch hot but not simmering water, slowly melt white chocolate, stirring occasionally. Set aside with top of double boiler still over bottom to keep chocolate slightly warm.

Thoroughly stir together flour, sugar, baking powder, and salt in a large mixer bowl. Add butter and ½ cup milk and beat on low speed until thoroughly incorporated but not over-mixed, being sure to scrape to bowl bottom. One at a time, beat in eggs and yolk, beating on medium speed for 15 seconds after each addition. Add vanilla and orange zest, beating for 15 seconds longer. Gradually beat in remaining milk and sour cream until incorporated. Raise speed to high and beat for exactly 1 minute; for best texture, take care not to underbeat or over-beat. Reduce speed to low. Beat in white chocolate just until evenly distributed throughout. Turn out batter into prepared pans, spreading to edges.

Bake for 25 to 30 minutes or until nicely browned and a toothpick in-

Cake

7 ounces top-quality white chocolate, very coarsely chopped

4 cups sifted cake flour

1½ cups granulated sugar

1 tablespoon plus 2 teaspoons baking powder

¾ teaspoon salt

1 cup (2 sticks) unsalted butter, very soft but not melted

1 cup whole milk, divided

3 large eggs, plus 1 large egg yolk

2½ teaspoons vanilla extract

¼ teaspoon very finely grated orange zest (orange part of skin)

5 tablespoons sour cream

serted in thickest part comes out moist but clean. Layers will also spring back when lightly pressed in center. Transfer pans to wire racks and let stand until cooled. Run a knife around pans to loosen layers. Remove from pans and gently peel off paper. Let stand, right side up, on wire racks until completely cooled. Layers are best used immediately, but may be made ahead and stored, tightly wrapped and frozen, for up to a week. Thaw thoroughly before frosting.

To prepare frosting: Very slowly melt white chocolate in the top of a double boiler, over about 1 inch hot but not simmering water, stirring frequently until completely smooth; do not allow any water to drip into chocolate. Remove from heat and set aside with top of double boiler still over bottom to keep chocolate slightly warm. Beat together butter, sour cream, and vanilla until very well blended and smooth. Beating on medium speed, add slightly warm white chocolate (warm enough that chocolate will not set and harden, but not so warm that it melts the butter). Continue beating until frosting is very smooth and fluffy. Taste frosting and if sweeter frosting is desired, beat in up to two tablespoons powdered sugar.

> **White Chocolate-Sour Cream Frosting**
> *12 ounces top–quality white chocolate,*
>   *broken or coarsely chopped*
> *¾ cup unsalted butter, soft but not melted*
> *½ cup sour cream*
> *1 teaspoon vanilla extract*
> *1 to 2 tablespoons powdered sugar*
>   *(optional)*

When cake is at room temperature, place a generous dab of frosting in the center of serving plate to anchor cake. Center one layer on plate and spread a scant fourth of frosting over top. Add a second layer and spread with another scant fourth of frosting. Using a long-bladed spatula or palette knife, add remaining layer and cover top and sides with frosting; reserve some frosting if decorative piping is desired. Swirl frosting attractively or smooth out surface if piping will be added. Add piping using a pastry bag fitted with an open-star tip. Add fresh flowers or piped icing flowers to cake as desired.

Cake will keep, covered and in a cool place (not refrigerated), for up to 24 hours, but tends to dry out if kept longer.   *Makes 12 to 15 servings*

This is an updated version of a traditional Italian flourless chocolate-and-almond cake. Almonds are used abundantly in Italian desserts, and many Italian bakers have a cake of this sort in their repertoire. ❖ Most of the work is done in a food processor, making this recipe somewhat easier to prepare than the original. The cake is left unfrosted and simply finished with a dusting of powdered sugar. The large quantity of ground almonds lends an unusual, slightly grainy and dense texture as well as a delicious, subtle flavor. ❖ The cake keeps extremely well and may be even better the second or third day.

CHOCOLATE ALMOND CAKE

Torta di Cioccolata e Mandorle

Position a rack in center of oven and preheat to 350°F. Very generously grease a 10-inch-by-at least 2½-inch springform pan. Line pan with a wax-paper round cut to fit. Grease wax paper generously. Evenly dust wax paper and pan sides with 1 tablespoon cocoa powder, tapping out any excess. (Reserve remaining cocoa for cake.)

Spread almonds in a roasting pan. Toast, stirring occasionally, for 6 to 8 minutes or until tinged with brown and fragrant. Set aside until thoroughly cooled. Do not turn off oven.

Finely grate chocolate in a food processor fitted with a grating disk. Set aside in a very large bowl. Combine almonds, remaining 3 tablespoons cocoa powder, and ¼ cup sugar in food processor fitted with a steel blade. Process until *very finely ground* but not oily. Stir almonds into grated chocolate until well mixed.

In processor bowl fitted with steel blade, process butter, 1 cup sugar, and almond extract in on/off pulses just until blended and smooth, about one minute. Add yolks, two at

Cake

4 tablespoons unsweetened cocoa powder, preferably Dutch process (European-style), divided

10 ounces (about 3¼ cups) sliced almonds, blanched or unblanched

8 ounces bittersweet (not unsweetened) or semisweet chocolate, coarsely chopped or broken into small pieces.

1¼ cups plus 3 tablespoons granulated sugar, divided

¾ cup (1½ sticks) unsalted butter, cool and firm but not hard

⅛ teaspoon almond extract

6 large eggs, separated (whites completely free of yolk)

⅛ teaspoon salt

⅛ teaspoon lemon juice

a time, through feed tube, continuing to process just until mixture is smooth and light but not at all runny.

In a completely grease-free large mixing bowl with grease-free beaters, beat egg whites, salt, and lemon juice at low speed until frothy. Raise speed to high and beat until soft peaks form. Gradually beat in remaining 3 tablespoons sugar. Continue beating until whites stand in smooth and firm but not dry peaks. Using a large wooden spoon, vigorously stir butter mixture into reserved almond-chocolate mixture until blended; mixture will be stiff and difficult to combine. Whisk about 1½ cups chocolate mixture into egg white mixture. Stir egg white mixture back into chocolate mixture and continue vigorously stirring or whisking until ingredients are evenly incorporated but not overmixed. Immediately turn out batter into prepared pan, spreading to edges. Shake pan to even surface.

> **D**ecoration
> *2 to 3 tablespoons powdered sugar*
> *1 cup heavy (whipping) cream, whipped and flavored with 1 tablespoon powdered sugar and 1 tablespoon Amaretto liqueur (optional)*

Bake cake for 15 minutes. Lower heat to 325°F. and continue baking, 40 to 50 minutes longer, or until the center springs back when lightly tapped and a toothpick inserted in the thickest part comes out clean but moist.

Transfer pan to wire rack and let stand until completely cooled, at least 1½ hours. (Cake will sink slightly.) Run a knife around edges to loosen. Release sides of springform pan. Carefully invert cake onto center of serving plate. Loosen and remove pan bottom. Carefully peel off wax paper. Brush any loose crumbs from surface. Garnish by sifting powdered sugar over surface. (Alternatively, lay a paper doily over cake surface and sift sugar over top to create a design. Carefully lift off doily and excess sugar.) Wipe away any powdered sugar from rim of plate. Cake may be stored, airtight and refrigerated, for up to 5 or 6 days, or in the freezer for up to 2 weeks.

Serve at room temperature or cool but not cold, cut into wedges. Add dollops of Amaretto-flavored whipped cream to servings, if desired.

Makes 9 to 12 servings

The attractive Bundt shape and the lustrous, mirror-like perfection of its glaze make this moist, dense, and fudgy cake look like the product of a fine European bake shop. Nevertheless, it is easy to prepare.

To prepare cake: Position a rack in center of oven and preheat to 350°F. Very generously grease a 10- to 12-cup Bundt pan. Dust pan with 1½ tablespoons cocoa powder, tapping out excess.

In top of a boiler over 1 inch of hot but not simmering water, melt chocolate, stirring occasionally, until smooth. Set aside with top of double boiler still over bottom to keep chocolate slightly warm. Sift together flour, ½ cup cocoa powder, baking powder, and salt.

In a large bowl with mixer set on medium speed, beat butter for 2 to 3 minutes until very light and fluffy. Add sugar, coffee powder, and eggs and egg yolk and beat about 2 minutes longer, until very light and well blended. With mixer on low speed, beat in half of dry ingredients, then sour cream, melted chocolate and vanilla, then remaining half of dry ingredients, just until evenly incorporated and smooth.

Turn out batter into pan, spreading to edges. Bake for 50 to 60 minutes, or until a toothpick inserted in the thickest part comes out clean and the top springs back when lightly pressed. Transfer pan to a wire rack and let stand until cake is *completely cooled.*

Very carefully run a knife around pan edges to loosen cake from sides and bottom. Rap pan sharply against counter several times to loosen completely. Holding cooling rack against pan, invert cake onto rack. Set rack over sheet of wax paper and brush off any loose crumbs from cake surface. Set rack and cake over a large tray or jelly-roll pan (to catch drips when cake is glazed).

Cake

½ cup plus 1½ tablespoons unsweetened cocoa powder, preferably Dutch-process

5½ ounces bittersweet or semisweet chocolate, coarsely chopped

2 cups all-purpose flour

1¾ teaspoons baking powder

⅛ teaspoon salt

½ cup (1 stick) unsalted butter, slightly softened

2 cups granulated sugar

½ teaspoon instant coffee powder

2 large eggs, plus 1 large egg yolk

1⅓ cups sour cream

2½ teaspoons vanilla extract

Dark and Shiny Chocolate Glaze

¼ cup granulated sugar

2 tablespoons unsweetened cocoa powder, preferably Dutch-process

⅓ cup coffee (or water if preferred)

2½ tablespoons light corn syrup

2½ ounces bittersweet or semisweet chocolate, chopped coarsely

5 tablespoons unsalted butter, slightly softened

½ teaspoon vanilla extract

CHOCOLATE-SOUR CREAM BUNDT CAKE

Schokoladenkuchen with Schokoladenguß

To prepare glaze: In a medium saucepan, stir together sugar and cocoa until completely blended and smooth. Stir in coffee, then corn syrup, until smoothly incorporated. Bring mixture just to a boil, stirring, over medium-high heat. Boil for 1½ minutes; remove from heat. Immediately add chocolate, stirring until completely melted and smooth. A chunk or two at a time, stir in butter until glaze is completely smooth. Stir in vanilla. Set glaze aside about 10 to 15 minutes until partially cooled and just slightly thickened.

Rotating cake as you work, slowly pour glaze over top, allowing it to drip, and completely coat surface. If necessary, reapply glaze that drips off cake to cover any unglazed areas, avoiding any crumbs so smooth surfaces will not be marred. Let cake stand about 15 minutes, until excess glaze has dripped from sides. Working carefully and using several wide spatulas, lift cake from rack to serving plate. Serve immediately or store, covered and in a cool place (not refrigerated), for a day or two.   *Makes 9 to 10 servings*

CHOCOLATE PUDDING CAKE

Position a rack in center of oven and preheat to 350°F. Generously grease a 2-quart or slightly larger soufflé dish, round baking dish, or square or round oven-proof casserole.

To prepare cake: In a food processor fitted with a steel blade, combine chocolate chips, sugar, cocoa powder, flour, baking powder, coffee powder (if used), and salt. Process until chocolate chips are very finely ground and mixture is well blended. Sprinkle butter over dry ingredients. Process in on/off pulses until butter is evenly incorporated and mixture resembles fine meal. Add sour cream, egg, and vanilla to processor and process just until evenly incorporated and smooth. If necessary, stop machine and stir to distribute ingredients once or twice. Turn out batter into prepared dish, spreading to edges with greased table knife.

To prepare sauce: Rinse out and drain processor bowl and reinsert rinsed blade. Add chocolate chips and sugar. Process until chips are finely chopped. With motor running, slowly add ¾ cup very hot tap water through feed tube, processing until mixture is very smooth and well blended. Continuing to process, slowly add ⅓ cup more hot tap water, then vanilla. Process until mixture is smooth (it will be thin). Pour sauce over batter; *do not stir.*

Bake for 45 to 55 minutes until top is puffy and springs back when lightly pressed in the center. Cool cake on wire rack for about 7 to 10 minutes. Spoon into bowls and serve immediately. Garnish with scoops of vanilla ice cream or heavy cream or whipped cream, if desired. Alternatively, for a more formal presentation, run a knife around cake edge to loosen from dish sides. Insert knife under edge of cake to lift and loosen from bottom. Center a rimmed serving plate over casserole. Holding casserole and plate firmly together, invert so cake rests on plate. Spoon any sauce remaining in casserole around cake edges. Cut into wedges, spoon sauce over each wedge, and serve immediately. Serve with ice cream or whipped cream, if desired.

Makes 5 to 6 servings

Cake
⅓ cup (2 ounces) semisweet chocolate chips
¾ cup granulated sugar
¼ cup unsweetened, nonalkalized, American-style cocoa powder (such as Hershey's)
1 cup all-purpose flour
1¼ teaspoons baking powder
½ teaspoon instant coffee powder or granules (optional)
⅛ teaspoon salt
½ cup (1 stick) unsalted butter, cut into chunks
¾ cup sour cream or ⅔ cup plain unsweetened yogurt
1 large egg
1 teaspoon vanilla extract

Sauce and Garnish
⅔ cup (4 ounces) semisweet chocolate chips
½ cup granulated sugar
1 teaspoon vanilla extract
Ice cream or whipped cream, for garnish (optional)

A German homemaker might serve this cake with afternoon coffee. It is easy and homey and has a delicate yet gratifying taste and a wonderfully tender crumb. It is reminiscent of some American pound cakes and 1-2-3-4 cakes but is not quite the same as either. The chocolate marbling adds not only visual interest but a nice flavor element. It tastes best the day it is made.

Position a rack in center of oven and preheat to 350°F. Generously grease, then flour a 12-cup or slightly larger Bundt pan (or tube pan). Put chocolate in the top of a double boiler over about 1 inch hot but not simmering water. Melt chocolate, stirring occasionally, then set aside with boiler top still over bottom so chocolate will stay warm. Stir together flour, sugar, baking powder, and salt in a large mixer bowl. In a medium bowl, using a fork, beat together eggs, yolk, milk, and vanilla, until blended.

Add butter and half of egg mixture to dry ingredients. Beat on low speed until thoroughly incorporated but not overmixed. Raise speed to high and beat for 1 minute. Add remaining egg mixture and beat on high speed 1 minute longer, until batter is fluffy and smooth. Stir together melted chocolate and 1¼ cups batter until well blended. Spoon out generous half of plain batter into five or six pools in prepared pan. Spoon pools of chocolate batter into spaces between pools of plain batter. Top with pools of remaining plain batter. Swirl table knife through batter until desired marbling is achieved.

> 3 ounces bittersweet (not unsweetened) or semisweet chocolate
> 3 cups cake flour, sifted after measuring
> 1½ cups granulated sugar
> 1¾ teaspoons baking powder
> ½ teaspoon salt
> 4 large eggs, plus 1 large egg yolk
> ⅓ cup whole milk
> 2½ teaspoons vanilla extract
> 1½ cups (3 sticks) unsalted butter, slightly softened
> Powdered sugar, for garnishing cake top (optional)

Bake cake for 55 to 65 minutes or until a toothpick inserted in the thickest part comes out clean. Transfer pan to wire rack and let stand until cake is completely cooled. Run a knife around pan edges to loosen. Invert pan and slide out cake. Reinvert cake onto serving plate. Dust with a little sifted powdered sugar, if desired.

This cake is good plain or served with a dollop of whipped cream. It is also excellent served like American pound cake, with vanilla ice cream and chocolate sauce.

Makes 10 to 12 servings

MARBLED BUNDT CAKE

Swartz-Weiß Butterkuchen

FRANCE

CHOCOLATE MOUSSE CAKE

Gâteau de Mousse au Chocolat

Position rack in center of oven and preheat to 325°F. Very generously grease a 8- to 8½-inch-by-2½- or 3-inch springform pan. Insert a wax-paper round cut to fit. Grease wax paper generously. Evenly dust pan bottom and sides with 1 tablespoon cocoa powder, tapping out excess.

Coarsely chop 8 ounces chocolate. Very finely chop remaining 1½ ounces chocolate and reserve separately. In the top of a double boiler, over hot but not simmering water, heat 8 ounces chocolate, stirring occasionally, until completely melted and smooth. Remove top of double boiler from bottom. Two or 3 tablespoons at a time, whisk butter into chocolate, until evenly incorporated and mixture is thick and smooth.

In a large mixer bowl with mixer on low speed, beat egg yolks, 1¼ cups sugar, and vanilla, until blended. Raise speed to high and beat 3 to 4 minutes or until mixture is thick, lightened, and fluffy. Beat in remaining 2 tablespoons cocoa powder until smoothly incorporated. With a rubber spatula, fold chocolate-butter mixture evenly into yolk mixture.

In a large, grease-free mixing bowl with grease-free beaters, beat egg whites on low speed until frothy. Gradually raise speed to high and beat just until soft peaks form. A bit at a time, beat in remaining ¼ cup sugar. Continue beating until whites stand in firm but not dry peaks. Using a rubber spatula, gently but thoroughly fold whites into yolk mixture until thoroughly and evenly incorporated.

Cake

3 tablespoons unsweetened cocoa powder, preferably Dutch-process (European-style), divided

9½ ounces bittersweet (not unsweetened) or semisweet chocolate, divided

⅔ cup (1 stick plus 2⅔ tablespoons) unsalted butter

9 large egg yolks

1½ cups granulated sugar, divided

2 teaspoons vanilla extract

7 large egg whites, completely free of yolk

Stabilized Whipped Cream and Garnish

½ teaspoon unflavored gelatin

1½ cups heavy (whipping) cream, divided

¼ cup powdered sugar

¼ teaspoon vanilla extract

Chocolate curls, shavings, or ruffles, for garnish

Cocoa powder for sifting over cake top (optional)

Immediately turn out two thirds of batter into prepared pan, spreading mixture to edges. Reserve remainder of mixture in a medium saucepan.

Bake cake for 15 minutes. Lower heat to 300°F. and continue baking 40 to 45 minutes longer, or until surface springs back when lightly tapped (cake will seem underdone and slightly moist in center).

Meanwhile, return reserved mousse mixture to burner over medium-low heat, stirring constantly and scraping entire pan bottom to prevent sticking, until mixture reaches 160°F. on a candy thermometer, about 6 minutes. (If thermometer is unavailable, heat until mixture is very hot to the touch, but not boiling, or eggs may curdle.) Immediately remove from heat and stir in 1½ ounces reserved chocolate until completely melted and smooth. Cover and refrigerate mousse until well chilled, at least 1 hour.

Let cake stand on wire rack until completely cooled, about 2 hours. (It will sink slightly in the middle and surface will be cracked.) Run a knife around edges to loosen. Release springform pan sides. Carefully lay a serving plate over mousse cake. Holding cake and plate firmly together, invert cake onto plate. Loosen pan bottom from wax paper with a paring knife; then lift pan from wax paper. Peel wax paper from cake. Brush off any loose crumbs from cake top. Using a long-bladed spatula or table knife, spread mousse over cake top almost to edge, working so surface is even. Cover loosely and refrigerate.

To prepare whipped cream: Sprinkle gelatin over ⅓ cup cream in a small saucepan. Stirring frequently and breaking up any lumps, set aside for about 5 minutes until gelatin softens. Bring mixture to a simmer over medium-high heat, and heat, stirring, until gelatin completely dissolves. Remove from heat and stir cream-gelatin mixture into remaining cream until well blended. Refrigerate until very well chilled. With mixer on high speed, whip cream until very soft peaks form. Add powdered sugar and vanilla, continuing to beat until firm peaks form. Spread cream smoothly over cake top and sides. Decorate bottom edge with piped whipped cream shells, if desired. Garnish cake top with chocolate curls, shavings, or ruffles (see page 246 for directions on creating and arranging ruffles). Cover and refrigerate for up to 24 hours (or freeze, undecorated, for up to a week), if desired. Just before serving, dust curls or ruffles with light sifting of cocoa powder, if desired.

Serve mousse cake lightly chilled but not cold, cut into wedges.

Makes 8 to 10 servings

This light yet rich dessert delivers the big raspberry-and-chocolate taste many fans of this wonderful flavor combination seek in a recipe. The basic components include a classic genoise cake, a raspberry-chocolate mousse, and a simple chocolate-cream glaze, or ganache. The gâteau is at its best and most beautiful when fresh raspberries are in season and can be tucked between the layers and used for garnish. However, even when fresh fruit is unavailable, a very fine, handsome cake with real raspberry appeal can still be produced. The secret is frozen raspberries in syrup, which are sold year-round.

To prepare cake: Position a rack in center of oven and preheat to 350°F. Grease an 8-inch springform pan. Line pan bottom with a wax-paper round cut to fit. Generously grease paper. Dust paper and pan sides with flour, tapping out excess.

Combine eggs, sugar, salt, and vanilla in a large mixer bowl. Over very low heat, set bowl over a pan of almost simmering water and warm mixture, stirring constantly, until almost hot to the touch. Remove bowl from pan of water; wipe off bowl. Beat mixture with mixer set on high speed for 4 to 5 minutes, until thick and about triple in volume. Lower mixer speed to medium and continue beating for 4 to 6 minutes longer; mixture will deflate slightly (which helps stabilize it). Combine flour and cocoa powder in a sifter and sift over beaten eggs. Using a rubber spatula, gently but quickly fold in flour mixture, turning bowl and scraping to the bottom to incorporate evenly. Add ½ cup of batter to butter and mix until blended. Add butter mixture back to batter and continue folding until just evenly incorporated but not overmixed, being sure to scrape to bottom of bowl. Immediately turn batter into pan, lightly spreading out to edges.

Quickly transfer to oven and bake for 27 to 33 minutes or until cake springs back when lightly pressed in center, and a toothpick inserted in thickest part comes out clean. Transfer pan to a wire rack. Let stand until thoroughly cooled. Run a knife around pan edges to loosen cake sides. Release springform sides. Place cake, with pan bottom attached,

Chocolate Cake (Genoise)

5 large eggs
⅔ cup granulated sugar
Pinch of salt
1½ teaspoons vanilla extract
⅔ cup all-purpose flour
⅓ cup unsweetened cocoa powder, preferably Dutch-process (European-style)
3 tablespoons melted and slightly cooled unsalted butter

(Continued on page 60)

SWITZERLAND

CHOCOLATE-RASPBERRY MOUSSE CAKE

Gâteau de Mousse au Chocolat et aux Framboises

cake-side down on rack. Carefully remove pan bottom, as the flat surface will be cake top. Cake is best made ahead and stored, wrapped airtight, for 8 hours (or refrigerated for up to 3 days and frozen for up to 2 weeks).

To prepare mousse and glaze: Sprinkle gelatin over 2½ tablespoons cold water in small bowl; let stand to soften. Set raspberries and syrup in a fine sieve over a bowl. Press syrup and pulp through; discard seeds. Put berry mixture in a 1-quart microwave-safe measure or bowl. Microwave, uncovered, 3 minutes on high, then 3 to 4 minutes on medium power until mixture reduces to ½ cup. (Alternatively, place in a medium saucepan and simmer very gently until reduced to ½ cup.) Add softened gelatin to berries, stirring until gelatin dissolves. Bring 1 cup cream to a boil over medium-high heat. Add chocolate, stirring until it completely melts and mixture is smooth. Stir in 1 tablespoon brandy. Measure out a generous ⅓ cup melted chocolate and stir into berry mixture. Cover remaining chocolate and set aside at room temperature. Refrigerate gelatin mixture until beginning to set but not firm, about 15 to 20 minutes.

To assemble cake: Whip remaining 1⅔ cups cream with granulated sugar until peaks are almost firm. Fold whipped cream and vanilla into gelatin mixture. Peel paper from cake bottom and discard, working carefully as this flat, smooth surface will serve as cake top. Using a large serrated knife, slice cake into three layers. (If desired, add cutting guides around cake by measuring and marking sides into thirds with toothpicks.) Return one layer (not the flat-surfaced bottom layer to be used for top) to washed and dried springform pan. Stir remaining 1

Chocolate-Raspberry Mousse and Glaze

2½ teaspoons unflavored gelatin
1 10-ounce package frozen raspberries in syrup, thawed
2⅔ cups heavy (whipping) cream, divided
8 ounces bittersweet (not unsweetened) or semisweet chocolate, finely chopped
2 tablespoons raspberry brandy, Grand Marnier, or kirsch, divided
¼ cup granulated sugar
1 teaspoon vanilla extract
¼ cup seedless red-raspberry jam or jelly
1 pint fresh red raspberries (optional)
Decorations (optional)
Fresh red raspberries
Lightly sweetened whipped cream

tablespoon brandy into raspberry jam. Evenly cover the cake layer in pan with half of raspberry jam. Spread half of chocolate-raspberry mousse evenly over layer. If fresh berries are used, sprinkle half of them over mousse. Top with second cake layer and press down evenly. Evenly spread layer with remaining jam, then with remaining mousse. Top with berries, if used. Brush any loose crumbs from flat surface of top layer. Center it, flat-side up over mousse, pressing down all over until cake is level. Cover and refrigerate for at least 1 hour, until cake is cold and mousse sets.

Carefully run a knife, dipped in hot water and then dried, around cake sides. Release cake from springform sides. Set cake, still resting on springform pan bottom, on a wire rack placed over a large plate or tray (to catch drips). Smooth out mousse on cake sides, if necessary. If the reserved chocolate mixture has cooled completely and stiffened, barely warm it over lowest heat, stirring gently, until it is pourable but not runny. Pour generous three fourths of glaze over cake top. Using a long-bladed spatula or large knife and working quickly, spread out glaze so it forms a thin layer and runs over edges and covers cake sides. For best appearance, use only a few light strokes and let excess chocolate drip off. Touch up sides with remaining glaze. Carefully lift rack and rap against counter several times so excess chocolate runs off. Let stand until glaze begins to set. Lift pan; wipe off any excess chocolate from pan edge. Add large dab of glaze to center of serving plate and press down pan bottom to anchor it. Refrigerate cake until glaze sets and mousse is well chilled, at least 2 hours.

Optional garnish: Arrange or scatter some perfect berries on cake top. If desired, also pipe whipped-cream rosettes at even intervals around edge of cake top.

Serve cake chilled. Cut with a large knife, wiping off blade between cuts. Gâteau prepared with fresh raspberries will keep 24 hours; without fresh berries, 48 hours.   *Makes 12 to 14 servings*

White Chocolate Fruit Fools

CHAPTER

**MOUSSES,
PUDDINGS AND
SOUFFLES**

FOUR

Fools are simple, fruit-swirled whipped cream desserts that originated in Great Britain. They were introduced into America by British settlers and became very popular in the South. ❖ In the following updated version, the whipped cream is enlivened with lemon zest and white chocolate. The recipe also includes several different fruit possibilities —traditional blackberry, plus papaya-orange, strawberry-raspberry, and kiwi-lime. To serve an appealing variety of fools at one time, prepare at least three of the four fruit combinations suggested here, or devise three choices of your own using whatever berries or fruits you have on hand.

WHITE CHOCOLATE-FRUIT FOOLS

To prepare fool: Sprinkle gelatin over lemon juice in a small saucepan. Let stand for about 5 minutes, until gelatin softens. *Slowly melt* white chocolate in top of a double boiler over about 1 inch of slightly hot water, stirring occasionally. With top still over bottom, set melted chocolate aside. Stir together sour cream, sugar, lemon zest, and vanilla in a small bowl; set aside. Heat gelatin mixture over medium heat, stirring until gelatin completely dissolves. Stir gelatin into sour cream mixture.

In a large mixer bowl, beat cream to firm but not stiff peaks. Stir white chocolate into sour cream mixture, until smoothly incorporated. Using a wire whisk, whisk white chocolate mixture into whipped cream, until evenly incorporated. Fool is best placed in serving dishes or chocolate cups with fruit coulis, then chilled for 2 to 3 hours before serving. (Alternatively, it may be held, covered and refrigerated, for up to 24 hours before assembling with fruit.)

Strawberry-raspberry and blackberry fruit mixtures may be prepared 24 hours ahead of assembly; papaya-orange and kiwi-lime should be prepared only an hour or so ahead to preserve fresh taste and bright color.

White Chocolate Fool

$1/4$ teaspoon unflavored gelatin

2 teaspoons fresh lemon juice

$31/2$ ounces top-quality white chocolate, chopped

$1/4$ cup sour cream

$1/4$ cup granulated sugar

Generous $1/8$ teaspoon very finely grated lemon zest (yellow part of skin)

$1/2$ teaspoon vanilla extract

$11/2$ cups heavy (whipping) cream

For blackberry coulis: In a medium saucepan, stir together 3 tablespoons sugar and cornstarch, until well blended. Stir in blackberries until coated with mixture. Bring mixture to a simmer over medium-low heat, stirring. Simmer 3 to 4 minutes longer, until berries exude their juice and mixture thickens just slightly. Press mixture through a fine sieve into a storage bowl. Taste and stir in a bit more sugar, if necessary; mixture should be tart.

For papaya (or mango)-orange coulis: No more than an hour or so before assembling desserts, combine papaya (or mango), orange segments, lemon juice, and orange zest in a blender (or food processor). Blend until completely smooth. Transfer mixture to a storage container. Stir in sugar to taste.

For strawberry-raspberry coulis: Combine strawberries and raspberries in a blender (or food processor). Blend until completely pureed. Press mixture through a very fine sieve into a storage bowl. Stir in sugar to taste; coulis should be tart.

For kiwi-lime coulis: Combine kiwi fruit and lime juice in a food processor. Process in on/off pulses *just until pulpy* but *do not process further or seeds may be ground up and discolor mixture.* Press mixture through a very fine sieve into a storage bowl, discarding seeds. Stir in lime zest and sugar to taste; mixture should be tart.

Cover fruit mixtures and refrigerate until well chilled, before serving.

To assemble desserts: Spoon about a third of white chocolate fool into chocolate cups, serving dishes, or parfait glasses. Divide about half of each coulis among three or four servings, swirling mixtures slightly. Repeat process, adding another third of fool, then most of remaining coulis (reserve a small amount for garnishing servings), and swirling slightly. Cover with remaining fool. Top each serving with a small decorative swirl of coulis. Cover and refrigerate until well chilled, about 2 hours.   *Makes 9 medium-sized or 12 small servings*

Blackberry Coulis

3 to 4 tablespoons granulated sugar

½ teaspoon cornstarch

2 cups fresh or dry-pack (unsweetened) frozen blackberries

Papaya- or Mango-Orange Coulis

1¼ cups ripe papaya or mango chunks

Membrane-free, seeded segments of 1 medium orange

1 teaspoon fresh lemon juice

⅛ teaspoon very finely grated orange zest (orange part of skin)

2 to 4 teaspoons granulated sugar

Strawberry-Raspberry Coulis

1¼ cups coarsely sliced fresh strawberries

⅔ cup fresh raspberries

1 to 2 tablespoons granulated sugar

Kiwi-Lime Coulis

1¼ cups fully ripe kiwi-fruit chunks (3 to 4 medium, peeled kiwi fruit)

¼ teaspoon fresh lime juice

Very finely grated zest (green part of skin) of 1 medium lime

2 to 3 tablespoons granulated sugar

Chocolate mousse is a French classic, and one of the hallmark recipes of French restaurants around the world. Of course, it has also become an international favorite, and turns up on dessert carts wherever fine sweets are enjoyed. ❖ *This is a slightly dense, very smooth, chocolatey mousse. Since the flavor of any mousse depends so much on the special character of the chocolate used, it is worth selecting a high-quality brand. My personal favorite for this recipe is Lindt Excellence.*

❖ *For a mousse with a hint of orange, add orange zest and Grand Marnier. For a pure, smooth chocolate flavor, omit the orange zest and use crème de cacao instead of Grand Marnier.*

CHOCOLATE MOUSSE

Mousse au Chocolat

In the top of a double boiler, over about 1 inch hot but not simmering water, heat chocolate and butter, stirring occasionally, until melted and smooth. Set aside with top of double boiler still over bottom to keep chocolate warm.

In a medium, non-aluminum saucepan, over medium-low heat, whisk together sugar, egg yolks, orange zest (if used), and 2½ tablespoons hot tap water, until blended. If using a candy thermometer to gauge doneness, clip it to pan side, inserting so tip is completely submerged but not touching pan bottom. Continuously whisking and scraping pan bottom, adjust burner and cook so mixture heats efficiently but gently enough so that it *does not near the boiling point* (which might cause the yolks to curdle). If mixture begins to overheat, lift from burner, whisking a few seconds. Continue whisking for about four minutes, until mixture is slightly hot to the touch, light, and slightly thickened (or until it registers 160° to 161°F. on candy thermometer).

Immediately remove pan from heat and whisk in crème de cacao (or Grand Marnier), vanilla, and ⅓ cup hot tap

> 8 ounces bittersweet (not unsweetened) chocolate
>
> 3 tablespoons unsalted butter
>
> ⅓ cup granulated sugar
>
> 4 large egg yolks
>
> Generous pinch of very finely grated orange zest (orange part of skin) add only if Grand Marnier is used
>
> 1 tablespoon crème de cacao (or coffee), or Grand Marnier
>
> 1 teaspoon vanilla extract
>
> 1½ cups heavy (whipping) cream
>
> Whipped cream or crème fraîche, for garnish (optional)

water. Strain mixture through a fine sieve into chocolate. Whisk mixture into chocolate until well blended and smooth. Immediately whip cream in a larger mixer bowl with mixer on high speed, until cream stands in soft peaks. Whisk about 2 tablespoons cream into slightly warm chocolate mixture. Then whisk chocolate mixture into cream until completely smooth and well blended.

Spoon mousse into individual bowls, demitasse cups, or sherbet dishes; mousse is rich so keep servings fairly small.

Chill thoroughly, at least 4 hours, before serving. Garnish servings with dollops of whipped cream or crème fraîche, if desired. Do not allow mousse to stand unrefrigerated for more than a few minutes before serving, or it will become too soft. *Makes 9 to 12 servings*

This is a very smooth, creamy mousse with a subtle mocha flavor. Unlike classic French mousse, which is aerated with egg whites, this version is lightened with whipped cream. The result is a rich but not too heavy dessert.

CHOCOLATE MOCHA MOUSSE

Mousse au Chocolat et au Café à la Crème Fouettée

In the top of a double boiler, over about 1 inch hot but not simmering water, heat chocolate, stirring occasionally, until melted and smooth. Set aside with double boiler top still over pan bottom to keep chocolate warm.

Combine sugar and coffee in a 1-quart saucepan over high heat, heating just until sugar dissolves and mixture just comes to a boil. Meanwhile put yolks, instant coffee powder, 1 tablespoon hot tap water, and salt in a large mixer bowl. Beat on high speed for about 5 minutes, until lightened and very fluffy. Continuing to beat on high speed, pour boiling coffee syrup in a thin stream down bowl sides (avoiding beaters), until completely incorporated. Continue beating about 5 minutes longer, until mixture is very light, thickened, and greatly increased in volume.

Transfer mixture to a medium saucepan over medium-low heat. Adjusting heat as needed so mixture warms efficiently, but gently, and continuously whisking and scraping pan bottom with a wire whisk, heat for about 4 to 5 minutes, until mixture is hot to the touch but *not near the boiling point.* (If using a candy thermometer to gauge doneness, clip it to pan side, inserting so tip is completely submerged but not touching pan bottom. Cook mixture, stirring and scraping pan bottom, until the thermometer registers 160°F.) Immediately remove mixture from heat, continuing to whisk about 3 minutes longer, until mixture cools slightly. A bit at a time, whisk slightly warm chocolate into egg mixture just until thoroughly incorporated. Whisk in coffee liqueur (if used).

Immediately whip cream in a large mixer bowl with mixer set on high speed, until it stands in firm but not stiff peaks. Whisk about ¼ cup whipped cream into chocolate mixture. Whisk chocolate mixture back into cream until completely smooth and well blended. Spoon mousse into individual bowls, mousse cups, or sherbet dishes.

Chill at least 3 hours and up to 48 hours before serving. Garnish servings, chilled, with dollops of whipped cream, if desired. *Makes 8 to 12 servings*

9 ounces bittersweet (not unsweetened) or semisweet chocolate, coarsely chopped
⅓ cup plus 1 tablespoon granulated sugar
⅓ cup coffee
6 large egg yolks
Scant ½ teaspoon instant coffee powder or granules
Pinch of salt
1 tablespoon Kahlúa or other coffee-flavored liqueur (optional)
2 cups heavy (whipping) cream
Whipped cream for garnish (optional)

CHOCOLATE SOUFFLÉ

Soufflé au Chocolat

Position rack in lower third of oven and preheat to 400°F. Generously grease or spray with nonstick vegetable cooking spray a 1½-quart soufflé dish. Fit soufflé dish with a 4-inch-wide aluminum foil collar. (To prepare collar, tear off a sheet of foil long enough to fit around and slightly overlap rim of dish. Fold over foil several times to form a 4-inch-wide band. With band extending at least 2 inches above rim, wrap it around outside edge of dish, overlapping ends and fastening securely with straight pins or by tying with natural-fiber string.)

Combine butter and flour in a medium-sized, heavy saucepan. Heat mixture over medium heat, stirring, until butter melts and mixture is smooth. Cook, stirring, for one minute. Stirring vigorously, add milk until well blended and smooth. Bring mixture to a boil, stirring vigorously and scraping pan bottom. Immediately remove from heat. Add chocolate to milk mixture, stirring until completely melted and smooth. Stir in vanilla. Set aside.

> 3 tablespoons unsalted butter, cut into pats
> 3½ tablespoons all-purpose flour
> ¾ cup whole milk
> 3½ ounces bittersweet chocolate, chopped moderately fine
> 1½ teaspoons vanilla extract
> 5 large eggs, separated
> Generous pinch of salt
> ⅔ cup granulated sugar, divided
> 1 tablespoon cognac or good brandy
> 1 tablespoon Grand Marnier
> Lightly sweetened whipped cream, for serving with soufflé (optional)

In a mixer bowl, beat egg yolks, salt, and half the sugar, until blended. Continue beating on high speed for 4 to 5 minutes, until mixture is light and thick and drops from beaters in slowly flowing ribbons. Adding a small amount at a time, stir yolk mixture into barely warm chocolate mixture until well blended and smooth. Stir in cognac and Grand Marnier.

In a large, completely grease-free mixer bowl with mixer set on medium speed, beat whites until very frothy. Raise speed to high and beat until whites begin to form peaks. Gradually add remaining sugar, continuing to beat on high speed until soft peaks form. Using a wire whisk, whisk about a cup of whites into chocolate mixture. Add chocolate mixture back to remaining egg whites, whisking until completely blended but not overmixed. Spoon mixture into prepared dish.

Set soufflé dish on a baking sheet. Bake for 25 minutes. Lower oven setting to 375°F. and continue baking six to 12 minutes, or until top is almost firm and puffy (center should still be moist and look underdone). Serve immediately, passing a bowl of lightly sweetened whipped cream, if desired. *Makes 4 to 5 servings*

TRI-COLOR
CHOCOLATE TERRINE
GRAND HÔTEL NATIONAL

La Terrine de Chocolat Trois Couleurs

Following is my adaptation of an elegant mousse recipe that I obtained from the Von Pfyffer Restaurant in the Grand Hôtel National in Lucerne, Switzerland. ❖ The terrine features contrasting ribbons of dark chocolate, white chocolate, and milk chocolate–mocha mousse. It is rich and smooth as silk. ❖ Though preparing the individual terrine layers is a bit time-consuming, the techniques involved are fairly easy.

Lightly grease an 11-by-4-inch French terrine (loaf) pan, 8½-by-4½-inch loaf pan, or other 1½-quart loaf pan. Line pan as follows: Cut a piece of wax paper the same *width* as the pan and long enough to cover pan bottom and overhang its *longer sides* by at least 1 inch. Insert wax paper into pan, adjusting and smoothing to remove any wrinkles. Grease bottom surface lightly. Cut a piece of wax paper the *width* of the *pan ends* and long enough to cover bottom and *overhang shorter sides* by at least 1 inch. Insert paper into pan, adjusting and smoothing to any wrinkles. Set aside.

1¾ teaspoons unflavored gelatin, divided
½ cup whole milk
1 teaspoon vanilla extract
9 large egg yolks
5 ounces top-quality Swiss bittersweet (not unsweetened) chocolate, coarsely chopped
3 cups heavy (whipping) cream, divided
1½ tablespoons cognac (or water if preferred)
6 ounces top-quality Swiss white chocolate, coarsely chopped
6 ounces top-quality Swiss milk chocolate, coarsely chopped
Generous ½ teaspoon instant espresso coffee powder (if unavailable, substitute regular instant coffee powder)
Dark- and white-chocolate curls, for garnish (optional)
Caramel-Chocolate Sauce (page 234), for serving (optional)

Sprinkle 1¼ teaspoons gelatin over milk in the top of a double boiler. Let stand about 5 minutes until gelatin softens. With double boiler top placed directly over medium-high heat, heat milk just to a boil, stirring until gelatin dissolves. Stir in vanilla. Place egg yolks in a bowl and slowly whisk in about half of milk mixture. Whisk egg yolk mixture back into top of double boiler. Set double boiler top over a bottom filled with about 1 inch hot but not simmering water. Heat mixture over medium-low heat, stirring constantly and scraping pan sides and bottom until mixture reaches 160°F. (or is very hot to the touch and coats the spoon), about 5 minutes; be careful not to overheat mixture or it may curdle. Immediately remove double boiler top from bottom. Strain mixture through a fine sieve into a measuring cup.

For bittersweet chocolate layer: Melt bittersweet chocolate in the top of a double boiler over about 1 inch hot but not simmering water, until completely melted, stirring occasionally. Set aside with double boiler top still over pan bottom to keep chocolate warm. In a mixer bowl with mixer on high speed, beat a third of yolk mixture for about 1 minute, until very frothy. Gradually add chocolate, beating until well blended and smooth. Scrape down bowl sides several times. In a separate mixer bowl with mixer on high speed, beat 1 cup cream until it stands in firm but not dry peaks. Using a whisk, beat a generous dollop of cream into chocolate mixture until evenly incorporated. Whisk in remaining whipped cream until evenly incorporated but not overmixed. Turn out mousse into terrine pan, being careful not to dislodge wax-paper lining. Rap pan on counter and shake to even surface. Cover and freeze for about 30 minutes, or until layer is firm enough to hold when topped with another layer.

For white chocolate layer: Sprinkle remaining ½ teaspoon gelatin over cognac in a small heat-proof bowl or cup. Let stand for 5 minutes. Set gelatin container in a larger saucepan. Add a little hot water to larger pan. Place larger pan over medium heat and heat gelatin, stirring, until smooth and syrupy. Let cool slightly. (Alternatively, place gelatin in microwave-safe container and microwave on 50-percent power, turning and stirring every 10 seconds, until completely smooth and syrupy.) Meanwhile, *very slowly* melt white chocolate in the top of a double boiler, over about 1 inch hot but not simmering water, until completely melted, stirring occasionally (do not overheat or white chocolate may lump). Set aside with double boiler top still over pan bottom to keep chocolate warm. In a mixer bowl with mixer on high speed beat another third of egg yolk mixture with warm cognac mixture until very frothy. Gradually add white chocolate, beating until well blended and smooth. Scrape down sides of bowl several times. In a separate mixer bowl with mixer on high speed, beat 1 cup cream until it stands in firm but not dry peaks. Using a whisk, beat several dollops of cream into white chocolate mixture until evenly incorporated. Whisk in remaining whipped cream until evenly incorporated but not overmixed. Turn out mixture over bittersweet layer in terrine pan. Rap pan on counter and shake to even surface. Cover and freeze for at least 35 to 45 minutes or until firm enough to hold when topped with another layer.

For milk chocolate–coffee layer: Melt milk chocolate in the top of double boiler over about 1 inch hot but not simmering water, until completely melted, stirring occasionally. Set aside with double boiler top still over pan bottom to keep chocolate warm. In a mixer bowl with mixer on high speed, beat in remaining egg yolk mixture with coffee powder until coffee dissolves and mixture is very frothy. Gradually add milk chocolate, beating until well blended and smooth, and scraping down bowl several times. In a separate mixer bowl with mixer on high speed, beat remaining 1 cup cream until it stands in firm peaks. Using a whisk, beat a generous dollop of cream into chocolate mixture until smoothly incorporated. Whisk in remaining whipped cream until evenly incorporated but not overmixed. Turn out mixture over white chocolate layer in terrine pan. Rap pan on counter and shake to even surface. Cover and refrigerate for at least four hours or until terrine is thoroughly chilled (or wrap airtight and freeze for up to three days, allowing to thaw in refrigerator before serving).

To unmold terrine, dip pan in hot water for about 5 seconds. Carefully slip a knife between wax paper and pan edge to loosen paper and terrine. Pulling on overlapping ends of paper, invert terrine and release onto serving plate (or onto cutting board if serving individually plated slices). Gently peel off wax paper. If surface is soft from unmolding, immediately return terrine to refrigerator until firm.

To serve, slice terrine at the table, or cut terrine into slices and arrange individually on chilled dessert plates. Slice using a large knife wiped clean between each cut. If desired, serve slices garnished with dark- and white-chocolate curls or fresh flower petals, as shown. Whole terrine or slices may also be presented on Caramel-Chocolate Sauce, if desired. *Makes 9 to 11 slices*

This delicious, mildly flavored bavarian cream is accented with tiny bits of bittersweet chocolate and garnished with white chocolate–enriched whipped cream. ❖ *For a particularly dramatic and appealing presentation, serve the bavarian with a strawberry sauce and wild strawberries. Also called fraises des bois, these small, flavorful berries can sometimes be purchased frozen, in which case arrange them, still partially frozen, around the dessert just before serving. If fresh or frozen wild strawberries are unavailable, substitute small, perfect fresh strawberries.*

To prepare bavarian: Sprinkle gelatin over rum and ½ tablespoon cold water in a small bowl. Place egg whites in a grease-free bowl; cover and set aside. Put yolks in a small non-aluminum bowl. In a medium-sized, heavy saucepan bring milk just to a boil over medium-high heat. Immediately remove from heat. Pour a scant third of milk over white chocolate in a medium bowl, stirring until chocolate partially melts and mixture is very well combined. Stir in another 2 tablespoons hot milk until mixture is completely melted and smooth. Set aside.

Add 3 tablespoons sugar and lemon (or orange) zest to egg yolks, whisking with a fork until blended. Immediately whisk about half of remaining milk into yolk mixture until well blended. Then pour yolk mixture back into milk in saucepan. (If using a candy thermometer, clip to pan side, inserting so tip is completely submerged but not touching pan bottom.) Return pan to stove, continuously stirring and scraping pan bottom and adjusting burner so mixture heats efficiently but gently enough that it *does not near the boiling point* or eggs may curdle. Watch carefully; if mixture begins to heat rapidly, immediately lift pan from heat and stir vigorously, as overheating may cause it to curdle. Continue cooking until mixture thickens just slightly and coats the spoon (a line drawn across spoon with a finger should remain visible) or until mixture registers 160° to 161°F. on candy thermometer. Immediately remove pan from heat, continuing to stir for 15 seconds. Stir

2¼ teaspoons unflavored gelatin (see Note)
3 tablespoons light rum
4 large eggs, separated (whites completely free of yolk)
1 cup whole milk
5½ ounces top-quality white chocolate, coarsely chopped
5 tablespoons granulated sugar, divided
⅛ teaspoon coarsely grated lemon or orange zest (colored part of skin)
1½ cups heavy (whipping) cream
1½ teaspoons vanilla extract
Pinch of salt
3 ounces bittersweet (not unsweetened) or semisweet chocolate, chopped by hand into scant ⅛-inch pieces
1 10-ounce package frozen strawberries in syrup, thawed (for optional sauce)
1 to 1½ cups fresh or frozen wild strawberries or small regular strawberries (for optional garnish)

WHITE CHOCOLATE BAVARIAN CREAM

Bavaroise aux Chocolats Blanc et Noir

FRANCE

white chocolate mixture and softened gelatin into milk mixture until gelatin dissolves and mixture is completely smooth. Pour mixture through a fine sieve into a large bowl.

Refrigerate mixture, covered and stirring occasionally, until partially set but not at all firm, about 20 to 30 minutes. (If mixture sets too much, place bowl over warm water and whisk until just slightly softened.) Using a wire whisk, lightly whisk chilled mixture until smooth and well blended.

In a mixing bowl, beat heavy cream and vanilla with mixer on high speed until stiff peaks form. Remove ¾ cup whipped cream from mixer bowl. Measure out 2 tablespoons white chocolate mixture and whisk into ¾ cup whipped cream. Cover and refrigerate whipped cream–white chocolate mixture to use as garnish. With completely grease-free beaters in a grease-free mixing bowl, beat egg whites until frothy and opaque. Add salt and beat on high speed until soft peaks begin to form. Add remaining 2 tablespoons sugar and continue beating on high speed until firm, but not dry, peaks form.

Add remaining whipped cream, egg whites, and chopped chocolate to white chocolate mixture. Using a wire whisk, whisk until ingredients are lightly blended. Fold together ingredients with a rubber spatula, until completely blended but not overmixed. Turn out mousse into oiled 6-cup or larger turban, Bundt pan, or ring mold. Chill for at least 5 hours or until cold and completely set.

To prepare sauce: Place thawed strawberries in a fine sieve and press out as much strawberry juice and pulp as possible, discarding seeds. Refrigerate until serving time.

To unmold bavarian and decorate: Dip mold in hot water for about 10 seconds. Loosen edges with a small knife and slide out onto a wide-rimmed platter. Return to refrigerator briefly if necessary to firm up surface melting caused by unmolding. If desired use a ¼- to ½-inch diameter open-star tip, to pipe reserved whipped cream mixture in decorative vertical lines around bavarian sides or in rosettes and shells around top and bottom. (Alternatively, pass whipped cream separately.) If desired, just before serving, spoon strawberry sauce around bavarian, wiping away any drips from edge of plate. Arrange fresh or partially frozen wild strawberries around bavarian center and base, if desired. Serve bavarian cut into slices with sauce spooned over each slice. *Makes 8 to 10 servings*

Note: If the bavarian will be standing at room temperature before serving (for example, on a buffet table) or if served in very hot weather, increase gelatin to 2½ teaspoons.

This recipe was inspired by a bread pudding I tasted in England. Fine-quality bread, raisins, and chocolate, plus the seemingly insignificant amounts of cinnamon and mace, make it exceptionally good. The filling is smooth and custardy and the top is slightly crusty because of the crisping of the bread.

CHOCOLATE BREAD PUDDING

Position rack in center of oven and preheat to 350°F. Lightly grease a 12-by-7½-inch flat baking dish, 2-quart oval gratin dish, or similarly sized casserole. Heat cream in a medium saucepan over medium-high heat just until boiling. Remove pan from heat. Add chocolate and stir until *completely blended and smooth*. Return pan to burner over medium heat. Stirring constantly, very slowly add 1 cup milk to chocolate mixture. Continue stirring until completely blended and smooth. Add ¼ cup butter and sugar, stirring until butter melts. Remove pan from heat and set aside. Using a fork, beat together eggs, yolks, mace, cinnamon, and vanilla in a medium bowl, until well blended. Stir remaining 1⅓ cups milk into eggs. Add egg mixture to chocolate mixture, stirring until thoroughly blended.

Generously butter *one side* of bread slices with remaining ¼ cup butter. Cut slices in half diagonally. Overlapping the slices by about ½ inch, arrange, buttered side up, in rows in baking dish. Sprinkle raisins over slices. Slowly pour chocolate mixture through a fine sieve over bread, being sure to moisten all slices. Let pudding stand for 15 minutes. Set pudding in a larger roasting pan on center oven rack. Fill roasting pan about 1 inch deep with lukewarm water.

⅔ cup light cream

5½ ounces bittersweet (not unsweetened) or semisweet chocolate, coarsely chopped

2⅓ cups whole milk, divided

½ cup (1 stick) unsalted butter, slightly softened (divided)

¾ cup granulated sugar

3 large eggs, plus 2 large egg yolks

Generous pinch of mace

Generous pinch of cinnamon

1 teaspoon vanilla extract

About 10 slices (6 to 7 ounces) fresh, flavorful Italian-style bread, crusts removed

⅓ cup dark seedless raisins

About 1 tablespoon powdered sugar, for garnish (optional)

Heavy cream or whipped cream, for garnish (optional)

Bake pudding for 40 minutes. Lower oven temperature to 325°F. Remove baking dish from water bath. Cover pudding with foil and return dish to oven (without water bath) just until pudding puffs slightly and center feels set when lightly tapped, about 10 minutes longer. Cool pudding about 10 minutes on wire rack before serving. (Or cool, refrigerate, and reheat to very warm but not hot, just prior to serving.)

Just before serving, garnish pudding with light sifting of powdered sugar, if desired. Serve pudding with heavy cream or whipped cream, if desired. *Makes 8 to 10 servings*

QUEEN'S DARK- AND WHITE- CHOCOLATE CHARLOTTE

Charlotte aux Chocolats Noir et Blanc à la Reine

FRANCE

Dramatic and delectable, this classic French dessert boasts layers of creamy white- and dark-chocolate mousse encased in strips of chocolate and vanilla cake. It is the brilliant royal red color of the crowning touch—fresh strawberries set in a raspberry glaze—that gives the Queen's Charlotte its name.

To prepare cake: Position rack in center of oven and preheat to 350°F. Grease bottom and sides of a 10½-by-15-inch (or similar) jelly-roll pan. Line pan with baking parchment (or wax paper). Grease parchment. Fold over a sheet of aluminum foil several times to produce a 1½-inch wide band. Insert band crosswise to divide pan in half and serve as barrier between dark and light cake batters.

With mixer on low speed, lightly beat together yolks, ½ cup sugar, and 1 tablespoon hot water in a large mixer bowl. Raise speed to high and beat for 4 to 5 minutes, until mixture is thick and about triple in volume. Beat in salt and vanilla. By hand, add flour, stirring until partially incorporated. Set aside.

In a grease-free large mixer bowl, beat whites on low, then medium speed, until foamy. Raise speed to high and continue beating just until soft peaks form. Beat in remaining sugar. Continue beating until whites stand in stiff but not dry peaks. Gently but quickly fold whites into batter, turning bowl and scraping to the bottom to incorporate ingredients evenly. Immediately turn out half of batter into one side of prepared pan, lightly spreading to edges. Whisk cocoa powder into remaining batter until evenly incorporated. Pour into other half of pan, spreading to edges.

Quickly transfer to oven and bake for 11 to 15 minutes, or until cake is tinged with brown and springs back when lightly pressed in center. Transfer pan to a wire rack. Lightly drape a clean, damp tea towel over surface of cake. Let cake stand until thoroughly cooled. Cake may be used immediately, but is easier

Cake
6 large eggs, separated (whites completely free of yolk)

¾ cup granulated sugar, divided

⅛ teaspoon salt

1½ teaspoons vanilla extract

½ cup minus 1 tablespoon all-purpose flour

1 tablespoon unsweetened cocoa powder, preferably Dutch-process (European-style)

Powdered sugar and cocoa powder for dusting cake surface and cutting board

Dark- and White-Chocolate Mousses
6 ounces top-quality white chocolate, finely chopped

4½ ounces bittersweet (not unsweetened) chocolate, finely chopped

2½ teaspoons unflavored gelatin

3 tablespoons light rum (or water, if preferred)

¾ cup whole milk

10 large egg yolks

2 teaspoons vanilla extract

2¾ cups heavy (whipping) cream

¼ cup powdered sugar

Garnish
About 3 cups fresh small or medium whole strawberries

1 10-ounce package frozen raspberries in syrup, thawed

½ teaspoon unflavored gelatin

Lightly sweetened whipped cream, for garnish (optional)

to handle if allowed to stand (dust light side with powdered sugar and dark side with cocoa powder, then cover with wax paper and foil) for a few hours (or overnight, if preferred).

Assemble cake as follows: Very generously butter a 9-by-2½- or 3-inch springform pan. Cut through parchment to separate dark and light cake portions. With parchment facing up, transfer vanilla cake portion to a cutting board dusted with powdered sugar; transfer cocoa cake to a cutting board dusted with cocoa powder. Peel off and discard parchment from layers. Trim off any dry edges from portions. Using a sharp knife, cut dark and light portions crosswise into 2¾-inch bands. (If cake sticks, brush knife frequently with vegetable oil and wipe off cake build-up with paper towels.) Then cut bands lengthwise at ¾-inch intervals to yield ¾-inch strips. Alternating dark and light strips, arrange, upright with smooth (bottom) sides out, around perimeter of pan, spacing tightly together and pressing against pan sides so strips stay in place. Set aside.

For mousses: Place white and dark chocolates in separate medium-sized, heat-proof bowls over small saucepans containing about 1 inch of hot but not simmering water. Slowly heat, stirring occasionally, until chocolates are melted and smooth. Remove from heat and set chocolates aside. Sprinkle gelatin over rum in a small bowl or cup. Let stand at least five minutes, until gelatin softens.

Heat milk just to simmering in a double boiler top set over direct heat. Add gelatin mixture to milk, stirring until dissolved. Whisk about half of milk into egg yolks, then whisk yolks back into remaining milk. Set double boiler top over a bottom filled with about 1 inch of gently simmering water. Heat over medium heat, stirring constantly and scraping pan bottom, until mixture reaches 160°F. or is very hot (but not boiling) and coats the spoon, about 3 to 5 minutes. Immediately remove from heat. Stir in vanilla. Strain half of mixture through a fine sieve into white chocolate, and the other half into dark chocolate; stir until both mixtures are well blended. Set white chocolate mixture aside at room temperature. Refrigerate dark chocolate mixture, covered, until just beginning to jell but still fluid, about 10 minutes.

In a large mixer bowl with mixer set on high speed, beat cream until it stands in soft peaks. Add powdered sugar and continue beating until firm peaks form. Using a whisk, fold half of cream into dark chocolate mixture. Pour into pan that is lined with strips of cake, rapping on counter to even surface. Transfer to freezer until surface of mousse firms enough to support second mousse layer, about 15 minutes. Meanwhile, whisk remaining cream into white chocolate mixture; set aside at room temperature, whisking occasionally. When dark chocolate mousse is set, pour white chocolate mousse over top. Rap pan on counter to even surface. Arrange strawberries on mousse, imbedding slightly. Refrigerate for about 20 to 30 minutes, until mousse partially sets.

To prepare raspberries, press them through a fine sieve, reserving pulp and juice in a small saucepan and discarding seeds. Sprinkle gelatin over berry pulp and juice. Let stand about five minutes until gelatin softens. Heat mixture over medium heat, stirring until gelatin dissolves. Set mixture aside for about 10 minutes, until cool to the touch and slightly thickened but not set. Slowly pour raspberry puree over strawberries, being sure to top all berries and gently tipping pan until entire surface is covered. Cover and refrigerate for at least 5 hours and up to 24 hours, until mousse is well chilled and completely set.

To serve: Wrap a damp, hot tea towel around springform pan sides and let stand for a few minutes to soften butter. Carefully remove springform pan sides. Transfer charlotte to serving plate. If desired, pipe a ring of whipped cream shells around top (just inside cake) and bottom of charlotte. Serve immediately. *Makes 12 to 14 servings*

Steamed puddings are a great favorite in the British Isles, where they appear on menus at country inns and charming old hotel restaurants. They are also popular among home cooks. ❖ Served warm, with a dollop of rum hard sauce, this mild, mellow chocolate dessert (more like a moist, light sponge cake than an American-style pudding) makes a gratifying finish to a cool-weather meal. If prepared in a pretty mold or Bundt pan, it is also quite attractive.

STEAMED CHOCOLATE PUDDING WITH RUM HARD SAUCE

To prepare pudding: Generously grease or spray with nonstick vegetable cooking spray an 8-cup tubed pudding mold (or Bundt pan). Set out a deep stockpot or other pot large enough to hold the pudding mold.

Melt butter and chocolate in a medium-sized, heavy saucepan over very low heat, stirring constantly, until well blended and smooth. Remove pan from heat and cool until barely warm to the touch. In a small bowl, beat egg yolks, ½ cup sugar, vanilla, and salt, until blended. Continue beating on high speed for 4 to 5 minutes, until mixture is light and thick and drops from beaters in slowly flowing ribbons. Adding a small amount at a time, stir egg mixture into barely warm chocolate mixture until well blended and smooth. Thoroughly stir together flour and baking powder. Sift dry mixture over chocolate mixture. Using a whisk, fold together very lightly but do not fully incorporate.

In a large, completely grease-free mixer bowl, beat whites with mixer on medium speed, until very frothy. Raise speed to high and beat until whites begin to form peaks. Gradually add remaining sugar, continuing to beat until soft peaks form. Using a wire whisk, whisk about a cup of whites into chocolate mixture. Add chocolate mixture back to remaining egg whites, whisking until completely blended but not over-

Pudding
½ cup unsalted butter, cut into chunks
6 ounces bittersweet (not unsweetened) chocolate, coarsely chopped
6 large eggs, separated (whites completely free of yolk)
1 cup granulated sugar, divided
2½ teaspoons vanilla extract
⅛ teaspoon salt
1 cup all-purpose flour
¾ teaspoon baking powder
Powdered sugar for dusting pudding top (optional)

Rum Hard Sauce
⅔ cup (1 stick plus 2⅔ tablespoons) unsalted butter, slightly softened
½ cup powdered sugar
3 tablespoons light rum
¼ teaspoon vanilla extract

mixed. Spoon mixture into prepared mold, carefully smoothing surface with a knife. Cover mold tightly with lid or heavy-duty foil. Set mold in pot and add enough boiling water to come halfway up mold sides. Cover pot and adjust burner so water simmers gently. (If pot is not deep enough to completely cover mold, enclose mold by making an aluminum foil tent and shaping and crimping it to fit snugly against pot rim.)

Replenishing water once or twice if necessary, steam pudding for 2½ hours, or until top springs back when tapped and a toothpick inserted in thickest part comes out moist but clean. Run a knife around mold to loosen pudding. Unmold onto a serving plate. Dust top of pudding with a very light sifting of powdered sugar, if desired. Serve, cut into slices, while still warm; pass a bowl of hard sauce separately. (If necessary, pudding may be made ahead and rewarmed in a low oven. Cover pudding tightly with aluminum foil and place a pan of hot water on oven floor to keep pudding from drying out.)

To prepare hard sauce: In a mixer bowl with mixer on medium speed, beat together butter, powdered sugar, rum, and vanilla, until completely blended and fluffy. Transfer to storage container or small serving dish. Cover and refrigerate at least 1½ hours and up to a week before serving. Let warm up slightly before serving. *Makes 7 to 8 servings*

This recipe was graciously shared with me by Dietmar Fercher, head pastry chef at the historic Café Central in Vienna's First District and one of the best (some say the best) pastry chefs in the city. Considering Vienna's undisputed reputation as a dessert and pastry capital, this is high praise indeed. ❖ These traditional Austrian puddings are prepared in little oven-proof molds (old-fashioned custard cups work well also) and are served, unmolded, with warm chocolate sauce and whipped cream.

AUSTRIAN CHOCOLATE PUDDINGS

Mohr im Hemd

To prepare puddings: Position rack in center of oven and preheat to 350°F. Generously butter 5 or 6 ¾- to 1-cup heat-proof baking cups or ramekins.

Melt butter and chocolate in a medium-sized, heavy saucepan over very low heat, stirring constantly, until well blended and smooth. Remove pan from heat and cool until barely warm to the touch. In a small bowl, beat egg yolks, salt, and vanilla until blended. Adding a small amount at a time, stir egg mixture into barely warm chocolate mixture, until well blended and smooth. Chop hazelnuts and combine with 2 tablespoons sugar in a blender or food processor. Grind hazelnuts until *very fine* but not oily. (If blender is used, stop motor and stir to redistribute contents several times.)

In a large, completely grease-free mixer bowl, beat egg whites on medium speed until very frothy. Raise speed to high and beat until whites are opaque and begin to form peaks. Gradually add remaining 2 tablespoons sugar, continuing to beat until soft peaks form. Using a wire whisk, whisk about a cup

¼ cup (½ stick) unsalted butter, cut into chunks

2 ounces bittersweet (not unsweetened) chocolate, coarsely chopped

3 large eggs, separated, (whites completely free of yolk)

Pinch of salt

1 teaspoon vanilla extract

½ cup (about 2 ounces) toasted and hulled hazelnuts (see Note)

¼ cup granulated sugar, divided

1 tablespoon very fine breadcrumbs

Thin Chocolate Sauce and Garnishes

⅓ cup granulated sugar

3½ ounces bittersweet chocolate, chopped

½ teaspoon vanilla extract

1 tablespoon light or dark rum

Very lightly sweetened whipped cream, for garnish

Chocolate curls, for garnish (optional)

of whites into chocolate mixture. Add chocolate mixture, hazelnut mixture, and breadcrumbs to remaining egg whites, whisking until completely blended but not overmixed. Divide mixture among baking cups, filling each ½ to ⅔ full. (Old-fashioned 1-cup containers will be about ½ full, smaller containers fuller.)

Set cups in a baking pan and add enough hot water to rise 1¼ inches up sides of cups. Bake for 25 to 30 minutes or until puddings are puffed and springy but not completely firm when tapped on top. Serve warm from the oven, as the puddings will gradually deflate upon standing.

To prepare sauce: Combine 3 tablespoons hot tap water and ⅓ cup sugar in medium saucepan over medium heat, stirring until sugar completely dissolves and mixture comes to a full boil. Boil for 30 seconds. Remove pan from heat and add chocolate, stirring until it completely melts. Stir in 1 tablespoon more hot water, vanilla, and rum until well blended

To serve: Spoon several tablespoons sauce into center of individual serving plates. Tip plates back and forth so sauce forms a pool in center of each. Run knife around still-warm puddings to loosen. Unmold puddings on sauce. Garnish each serving with a dollop of whipped cream, or pipe a collar of cream around the bottom of each dessert. Garnish servings with chocolate curls, if desired. Pass leftover sauce separately.

Makes 5 or 6 servings

Note: To toast and hull hazelnuts: Preheat oven to 350°F. and spread nuts in a baking pan. Toast for 13 to 16 minutes, stirring occasionally, or until hulls loosen and nuts are tinged with brown. Set nuts aside until cool. Rub in a kitchen towel or between fingers, loosening and discarding any loose bits of hulls.

Pots de crème is an apt name for these classic little French desserts. Baked and served in individual custard pots, or cups, they are as rich as chocolate mousse, softer and creamier than good pudding, and more tender and elegant than old-fashioned baked custard. These particular "pots of cream" also have a deep, satisfying chocolate flavor. And they are easy to make!

Preheat oven to 325°F. Set out eight 3-ounce pots de crème baking cups or similar oven-proof custard cups or ramekins. Also set out a large roasting pan (or several pans) large enough to hold baking cups.

Combine milk and cream in a 2-quart or larger saucepan over medium-high heat and bring almost to a full boil. Immediately remove pan from heat. Pour ¼ cup hot milk-cream mixture over chocolate, stirring until chocolate partially melts and mixture is very well blended. Pour ¼ cup more hot mixture over chocolate, stirring until chocolate completely melts and mixture is thoroughly blended and smooth. Stir ½ cup more hot liquid into chocolate until completely incorporated and smooth. Set aside.

In a medium bowl, whisk together sugar and egg yolks until well blended. Whisking continuously, add about ½ cup hot milk-cream mixture to yolk mixture until well blended. Pour yolk mixture back into hot milk-cream mixture in the saucepan. Whisk chocolate, coffee, and vanilla back into saucepan until thoroughly incorporated.

1 cup whole milk
1¹/3 cups heavy (whipping) cream
6 ounces bittersweet (not unsweetened) or semisweet chocolate, chopped into ¹/4-inch or smaller pieces
Generous ¹/3 cup granulated sugar
7 large egg yolks
2 tablespoons coffee
1¹/2 teaspoons vanilla extract
Whipped cream, for garnish (optional)

Pour mixture through a fine sieve into a 4-cup measure. Divide mixture evenly among 8 cups (each cup shold be no more than a generous three-fourths full).

Set cups in larger pan. Carefully add enough hot water to larger pan to come halfway up sides of cups. Bake on center oven rack for 30 to 35 minutes or until the custards look almost set when cups are jiggled (don't tap surface, as custard surface will be marred). Transfer cups to wire racks and cool thoroughly. Cover custards with plastic wrap and refrigerate for at least 5 hours and up to 48 hours, if desired.

Serve baked custards with small dollops of whipped cream, if desired.

Makes 8 servings

DARK CHOCOLATE BAKED CUSTARDS

Pots de Crème au Chocolat Noir

FRANCE

This soothing baked dessert combines a smooth custardy bottom layer with a very tender soufflé-like top. One of my testers says it tastes like warm, soft, puffy brownies mixed up with chocolate custard sauce; this sums it up rather nicely, I think. ❖ Souffléd puddings are old-fashioned American desserts. In some old regional cookbooks they are called puff puddings or just puffs.

CHOCOLATE SOUFFLÉD PUDDING

Position a rack in center of oven and preheat to 350°F. Generously grease a 2½-quart casserole or soufflé dish. Set out a baking pan large enough to hold the casserole.

In a medium saucepan over medium-high heat bring cream just to a boil. Immediately remove from heat. Pour ¼ cup cream over chocolate in a small deep bowl, stirring until chocolate partially melts and mixture is well blended. Stir in ¼ cup more cream until chocolate completely melts and mixture is smooth. Stir chocolate mixture back into remaining cream until smoothly incorporated. Slowly stir milk into cream mixture until well blended and smooth.

In a large mixer bowl with mixer set on medium speed, beat butter and brown sugar for 2 to 3 minutes until very light and fluffy. Beat in cocoa powder until well blended. One at a time, beat in egg and yolks. Beat in flour and vanilla just until smoothly incorporated. Reduce mixer speed to low and slowly beat in

1¾ cups heavy (whipping) cream
4½ ounces bittersweet (not unsweetened) or semisweet chocolate, chopped into ¼-inch pieces
1 cup whole milk
6 tablespoons unsalted butter, slightly softened
⅔ cup packed light or dark brown sugar
1½ tablespoons unsweetened cocoa powder
1 large egg, plus 4 large egg yolks
⅓ cup all-purpose flour
2½ teaspoons vanilla extract
4 large egg whites, completely free of yolk
⅛ teaspoon salt
¼ cup granulated sugar
Lightly sweetened whipped cream, for garnish (optional)

chocolate mixture, scraping to bowl bottom to be sure mixture is thoroughly blended.

In a separate, completely grease-free mixer bowl with mixer set on medium speed, beat egg whites until frothy and opaque. Raise speed to high and continue beating until soft peaks just begin to form. Gradually beat in granulated sugar, continuing to beat until mixture stands in firm but not dry peaks. Add egg white mixture to chocolate mixture, folding with a wire whisk until evenly incorporated but not overmixed. Turn out mixture into soufflé dish. Immediately place dish in larger pan and transfer to oven. Add enough hot tap water to rise 1 inch up casserole sides.

Bake for 55 to 65 minutes or until mixture is set when tapped in center. Remove large pan from oven; let soufflé dish stand in water bath for 10 to 15 minutes. Serve souffléd pudding immediately, spooned into bowls. Add a dollop of whipped cream, if desired. Alternatively, cover and refrigerate; rewarm in a low oven before serving. (The pudding will firm up and become brownie-like when chilled, and some people will like it that way.)   *Makes 6 to 8 servings*

Fudge Brownie Pie à la Mode

CHEESECAKES, TARTS, TARTLETS AND PIES

These fudgy, chewy brownies are especially designed to be baked in a pie plate and served à la mode. The batter puffs up and then falls slightly in the center during baking, creating pie-shaped wedges ideal for cradling a scoop or two of homemade or store-bought ice cream. ❖ Brownie Pie à la Mode is great plain, but to make absolutely certain that it is irresistible, you can top off the slices with Hot Fudge Sauce.

FUDGE BROWNIE PIE À LA MODE

Position a rack in center of oven and preheat oven to 325°F. Generously grease a 9-inch deep-dish pie plate; set aside.

Place chocolate in top of a double boiler over about 1 inch of hot but not simmering water. Warm over medium-low heat, stirring occasionally, until chocolate melts. Remove top of double boiler from bottom and set chocolate aside to cool slightly. Thoroughly stir together flour, cocoa, baking powder, and salt.

Combine butter and sugar in a mixer bowl. Beat with mixer on medium speed until blended. Beat in egg and yolk, then vanilla. Beat for 2 to 3 minutes until mixture is very light and fluffy and sugar has dissolved. With mixer on low speed, beat in melted chocolate. Gently stir in flour mixture just until evenly incorporated. Turn out batter into pie plate, carefully spreading to edges.

Bake on center oven rack for 34 to 39 minutes or until a toothpick inserted in center comes out clean but moist. (Brownie will puff up, then fall slightly in center.) Transfer pie plate to wire rack. Let stand at least 1 hour or until thoroughly cooled. If desired, keep pie, tightly covered, for up to 24 hours (or freeze for several days, then thaw thoroughly).

Serve pie cut into wedges and topped with scoops of ice cream. Pass a pitcher of Hot Fudge Sauce, if desired.

4 ounces bittersweet (not unsweetened) or semisweet chocolate, coarsely chopped or broken into small pieces
1/3 cup plus 2 tablespoons all-purpose flour
2 tablespoons unsweetened cocoa powder
1/4 teaspoon baking powder
1/4 teaspoon salt
1/2 cup (1 stick) unsalted butter, slightly softened
3/4 cup plus 2 tablespoons granulated sugar
1 large egg, plus 1 large egg yolk
2 teaspoons vanilla extract
Scoops of vanilla, butter pecan, toffee bar crunch, or other ice cream flavor
Hot Fudge Sauce (page 232), optional

Makes 8 to 10 servings

This is a rich, smooth chocolate cream pie with an assertive but not overpowering chocolate taste. Some recipes for this classic call for covering the filling with baked meringue—perhaps simply to make use of all the extra egg whites—but I prefer this version, which is topped off with lots of whipped cream.

OLD-FASHIONED CHOCOLATE CREAM PIE

To prepare pastry shell: Set out a 9-inch pie plate. In a food processor fitted with a steel blade, combine flour and salt. Process a few seconds to blend. Sprinkle butter and shortening over flour. Process in on/off pulses until fat is cut into flour and mixture resembles coarse meal. Processing in on/off pulses, add 1 tablespoon cold water through feed tube, processing only until evenly incorporated and particles begin to hold together. If mixture is crumbly, sprinkle over a little more water, a teaspoon or two at a time and continue processing in on/off pulses until mixture holds together and is smooth; be careful not to overprocess. (Alternatively, in a medium bowl, using a pastry blender, forks, or your fingertips, cut butter and shortening into flour and salt, until mixture is consistency of coarse meal. Add 1 tablespoon water to flour mixture, blending with a fork just until particles hold together. If necessary, add a little more water, 1 teaspoon at a time, to moisten pastry enough to hold together.) Gather pastry into a ball. Working between two sheets of wax paper, roll pastry into a 12-inch round of even thickness, checking underside of dough frequently and smoothing out any wrinkles that form. Peel off one sheet of paper. Lay pastry, dough-side down, loosely in pie plate. With top sheet of wax paper still in place, refrigerate dough for 25 to 30 minutes.

Pastry
1 1/3 cups all-purpose flour
   Scant 1/2 teaspoon salt
5 tablespoons cold unsalted butter, cut into pats
1 1/2 tablespoons solid white vegetable shortening

Filling and Garnishes
1 large egg, plus 4 large egg yolks
1/4 cup heavy (whipping) cream
1 cup granulated sugar, divided
3 cups whole milk, divided
2 tablespoons unsweetened, non-alkalized, American-style cocoa powder (such as Hershey's)
3 tablespoons all-purpose flour
1/3 cup plus 1 tablespoon cornstarch
1/8 teaspoon salt
3 ounces bittersweet (not unsweetened) or semisweet chocolate, chopped into 1/4-inch pieces
1/4 cup unsalted butter, cut into small pieces
2 1/2 teaspoons vanilla extract
1 1/2 to 2 cups heavy (whipping) cream, lightly sweetened and whipped, for garnish
   Grated chocolate, chocolate shavings, or curls, for garnish

Let dough soften at room temperature for a few minutes. Peel off and discard paper. Smooth dough firmly into bottom and sides of pie plate, patching any tears. Trim overlapping dough to 1 inch. Press and crimp to form decorative edge, keeping edge evenly thick. Prick pastry all over with a fork. Neatly line pastry with heavy-duty aluminum foil, wrapping excess foil over pan edges so pastry is completely covered. Return to refrigerator to chill for at least 20 minutes and up to eight hours, if desired.

Position a rack in center of oven and preheat to 400°F. Bake foil-covered shell for 15 minutes. Carefully remove foil and continue baking until tinged with brown, six to 10 minutes longer. Transfer pie plate to wire rack and let stand until completely cooled. Use immediately or store, wrapped airtight, for up to 24 hours (or freeze for up to a week).

To prepare filling: In a small, deep bowl, beat together egg and egg yolks, cream, and half of the sugar with a whisk or fork, until well blended; set aside. In a 4-quart or larger heavy, non-aluminum saucepan, bring 2 cups milk just to a boil over high heat. Remove from heat. In a small, deep bowl, stir together remaining half of sugar, cocoa powder, flour, cornstarch, and salt, until well blended and smooth. Gradually stir or whisk remaining 1 cup cold milk into cocoa mixture, until mixture is *completely smooth*. Briskly stir cocoa mixture into hot milk until blended. Return mixture to burner over medium heat and cook, whisking vigorously and scraping pan bottom, until mixture comes to a boil, about two to three minutes. Boil mixture, stirring vigorously, for 1½ minutes. Remove pan from heat, stirring 30 seconds longer. Whisking, add about a third of cocoa mixture to reserved egg mixture, until well blended. Whisk egg mixture back into saucepan. Return to burner over medium heat, stirring vigorously. Cook until mixture returns to boiling and boil for one minute. Immediately remove from heat and stir in chocolate, butter, and vanilla, until completely melted and smooth. Strain filling through a fine sieve into a non-aluminum storage bowl. Lay a piece of plastic wrap on surface of filling. Refrigerate filling for 20 to 30 minutes, until it cools and thickens just slightly. Stir well, then spoon into pie shell. Cover and refrigerate pie for at least four hours, and preferably longer, until set.

Just before serving, pipe, swirl, or spread whipped cream over entire surface of pie (or over each slice). Garnish generously with chocolate curls or shavings or grated chocolate, if desired. Ungarnished pie will keep, covered and refrigerated, for 3 or 4 days.   *Makes about 8 servings*

OLD-FASHIONED CHOCOLATE CREAM PIE

If ever there were a case of gilding the lily successfully, this is it. Those who like the nutty, gooey goodness of traditional pecan pie usually love it studded with chocolate bits.

PECAN-CHOCOLATE CHIP PIE

To prepare pastry shell: Set out a 9-inch pie plate. In a food processor fitted with a steel blade, combine flour and salt. Process a few seconds to blend. Sprinkle butter and shortening over flour. Process in on/off pulses until fat is cut into flour and mixture resembles coarse meal. Operating processor in on/off pulses, add 1½ tablespoons cold water through feed tube, processing only until liquid is evenly incorporated and particles begin to hold together. If mixture is crumbly, sprinkle over more water a teaspoon or two at a time, and continue processing in on/off pulses until mixture holds together smoothly; be careful not to overprocess or overmoisten. Press pastry into a ball. (Alternatively, if processor is unavailable, in a medium bowl, using pastry blender, forks, or your fingertips, cut butter and shortening into flour and salt, until mixture is consistency of coarse meal. Add 1½ tablespoons cold water to flour mixture, blending with a fork just until particles hold together. If necessary, add a little more cold water, a teaspoon at a time, to moisten pastry enough to hold together well. Knead lightly to form pastry into a ball.) Between two sheets of wax paper, roll pastry into a 12-inch round of even thickness, checking underside of dough frequently and smoothing out any wrinkles that form. Refrigerate dough on a large tray or baking sheet for 25 to 30 minutes.

Pastry
1½ cups all-purpose flour
  Scant ½ teaspoon salt
¼ cup (½ stick) cold unsalted butter, cut
  into ½-inch pieces
¼ cup solid white vegetable shortening
Filling and Garnish
 5 tablespoons unsalted butter
 1 cup light corn syrup
⅓ cup packed light or dark brown sugar
⅛ teaspoon salt
1¼ teaspoons vanilla extract
 3 large eggs
1¼ cups (about 5 ounces) pecan halves
½ cup (3 ounces) semisweet chocolate chips

Let dough soften at room temperature for several minutes. Peel off one sheet of paper. Turn over dough; drape, centered, in pie plate. Peel off and discard second sheet of paper. Fit pastry into plate, smoothing over bottom and sides and patching any breaks or tears. Trim dough overhanging the rim so that it overlaps by about ½ inch all around. Fold excess dough into plate; pinch and smooth into place to build up an edge of even thickness. Press and crimp to form a decorative edge. Prick pastry all over using a fork. Cover loosely and refrigerate at least 30 minutes and up to 8 hours, if desired.

To prepare filling: Position a rack in center of oven and preheat to 375°F. Bring butter just to a simmer in a medium-sized, heavy saucepan over medium-low heat. Continue simmering 1 to 2 minutes longer, stirring, until butter solids turn light brown. Immediately remove from burner. Pour about half of butter into a heat-proof cup and reserve. Stir corn syrup, sugar, salt, and vanilla into butter in pan until well blended and smooth. Beat eggs into mixture using a fork.

Spread pecans, then half of chocolate chips in pastry shell. Slowly pour egg mixture over top. Sprinkle remaining chocolate chips over top. Drizzle reserved browned butter over surface. Bake for 35 to 40 minutes until golden brown and puffy on top. Transfer to wire rack; let stand until cooled. Store, refrigerated, up to 5 days. Serve at room temperature or slightly cool, with dollops of whipped cream for garnish, if desired.

Makes about 8 servings

White Chocolate-Grand Marnier Cheesecake

Mocha-White Chocolate Swirl Cheesecake

White chocolate and Grand Marnier meld wonderfully in this elegant and rich, yet surprisingly light and delicate cheesecake. The slight tanginess of cream cheese is a nice foil for the sweetness of the white chocolate, and beaten egg whites produce the lovely airy texture. ❖ While this cheesecake is excellent served plain, it is also good with sliced fresh strawberries or peaches.

WHITE CHOCOLATE-GRAND MARNIER CHEESECAKE

Position a rack in center of oven and preheat to 350°F. Very generously grease a 10-by-2½-inch springform pan.

To prepare crust: Combine coarsely broken graham crackers, butter, and lemon zest in a food processor and process for about 1 minute, or until mixture begins to hold together. (Alternatively, combine graham cracker crumbs, butter, and lemon zest in a bowl and stir with a fork until mixture begins to hold together.) Pat crust evenly and firmly into bottom of springform pan; crust will be thin. Bake in preheated oven for 7 to 9 minutes, until lightly browned. Set aside on rack until cooled. Reset oven temperature to 400°F.

To prepare filling: In the top of a double boiler, over about 1 inch hot but not simmering water, slowly melt white chocolate, stirring occasionally, until chocolate is completely melted and smooth. Remove double boiler from heat and set aside with top still over bottom to keep chocolate warm. Combine ⅓ cup sugar, cream cheese, eggs, and lemon zest in a large mixer bowl. Beat on high speed for 5 to 6 minutes, or until very light and fluffy. Add lemon juice, vanilla, and Grand Marnier and continue beating just

Crust
4 ounces (14 2½-inch squares) graham crackers, coarsely broken, or 1 cup graham cracker crumbs
2½ tablespoons unsalted butter, melted
⅛ teaspoon very finely grated lemon zest (yellow part of skin)

Filling
6½ ounces top-quality white chocolate, very coarsely chopped
⅔ cup granulated sugar, divided
1½ pounds cream cheese, at room temperature
2 large eggs
⅛ teaspoon very finely grated lemon zest (yellow part of skin)
1½ tablespoons fresh lemon juice
2 teaspoons vanilla extract
2½ tablespoons Grand Marnier
4 large egg whites, completely free of yolk

Sour Cream Topping
1 cup sour cream
1½ tablespoons granulated sugar
1 teaspoon vanilla extract

until blended. Beat in white chocolate until very well blended and smooth. In a grease-free mixer bowl, beat egg whites on medium speed until frothy. Raise speed to high and beat just until soft peaks begin to form. Gradually add remaining ⅓ cup sugar and continue beating until firm but not dry peaks form. Fold egg whites into cream cheese mixture until evenly distributed throughout, but not overmixed.

Turn out mixture into crust, spreading evenly to edges. Shake pan to level the surface. Bake for 10 minutes. Reset oven temperature to 225°F. and continue baking for 50 to 55 minutes longer, or until mixture is barely set in the center when lightly tapped.

To prepare topping (while cheesecake is baking) stir together sour cream, sugar, and vanilla, until well blended.

Remove cheesecake from oven and spread topping evenly over surface. Return to oven and bake 5 minutes longer or until topping is smooth and melted. Cool on a wire rack. Cover and refrigerate for at least 6 hours or until very cold. (Cheesecake may also be frozen, removed from pan sides, wrapped, and then refrozen for up to 2 weeks.) Carefully run a thin-bladed knife around cheesecake to loosen it from pan sides. Gently remove sides. Serve cheesecake directly from pan bottom. If desired, decorate with white chocolate curls, shavings, or white chocolate flowers as shown on page 98. If desired, pass fruit separately. *Makes 12 to 15 servings*

Exceptionally smooth and almost custard-like, this handsome and delectable cheesecake presents a creamy mocha–white chocolate swirl filling over a chocolate-hazelnut crust. The secret to the delicate texture is gently beating (never whipping) the ingredients, and baking the cake in a water bath.

MOCHA-WHITE CHOCOLATE *SWIRL* CHEESECAKE

Position a rack in center of oven and preheat to 350°F. Spread hazelnuts in a baking pan and toast, stirring occasionally, for about 15 minutes, or until nuts are slightly colored and their hulls are loosened. Set aside until cool enough to handle. Remove all loose bits of hulls by vigorously rubbing nuts between palms or in a clean kitchen towel, discarding bits as you work.

Generously grease bottom and sides of an 8- or 8½-inch-by-2½-inch springform pan. Around the bottom and outsides of the pan, wrap a sheet of heavy-duty aluminum foil that is about 2 inches larger on all sides than springform pan, being careful not to puncture foil. (It will keep water from seeping into the pan bottom when cheesecake is placed in a water bath for baking.)

Combine hazelnuts, wafers, and butter in a food processor and process for 1½ to 2 minutes or until nuts are finely ground and mixture begins to hold together. Press crust mixture evenly and firmly into bottom (not sides) of springform pan. Bake until lightly browned, 10 to 15 minutes. Set aside on wire rack until cooled. Reset oven to 325°F.

To prepare filling, *slowly melt* white chocolate, stirring frequently, in top of a double boiler set over about an inch of *hot but not simmering* water.

Crust
⅓ cup (about 1½ ounces) hazelnuts
4½ ounces (18 to 20) chocolate wafers, coarsely broken, or 1¼ cups fine chocolate wafer crumbs (see Note)
1 tablespoon unsalted butter

Filling and Garnish
2 ounces top-quality white chocolate, coarsely chopped
3½ ounces bittersweet (not unsweetened) or semisweet chocolate, coarsely chopped
2½ tablespoons Kahlúa or other coffee-flavored liqueur
2 teaspoons instant coffee powder or granules
1 cup granulated sugar
1½ pounds cream cheese, at room temperature
4 large eggs
2 teaspoons vanilla extract
¾ cup heavy (whipping) cream
Dark chocolate, white chocolate, or mocha-colored chocolate leaves, for garnish (optional)

Set aside with double boiler top still over bottom to keep white chocolate warm. Melt dark chocolate in a small, heat-proof bowl set over a saucepan of almost simmering water, stirring occasionally, until smooth. Set aside with bowl over saucepan to keep chocolate warm. Combine liqueur and coffee powder in a large mixer bowl, stirring until coffee dissolves. Add sugar and cream cheese and *with mixer set on low speed,* beat for 3 to 4 minutes, or until completely smooth, scraping down bowl sides and beaters several times. Continuing to beat on low speed, gradually add eggs, one at a time, then vanilla, beating after each addition. A bit at a time, beat in cream. Remove 1 cup of mixture and set aside. Add melted bittersweet chocolate to remaining mixture and continue beating just until well blended and smooth. Turn out mixture into prepared crust gently so as not to trap air bubbles. Rap the pan against counter several times to release any air bubbles near batter surface. Stir white chocolate into reserved 1 cup batter until evenly incorporated. Spoon 7 or 8 small pools of white chocolate batter over surface. Gently draw a knife through mixture, partially incorporating white chocolate but leaving some white swirls and ripples visible.

Set springform pan in a larger pan and carefully add enough lukewarm water to large pan to rise 1 inch up the sides of the springform pan. Bake cheesecake for 60 to 65 minutes or until the mixture is set in the center when lightly tapped. Carefully remove pan from oven and let stand in water bath for 30 minutes. Transfer springform pan to cooling rack and let cheesecake stand until completely cooled. Cover and refrigerate for at least 6 hours or until very cold before serving. (Cheesecake may also be frozen, removed from pan, wrapped, and then refrozen for up to 2 weeks.) Carefully run a small knife around the cheesecake to loosen it from the pan. Remove pan sides. If desired, decoratively arrange several chocolate leaves in cake center. Serve cheesecake directly from pan bottom.   *Makes 10 to 12 servings*

Note: Use commercial chocolate wafers, such as Nabisco Famous Chocolate Wafers, or the Dark Chocolate Wafers, page 160.

Sinfully rich, but not heavy, this recipe was inspired by a popular cheesecake served at Eli's Restaurant in Chicago. It has a velvety-smooth texture and deep, dark chocolate flavor (thanks to an entire pound of chocolate). It is a good choice when you are baking for a crowd as it is quite large.

BLACK VELVET CHEESECAKE

Position a rack in center of oven and preheat to 350°F. Very generously grease a 10- by 3-inch springform pan.

To prepare crust: Combine wafers, walnuts, butter, and cinnamon in a food processor and process for about 1 minute or until nuts are ground and mixture begins to hold together. Pat crust evenly and firmly into bottom of springform pan and about 1¼ inches up sides. Bake for 7 to 9 minutes, or until tinged with brown and slightly firm when touched. Cool on a wire rack. Do not turn off oven.

To prepare filling: Melt chocolate in top of a double boiler over about 1 inch hot but not simmering water, stirring occasionally. Set aside with double boiler top still over bottom to keep chocolate warm. Combine ½ cup plus 2 tablespoons sugar, cocoa powder, and cream cheese in a large mixer bowl. Beat on medium speed until very well blended. Separate eggs, keeping whites absolutely free of any yolk. Set whites aside. One at a time, add yolks to cream cheese mixture, beating on high speed until yolks are well blended and batter is very light and fluffy. Beat in sour cream, then melted chocolate and vanilla, until very well blended and smooth. In a completely grease-free mixer bowl, beat egg whites on medium speed until frothy. Raise speed to high and beat just until soft peaks form. Gradually add remaining ½ cup sugar and continue beating until firm but not dry peaks

Crust
8 ounces (24 to 26 2½-inch) chocolate
   wafers, coarsely broken (see Note)
½ cup (2 ounces) chopped walnuts
2½ tablespoons unsalted butter, melted
   Pinch of ground cinnamon

Filling
16 ounces bittersweet (not unsweetened) or
   semisweet chocolate, coarsely chopped
1 cup plus 2 tablespoons granulated sugar,
   divided
¼ cup unsweetened, non-alkalized,
   American-style cocoa powder (such as
   Hershey's)
2 pounds cream cheese, at room
   temperature
5 large eggs, plus 1 large egg white
½ cup sour cream
2½ teaspoons vanilla extract

form. Fold egg whites into cream cheese mixture until evenly distributed throughout but not overmixed.

Turn out mixture into prepared crust, spreading evenly to edges. Jiggle pan to level the surface. Bake cheesecake for 15 minutes. Reset oven temperature to 250°F. and continue baking for 50 to 60 minutes or until cheesecake barely set in the center when lightly tapped.

To prepare topping (while cheesecake is baking), stir together sour cream, sugar, and vanilla, until well blended.

Remove cheesecake from oven and spread topping evenly over surface. Return to oven and bake for 4 to 5 minutes or until topping is smooth and melted. Transfer to wire rack and let cheesecake stand until completely cooled. Cover and refrigerate for at least 6 hours or until very cold. (Cheesecake may also be frozen, removed from pan, wrapped and then refrozen, for up to 2 weeks.) Carefully run a thin-bladed knife around cheesecake to loosen it from pan sides. Gently remove pan sides. If desired, remove cheesecake from pan bottom using a wide spatula, or serve directly from pan bottom. Decorate entire top with a light, even sifting of cocoa powder. If desired, arrange some chocolate curls or leaves in cheesecake center and dust them lightly with powdered sugar. *Makes 12 to 15 servings*

> **Sour Cream Topping and Decorations**
> *1¹/₂ cups sour cream*
> *1 teaspoon vanilla extract*
> *3 tablespoons granulated sugar*
> *¹/₂ tablespoon unsweetened, non-alkalized, American-style cocoa powder (such as Hershey's), for garnish*
> *Chocolate curls or leaves, for garnish (optional)*
> *Powdered sugar, for garnish (optional)*

Note: Use Dark Chocolate Wafers (recipe on page 160), or commercial wafers such as Nabisco Famous Chocolate Wafers.

This very smooth, custardy cheesecake features a fragrant orange filling between two thin layers of dark chocolate ganache. It is elegant, sophisticated, and delicious. It is excellent served plain, but for an added burst of flavor and color, top it with the fresh orange sauce.

ORANGE-TRUFFLE CHEESECAKE

Position a rack in center of oven and preheat to 350°F. Very generously grease a 9-inch-by- at least 2½-inch springform pan. Wrap around pan bottom and up sides a sheet of heavy-duty aluminum foil that is about 1¼ inches larger on all sides than springform, being careful not to puncture foil. (It will keep water from seeping into pan bottom when cheesecake is baked in water bath.) Set out a roasting pan or jelly-roll pan that is large enough to hold springform pan.

To prepare crust: Combine graham crackers, butter, and orange zest in a food processor and process for about 1 minute or until mixture begins to hold together. (Alternatively, combine thoroughly crushed crumbs, butter, and orange zest in a bowl. Stir with a fork until mixture begins to hold together.) Pat crust evenly and firmly into bottom and ¼ inch up sides of springform pan (layer will be thin). Bake in preheated oven until lightly browned, 7 to 9 minutes. Set aside on rack until cooled to lukewarm.

To prepare ganache: Bring cream just to a boil in a small saucepan over medium-high heat. Immediately remove pan from heat. Add half of cream to chopped chocolate, stirring until chocolate partially melts and mixture is well blended. Stir remaining cream into chocolate until it completely melts and mixture is smooth. Stir in 1½ tablespoons Grand Marnier. Measure out ½ cup ganache; cover and set aside. Pour remaining ganache into prepared crust in springform pan, *spreading only to within ¼ inch of edge.* Cover and refrigerate until ganache is cold and firm, about 30 minutes. (Or freeze for about 15 minutes.)

To prepare filling: Reset oven to 350°F. Combine sugar and cream cheese in a large mixer bowl. Beat on *very low speed,* scraping down bowl sides several times, for 3 to 4 minutes, or until very smooth and well blended, but not at all fluffy. One at a time, add eggs and egg yolks

Crust
4½ ounces graham crackers (8 2½-by-5-inch crackers), coarsely broken, or scant 1 cup graham cracker crumbs
2½ tablespoons cold unsalted butter, cut into chunks
¼ teaspoon very finely grated *orange zest (orange part of skin)*

Chocolate Ganache
⅓ cup heavy (whipping) cream
8 ounces bittersweet (not unsweetened) or semisweet chocolate, chopped into about ¼-inch pieces
2½ tablespoons Grand Marnier liqueur (or orange juice if preferred), divided

until evenly incorporated. Continuing to beat on low speed, beat in orange zest, cream, lemon juice, vanilla, and Grand Marnier, until very well blended.

Slowly pour mixture over ganache in pan, working gently so as not to trap air bubbles. Rap pan on counter several times to release air bubbles near batter surface. Set pan in larger pan. Place cheesecake and larger pan on center oven rack. Add enough water to larger pan to come ½ inch up springform pan sides. Bake for 55 to 65 minutes, until mixture is set in the center when lightly tapped. Transfer cheesecake to wire rack. Let cool for 15 minutes.

Meanwhile, prepare glaze. Gently stir into the reserved ganache 1 tablespoon hot tap water, then remaining 1 tablespoon Grand Marnier, until glaze is fluid and well blended; work gently so as not to trap air bubbles. Slowly pour glaze over warm cheesecake. Tip cheesecake from side to side to evenly distribute glaze over top to edge. Rap pan on counter sharply several times to release any bubbles trapped near surface. Let cheesecake stand on rack until completely cooled, about 3 hours. Cover and refrigerate cheesecake for at least 6 hours and up to 48 hours before serving. (Cheesecake may also be frozen, removed from pan sides, wrapped and then refrozen, for up to 2 weeks, but glaze will lose some of its sheen because of condensation.)

Cheesecake Filling
1⅓ cups granulated sugar
1½ pounds cream cheese, at room temperature
3 large eggs, plus 2 large egg yolks
2 teaspoons very finely grated orange zest (orange part of skin)
¼ cup heavy (whipping) cream
1½ tablespoons fresh lemon juice
2 teaspoons vanilla extract
2 tablespoons Grand Marnier (or orange juice if preferred)
Orange Sauce (Optional)
4 large oranges, preferably seedless
¼ cup sugar
¼ cup cranberry juice cocktail (or orange juice)
2 teaspoons cornstarch

To prepare orange sauce: Using vegetable peeler or knife, strip orange part of peel from 1 orange; set aside. Remove all skin and pith (white part of skin that remains on fruit when peeled) from oranges. Cut away orange segments from membranes and reserve. Bring sugar, ¼ cup water, and reserved strips of peel to a boil over medium-high heat. Boil for 3 to 4 minutes or until liquid is bubbly and reduced to generous 2 tablespoons. Strain out peel and return liquid and orange segments (and any juice) to pan. Stir together cranberry juice and cornstarch until well blended. Stir into saucepan and boil a minute or two longer, just until mixture thickens and becomes clear. Cover and refrigerate for at least 45 minutes and up to 24 hours before serving.

To serve, carefully run a small knife around cheesecake to loosen it from pan sides. Gently remove sides. Serve cheesecake directly from pan bottom. If sauce is prepared, either pass separately at table, or use as a topping and spoon onto cheesecake center just before serving.

Makes 10 to 14 servings

The mellow combination of walnuts, caramel, and chocolate lends this tart a rich, autumnal flavor. I enjoyed the tart that inspired it during a trip along the picturesque Alsatian wine route—which winds down the Rhine river plain through the foothills of the Vosges mountains.

CHOCOLATE-WALNUT TART WITH CARAMEL GLAZE

Tarte de Chocolat et Noix au Sauce Caramel

To prepare pastry: Set out a 9-inch tart pan with removable bottom. In a mixer bowl with mixer on medium speed, beat together butter, sugar, and salt, until light and fluffy. Beat in egg and vanilla until evenly incorporated and smooth. On low speed, beat in flour just until evenly incorporated. Shape dough into a ball; it will be slightly sticky. Between two sheets of wax paper, roll pastry into an 11-inch round, making sure edges are as thick as interior. Transfer dough to tray or baking sheet. Refrigerate at least 30 minutes and up to 24 hours, if desired. Let dough warm up until slightly malleable before using.

Peel off and discard one sheet of paper. Drape layer, centered, in tart pan with second sheet of wax paper facing up. Gently peel off paper. Pat dough into bottom and up sides of pan; it will be crumbly. Fold excess dough back into pan, pressing it into pan flutes to produce a ¼-inch thick edge. Patch any tears and pinch any broken areas back together as necessary. Prick dough all over. Cover dough surface with a large sheet of greased heavy-duty aluminum foil (greased side facing dough), overlapping foil and folding it firmly over tart edges so dough is completely covered. Refrigerate for 15 minutes. Meanwhile, position a rack in center of oven and preheat to 400°F.

Bake shell as follows: Set tart pan on baking sheet. Bake for 18 minutes. Gently remove foil. Bake about 5 to 8 minutes longer, until

Pastry

6½ tablespoons butter, slightly softened
2 tablespoons granulated sugar
⅛ teaspoon salt
1 large egg
½ teaspoon vanilla extract
1½ cups all-purpose flour

Filling

1 cup heavy (whipping) cream
5 large egg yolks
3½ tablespoons granulated sugar
1½ teaspoons vanilla extract
4 ounces bittersweet (not unsweetened) chocolate or 4½ ounces semisweet chocolate, coarsely chopped
⅓ cup very finely chopped walnuts

Caramel Glaze

½ cup granulated sugar
1 tablespoon light corn syrup
¼ cup heavy (whipping) cream
4½ tablespoons unsalted butter, cut into pats
Generous pinch of salt
¼ teaspoon vanilla extract

tart is just barely tinged with brown in bottom and is nicely browned on edges. Immediately remove baking sheet from oven. Transfer tart to wire rack to cool. Reset oven temperature to 325°F.

To prepare filling: In a medium saucepan over medium heat (or in a heat-proof microwave-safe bowl in microwave oven), heat cream until hot but not boiling. In a medium bowl, using a fork, beat together eggs, sugar, and vanilla until very well blended and smooth. Pour ¼ cup cream over chocolate in a small deep bowl, stirring until chocolate is partially melted and smooth. Add ¼ cup more cream, stirring until chocolate is completely melted and smooth. A bit at a time, beat remaining cream into egg mixture until incorporated. Gradually stir chocolate into egg mixture until well blended and smooth. Spread chopped walnuts in tart shell. Pour filling into shell. Set tart pan on baking sheet. Return tart to oven and bake for 22 to 27 minutes or until crust is nicely browned and center seems set but still slightly soft when tapped. Remove pan to wire rack to cool slightly. Meanwhile, prepare caramel.

To prepare caramel: Combine sugar and corn syrup in a medium-sized, heavy saucepan. Measure out 2 tablespoons very hot tap water; set near stove. Measure out cream, set aside. Heat corn syrup–sugar mixture over medium-high heat, stirring constantly with a *very long-handled wooden* spoon. Mixture will look dry and lumpy at first, but gradually sugar will melt and begin to liquify. Continue cooking, stirring, until mixture turns a very pale yellow. Quickly remove from heat and *working carefully to avoid splatters and steam,* immediately add hot tap water. Wait several seconds for splattering to subside, then immediately stir until mixture is well blended. When bubbling subsides, stir in cream, butter, and salt. Return mixture to burner over medium heat and bring just to simmer again, stirring. Simmer, stirring, about 1½ to 2 minutes longer, until caramel completely dissolves and mixture becomes clearer and turns a rich caramel color. Immediately remove from heat and stir in vanilla. Strain caramel through a fine sieve into a heat-proof bowl. Let stand until thickened slightly, about 30 minutes. Very slowly pour over tart top; for smooth appearance, do not stir or agitate caramel before pouring. Tip pan back and forth to even surface. Let stand until caramel cools to barely warm.

Refrigerate, covered, for at least 3 hours and up to 48 hours, if desired. Allow tart to warm up just slightly before serving. To cut slices cleanly, dip knife in hot water and wipe off between each cut.

Makes about 8 servings

RASPBERRY (OR STRAWBERRY) TRUFFLE TARTLETS

Tartelettes Chocolatée aux Framboises

There is a jewel-like perfection to many of the fresh fruit tartlets in French and Belgian pastry shops. Studded with plump, ripe berries (or other seasonal fruits) and lightly glazed with jelly, they look spectacular and usually taste just as good. The following recipe, which combines sweet-tart raspberries (or strawberries), a silky chocolate ganache, and crisp, short pastry, is particularly enticing.

To prepare pastry: Set out eighteen 2½- to 3-inch tartlet pans (or two 12-muffin 2½-inch or similarly sized muffin tins.) Lightly grease tartlet pans or muffin tins or spray with nonstick cooking spray. In a small bowl or cup, using a fork, beat together egg, sugar, and 1 tablespoon plus 2 teaspoons cold water, until evenly incorporated.

In a food processor fitted with a steel blade, combine flour and salt. Process a few seconds to blend. Sprinkle butter and oil over flour. Process in on/off pulses until fat is cut into flour and mixture resembles coarse meal. Processing in on/off pulses, add egg mixture through feed tube, processing only until liquid is evenly incorporated and particles begin to hold together. If mixture is crumbly, sprinkle over a teaspoon or two of cold water and continue processing in on/off pulses until mixture holds together, being careful not to overprocess or overmoisten. (Alternatively, in a medium bowl, using a pastry blender, forks, or your fingertips, cut butter into flour and salt, until mixture is consistency of coarse meal. Add egg mixture to flour mixture, blending with a fork, then kneading with fingertips just until particles hold together. If necessary, add a little cold water, a teaspoon at a time, to moisten pastry just enough to hold together.) Divide pastry into two portions; shape into balls. One at a time, place dough portions between two sheets of wax paper and roll out to a 3/16-inch thickness, checking underside of dough frequently and smoothing out any wrinkles that form. Stack dough sheets on a large baking sheet. Refrigerate for 25 to 30 minutes.

Pastry
1 large egg
1½ tablespoons granulated sugar
2¼ cups all-purpose flour
¼ teaspoon salt
¾ cup (1½ sticks) cold unsalted butter, cut into ½-inch pieces
1 tablespoon corn oil or other flavorless vegetable oil

Filling and Berries
1½ cups heavy (whipping) cream
2 tablespoons cold unsalted butter, cut into ¼-inch pieces
2 large egg yolks
¼ cup granulated sugar
6 ounces bittersweet (not unsweetened) or semisweet chocolate, chopped into ¼-inch pieces
½ teaspoon vanilla extract
1 tablespoon raspberry liqueur, Grand Marnier, kirsch, or cognac (optional)
4 to 5 cups fresh red raspberries (or small strawberries)
⅓ to ½ cup red-raspberry, red-currant or apple jelly, heated until melted, then cooled slightly

Transfer one dough sheet (leave second sheet refrigerated) to work surface. Peel off one sheet of paper and replace it. Turn over dough; peel off and discard second sheet. Cut out pastry rounds using a round cutter, rim of a drinking glass, or tin can that is about 1 inch larger in diameter than tartlet pans. (For muffin tins, cut out rounds large enough to form shells with 1-inch-high rims when inserted in tins.) Lay rounds in tartlet pans; then let rest a few minutes until dough is soft enough to smooth into pans without breaking. Push rounds down into tartlet pans (or muffin-tin cups), smoothing over bottoms and sides and trimming off any excess dough. (Decorate edges of dough in muffin cups by pressing with tines of fork.) Prick pastry all over using a fork. Repeat procedure with second dough sheet. Neatly line each pastry shell with heavy-duty aluminum foil, working so pastry is completely covered. Set tartlet pans on baking sheets and return to refrigerator to chill for at least 30 minutes and up to 8 hours, if desired.

Position a rack in center of oven and preheat to 400°F. With tartlet pans set on baking sheets, bake for 12 minutes. Carefully remove foil and continue baking shells until golden, about 4 to 10 minutes, depending on size of tartlets. Transfer tartlets to wire racks and let stand until shells are completely cooled. Lift shells from pans (or muffin tins), using tip of paring knife, if necessary. Use shells immediately or store, wrapped airtight, for up to 24 hours (or freeze for up to a week).

To prepare ganache filling: In a medium saucepan oven medium-high heat, bring cream and butter to a boil; boil just until butter completely melts. Immediately remove from heat. Using a fork or whisk, whisk together egg yolks and sugar in a medium bowl. Continuing to whisk, add about half of hot cream to egg mixture in a thin stream. Add egg mixture back to saucepan. Heat over medium heat, stirring constantly, several minutes longer, until mixture is very hot to the touch but not boiling, and slightly coats the spoon (160°F. on a candy thermometer); lift pan from burner, stirring, if mixture heats too rapidly. Do not allow it to come near the boiling point or egg yolks may curdle. Transfer 1 cup of mixture to a food processor fitted with a steel blade. With motor running, gradually add chocolate through feed tube until all is added and mixture is smooth. Stop processor and scrape down sides. Continuing to process, add remaining cream and vanilla, then liqueur (if used), until evenly incorporated. Refrigerate until mixture is cool and slightly thickened, at least 1½ hours and up to 24 hours, if desired.

Divide ganache among tartlet shells. Smooth out ganache surface using a table knife. Cover ganache with raspberries (or strawberries), arranging attractively. Cover and return to refrigerator for up to 8 hours, or serve immediately. Allow to warm up slightly before serving. Just before serving, lightly brush tops of berries with jelly.

Makes 15 to 18 2¾- to 3-inch tartlets or about 24 2½-inch tartlets

WHITE CHOCOLATE-STRAWBERRY TART

To prepare pastry shell: In a large mixer bowl with mixer set on medium speed, beat butter, oil, sugar, and salt until light and well blended. Add egg and vanilla, beating until thoroughly incorporated. With mixer on low speed, beat in half of flour just until incorporated. By hand, stir in remaining flour until evenly incorporated but not overmixed. Refrigerate dough for 15 to 20 minutes, until cool but not firm. Lay dough between two sheets of wax paper. Roll into an even 12-inch round, checking underside of dough and smoothing out any wrinkles that form. With paper in place, refrigerate dough on baking sheet for at least 1 hour and up to 48 hours, if desired. Allow dough to warm up until slightly pliable but *not soft* before using.

Position a rack in center of oven and preheat to 375°F. Peel off wax paper and lay dough in 11-inch scalloped tart pan, preferably with removable bottom (or 10-inch pie plate). Smooth dough firmly and evenly into bottom and sides of pan, patching any tears as necessary. Trim off excess dough so it is even with pan edge. Prick shell all over with a fork. Grease a 14-inch or slightly larger square of heavy-duty aluminum foil. Lay foil, greased side down, in pan, smoothing against bottom and sides and folding over outer edge of pan so dough is completely covered. Bake for 15 minutes. Gently remove foil. Lower heat to 350°F. and continue bak-

Pastry Shell

1/2 cup (1 stick) unsalted butter, slightly softened

1 tablespoon corn oil or other flavorless vegetable oil

3 1/2 tablespoons granulated sugar

1/8 teaspoon salt

1 large egg

1 teaspoon vanilla extract

Generous 1 1/2 cups all-purpose flour

Filling and Garnish

1 teaspoon unflavored gelatin

2 tablespoons light rum (or water if preferred)

1 cup heavy (whipping) cream, divided

6 ounces top-quality white chocolate, coarsely chopped

3 ounces cream cheese, cut into small chunks and slightly softened

1/8 teaspoon finely grated lemon zest (yellow part of skin)

2 large egg whites, completely free of yolks

1 tablespoon granulated sugar

2 teaspoons vanilla extract

About 4 cups (1 1/4 pounds) fresh, uniformly sized strawberries, sliced

2 to 3 tablespoons red-currant or raspberry jelly, heated to boiling and cooled to syrupy

Melted white chocolate, for garnish (optional)

WHITE CHOCOLATE-STRAWBERRY TART

ing for 9 to 14 minutes longer until shell is firm in center and lightly tinged with brown. (If edges brown too rapidly, wrap with narrow strips of foil and continue baking until center is just tinged with brown.) Transfer pan to wire rack until shell is completely cooled. Use immediately or store, in pan and wrapped airtight, for up to 24 hours.

To prepare filling: Sprinkle gelatin over rum in a small bowl. Set aside until gelatin softens. In a medium saucepan over medium-high heat, bring ¼ cup cream just to a boil. Immediately remove from heat. Add softened gelatin mixture, stirring until gelatin dissolves. Stir in white chocolate, continuing to stir until chocolate melts. Stir in cream cheese and lemon zest. Return pan to burner over lowest heat, stirring until cream cheese just melts. Set mixture aside to cool to room temperature.

Using completely grease-free beaters and mixer bowl, beat egg whites until soft peaks begin to form. Gradually add sugar, beating until peaks are just slightly stiff. Turn out beaten whites and vanilla into chocolate mixture, but do not stir. Put remaining cream in bowl used for whites and beat to soft peaks. Add chocolate mixture and egg whites to whipped cream, whisking lightly until ingredients are thoroughly blended but not overmixed. Carefully lift pastry shell from pan and transfer to serving plate. Turn out filling into pastry shell. Working from outer edge, arrange strawberries, cut side down, in concentric circles on top of filling. Carefully cover and refrigerate at least 3 hours and up to 8 hours if preferred. Just before serving, generously brush berry tops with jelly and, if desired, garnish top with a light zig-zag drizzling of melted white chocolate as shown in photograph. Cut slices with a large sharp knife.

Makes 8 to 10 servings

CHOCOLATE TART WITH AMARETTI

Schokoladenkuchen mit Amaretti

Murbteig Pastry

1½ cups all-purpose flour

2½ tablespoons granulated sugar

⅛ teaspoon salt

½ cup (1 stick) very cold unsalted butter, cut into 1-inch chunks

2 large egg yolks

1½ to 3 tablespoons whole milk

Filling

¾ cup whole milk

3 large eggs

3 tablespoons granulated sugar

½ teaspoon vanilla extract

2 teaspoons Amaretto (almond-flavored liqueur), rum, or orange juice

1¼ cups (about 3 ounces) chopped Amaretti cookies

3½ ounces bittersweet (not unsweetened) or semisweet chocolate, chopped into ¼-inch pieces

About 1 tablespoon powdered sugar, for garnish

1 cup heavy cream whipped with 1 tablespoon Amaretto, for garnish (optional)

To prepare pastry: Wrap outside of a 9-inch springform pan with heavy-duty aluminum foil, covering bottom and extending foil up sides about 1 inch. (This protects against leakage if pan bottom does not seal tightly.)

In a food processor fitted with a steel blade, combine flour, sugar, and salt. Process a few seconds to blend. Sprinkle butter over flour. Process in on/off pulses until fat is cut into flour and mixture resembles coarse meal. In a small bowl or cup, using a fork, beat together egg yolks and 1½ tablespoons cold milk, until evenly incorporated. Processing in on/off pulses, add egg mixture through feed tube, processing only until liquid is evenly incorporated and particles begin to hold together. If mixture is crumbly, sprinkle over a teaspoon or two of cold milk and process in on/off pulses, continuing to moisten until mixture holds together, being careful not to overprocess or overmoisten. (Alternatively, if processor is unavailable, in a medium bowl, using a pastry blender, forks, or your fingertips, cut butter into flour, sugar, and salt, until mixture is consistency of coarse meal. Beat together egg yolks and 1½ tablespoons milk. Add yolk mixture to flour mixture, blending with a fork, then kneading with fingertips, just until particles hold together. If necessary, add a little more milk, a teaspoon at a time, to moisten pastry enough to hold together.) Shape dough into a ball. Between two sheets of wax paper, roll dough into a 12-inch round of even thickness; be sure edges are as thick as interior of round. Transfer to tray or baking sheet. Refrigerate for at least 30 minutes and up to 24 hours, if desired. Let dough warm up until slightly malleable before using.

Peel off and discard one sheet of paper. Drape layer, with second sheet of wax paper facing up, in springform pan. Gently peel off paper. Pat dough into bottom and up sides of pan, smoothing out creases and pressing dough into place. Cover and return to refrigerator for 10 minutes. Meanwhile, position a rack in center of oven, preheat to 400°F., and prepare filling.

To prepare filling: In a small saucepan over medium heat (or in a heatproof microwave-safe bowl in a microwave oven), heat milk until hot but not boiling. In a medium bowl, using a fork, beat together eggs, sugar, and vanilla, until very well blended and smooth. A bit at a time, beat in milk until incorporated. Stir in Amaretto.

Using a small paring knife, trim off uneven dough edge so sides are 1½ inches deep. Prick dough lightly. Spread Amaretti evenly in pan. Sprinkle chocolate over cookies. Pour milk mixture evenly over chocolate.

Bake kuchen for 28 to 33 minutes, until crust is golden and center is puffed and just firm when tapped; if surface browns too rapidly, cover with foil for the last 15 minutes of baking.

Remove pan to wire rack. Uncover and let stand until completely cooled. Refrigerate until well chilled, at least 2 hours, and up to 48 hours before serving, if desired. Sift powdered sugar over top of kuchen just before serving. Kuchen may be served with dollops of Amaretto-flavored whipped cream, if desired. *Makes about 8 servings*

Note: If puff pastry dough is used: Grease springform pan heavily so pastry will adhere to pan sides. Complete dough preparation as directed in your recipe. Roll into a 13½-inch round on a floured board and make sides of crust 2 inches high to compensate for the extra puffing of the dough.

Orange-Chocolate-Hazelnut Tart

Cherry-Chocolate Tart

Whole, thin slices of orange are freshly candied and used to lend both vivid color and intense orange flavor to this easy yet sophisticated chocolate-hazelnut tart.

ITALY

ORANGE-CHOCOLATE-HAZELNUT TART

Crostata di Cioccolato e Nocciole con Arance

For candied orange slices: With a large, sharp serrated knife, slice oranges crosswise into scant ⅛-inch thick slices, discarding smaller end-pieces or imperfect slices. Combine corn syrup, ½ cup hot tap water, and sugar in a 12-inch skillet over medium heat, stirring until well blended. Bring mixture to a simmer. Lay orange slices in pan. Adjust heat so mixture simmers gently and cook, uncovered, for 20 to 30 minutes, or until slices are translucent and tender. Using a slotted spoon, gently lay slices, slightly separated, on a large sheet of wax paper. If necessary, boil down cooking syrup until just slightly thickened. Reserve syrup for garnishing tart top.

For pastry shell: Set out a 10-by-1-inch tart pan with removable bottom. In a food processor fitted with a steel blade, combine flour, sugar, and salt. Process a few seconds to blend. Sprinkle butter over flour mixture. Process in on/off pulses until butter is cut into flour and mixture resembles coarse meal. Processing in on/off pulses, add 1 tablespoon cold water through feed tube, processing only until liquid is evenly incorporated and particles begin to hold together. If mixture is crumbly, continue sprinkling water, a teaspoon at a time, and processing in on/off pulses, until mixture holds together smoothly, being careful not to overprocess or overmoisten. Press pastry into a ball. (Alternatively, if processor is unavailable, in a medium bowl, using pastry blender, forks, or your fingertips, cut butter into flour mixture, until mixture resembles coarse meal. Add 1 tablespoon cold water to flour mixture, blending with a fork, just until

Candied Oranges Slices

3 to 4 medium-sized, juicy oranges (preferably seedless)

3 tablespoons corn syrup

1¼ cups granulated sugar

Pastry

1¼ cups all-purpose flour

2½ tablespoons granulated sugar

¼ teaspoon salt

6½ tablespoons cold unsalted butter, cut into ½-inch pieces

Filling

¼ cup unsalted butter, cut into chunks

4 ounces bittersweet (not unsweetened) or semisweet chocolate, coarsely broken or chopped

1 tablespoon all-purpose flour

3 tablespoons heavy (whipping) cream

2 large eggs

3½ tablespoons clover honey

1¼ teaspoons vanilla extract

Finely grated zest (orange part of skin) of 1 large orange

¾ cup (about 3½ ounces) finely chopped, toasted and hulled hazelnuts (or finely chopped walnuts, if preferred); see Note

particles hold together. If necessary, add a little more cold water, a teaspoon at a time, to moisten pastry enough to hold together well. Knead lightly to form pastry into a ball.) Place pastry between two sheets of wax paper and roll into an even 12-inch round, checking underside of dough frequently and smoothing out any wrinkles that form. Refrigerate dough on a large tray or baking sheet for 25 to 30 minutes.

Let dough soften at room temperature for several minutes. Peel off one sheet of paper. Turn dough over and drape, centered, in pie plate. Peel off and discard second sheet of paper. Fit pastry into plate, smoothing over bottom and sides and patching any breaks or tears. Trim off dough at pan rim. Prick pastry all over using a fork. Grease a sheet of heavy-duty aluminum foil and press, greased side down, into pastry shell; fold foil out over pan edges to completely cover pastry. Refrigerate at least 30 minutes and up to 8 hours, if desired.

Partially bake shell by preheating oven to 400°F. and baking with foil in place for 12 minutes. Gently remove foil and bake 5 minutes longer. Set aside on wire rack. Reset oven to 375°F.

For filling: Combine butter and chocolate in a small, heavy saucepan over lowest heat, stirring until melted and smooth. Set aside. In a medium bowl, beat together flour and cream, until well blended. Using a fork, beat in eggs, then honey, vanilla, and orange zest. Add chocolate mixture and toasted hazelnuts and continue beating with a fork until evenly incorporated.

Pour mixture into prepared tart shell. Set tart pan on baking sheet. Bake on center oven rack for 22 to 27 minutes, until mixture is slightly puffed and set when tapped on top. Transfer to wire rack. Brush a little reserved orange cooking syrup over tart surface (if it is too stiff to work with, warm it slightly first). Select the prettiest, most perfect candied orange slices (reserve remainder for another use or discard), and arrange, overlapping as shown, or as desired, over tart surface. Drizzle slices with several tablespoons of orange cooking syrup. Refrigerate tart until thoroughly cooled, at least 1½ hours, before serving. Store, refrigerated, up to 5 days. Serve at room temperature or slightly chilled. Cut into wedges with a very sharp knife.

Makes about 8 servings

Note: To prepare hazelnuts: Toast in a preheated 350°F. oven for 12 to 15 minutes, until nuts brown and hulls loosen. Rub cooled nuts in kitchen towel or between your fingers, discarding loose bits of hull. Chop nuts finely.

This appealing pie-like dessert, or kuchen, is best if made with imported, flavorful cherries (either dark sweet, or sour varieties) packed in syrup. I have tried both French griottine and Hungarian morello cherries with excellent results. Another possibility is imported or American "gourmet" brandied cherries in syrup, or fresh, pitted, dark sweet cherries that have been simmered in sugar, a little kirsch, and their own juice. ❖ A layer of chocolate applied over the pastry shell not only adds visual appeal and flavor, but also keeps the pastry crisp and the cherries in place while the custard-kirsch filling sets up.

CHERRY-CHOCOLATE TART

Kirsch-Schokoladenkuchen

To prepare pastry: Wrap outside of a 9-inch springform pan with heavy-duty aluminum foil, extending foil over bottom and up sides about 1 inch. (This ensures against leakage if pan bottom does not seal tightly.) In a food processor fitted with a steel blade, combine flour, sugar, and salt. Process a few seconds to blend. Sprinkle butter over flour. Process in on/off pulses until fat is cut into flour and mixture resembles coarse meal. In a small bowl or cup, using a fork, beat together egg yolk, kirsch, and 1 tablespoon milk, until evenly incorporated. Operating processor in on/off pulses, add egg mixture through feed tube, processing only until liquid is evenly incorporated and particles begin to hold together. If mixture is crumbly, sprinkle a bit more milk over it, a teaspoon or two at a time, and continue processing in on/off pulses, until mixture holds together; be careful not to overprocess or overmoisten. (Alternatively, if processor is unavailable, in a medium bowl, using pastry blender, forks, or your fingertips, cut butter into flour, sugar, and salt, until mixture is consistency of coarse meal. Beat together egg yolk, kirsch, and 1 tablespoon milk. Add yolk mixture to flour mixture, blending with a fork, then

Murbteig Pastry

1½ cups all-purpose flour

2 tablespoons granulated sugar

⅛ teaspoon salt

½ cup (1 stick) very cold unsalted butter, cut into 1-inch chunks

1 large egg yolk

1 tablespoon kirsch (cherry brandy)

1 to 2 tablespoons whole or lowfat milk

Chocolate and Cherries

¼ cup heavy (whipping) cream

4½ ounces bittersweet chocolate, chopped moderately fine

1 tablespoon kirsch (cherry brandy)

1 pound sour or dark, sweet cherries in syrup (preferably imported), very well drained

Filling and Garnish

2 large eggs plus 2 large egg yolks

½ cup granulated sugar

2 tablespoons kirsch (cherry brandy)

1½ teaspoons vanilla extract

¾ cup heavy (whipping) cream

1 cup heavy cream, whipped with 1 tablespoon kirsch and 1 tablespoon granulated sugar, for garnish (optional)

kneading with fingertips just until particles hold together. If necessary, add a little more milk, a teaspoon at a time, to moisten pastry enough to hold together.) Shape dough into a ball. Roll out between two sheets of wax paper into a 12-inch round of even thickness; be sure edges are as thick as interior of round. Transfer to tray or baking sheet. Refrigerate for at least 30 minutes and up to 8 hours, if desired. Let dough warm up until slightly malleable before using.

Peel off and discard one sheet of paper. Drape layer, centered, in spring-form pan with second sheet of wax paper facing up. Gently peel off paper. Pat dough into pan, smoothing and pressing into bottom and sides to form a crust of even thickness. Cover and return to refrigerator for 10 minutes or until dough firms up. Using a small paring knife, trim off uneven dough edge, leaving a 1¼-inch-high edge. Prick dough lightly all over.

To prepare chocolate mixture and cherries: Bring cream just to a boil in a medium saucepan over medium-high heat. Remove from heat and stir in chocolate. Continue stirring until completely melted and smooth. Stir in kirsch. Pour mixture into pastry shell, spreading evenly out to pan edges. Sprinkle very well-drained cherries evenly over chocolate. Cover and refrigerate for at least 40 minutes (or speed chilling by freezing for 20 minutes), or until chocolate is very cold and firm (but not frozen).

To prepare filling: Position a rack in center of oven and preheat to 350°F. In a medium bowl, using a fork, beat together eggs and yolks, sugar, kirsch, and vanilla, until very well blended and smooth. Beat in heavy cream with fork until incorporated. Pour custard mixture evenly over cherries.

Bake kuchen for 45 to 55 minutes until crust is golden at edges and center is just firm when tapped.

Remove pan to wire rack and let stand until completely cooled. Refrigerate until well chilled, at least 2 hours, and up to 48 hours before serving. Allow it to come almost to room temperature before serving. Kuchen may be served with dollops of whipped cream, if desired.

Makes about 8 servings

A perennial favorite at the Hampton Square Restaurant in Westhampton Beach, Long Island, this sinfully rich tart matches a flaky-crisp shell with a mellow, macadamia-studded caramel filling and bittersweet chocolate glaze. The recipe, which I've altered slightly for home use, was shared with me by the restaurant's pastry chef, Elizabeth Esterling. For an equally delicious dessert, Chef Esterling likes to substitute coarsely chopped pecans for the macadamia nuts.

CHOCOLATE-CARAMEL MACADAMIA TART

To prepare pastry shell: Set out a 9-inch tart pan with removable bottom. In a measuring cup, mix together egg yolk, sugar, and salt. Add enough cold water to measure a scant ¼ cup. Beat in vegetable oil using a fork. In a medium bowl, using pastry blender, forks, or fingertips, cut butter into flour until mixture is consistency of coarse meal. Add egg mixture to flour mixture, blending with a fork just until particles hold together. If necessary, add a little cold water, a teaspoon at a time, to moisten pastry just enough to hold together. Form pastry into a ball; cover and refrigerate for at least 30 minutes and up to 24 hours.

Roll out dough on lightly floured board or between 2 sheets of wax paper into an 11-inch round of even thickness. (If paper is used, check underside of dough frequently and smooth out any wrinkles that form.) Peel off sheets of paper (if used). Loosely drape pastry in tart pan. Cover and refrigerate for 20 to 30 minutes.

Position a rack in center of oven and preheat to 400°F. Fit pastry into tart pan, trimming off excess at edges. Prick shell surface several times with a fork. Neatly line shell with heavy-duty aluminum foil, wrapping excess foil out over edges so shell is completely covered. Place pie weights or beans in foil-covered shell. Bake shell for 20 minutes. Carefully

Pastry Shell
1 small egg yolk
½ teaspoon granulated sugar
⅛ teaspoon salt
1½ teaspoons corn oil or other flavorless vegetable oil
½ cup (1 stick) cold unsalted butter, cut into ½-inch pieces
1¾ cups all-purpose flour

Caramel Filling and Nuts
⅔ cup heavy (whipping) cream
6 tablespoons unsalted butter, cut into chunks
½ vanilla bean, halved lengthwise (or ¾ teaspoon vanilla extract)
3 tablespoons light corn syrup
1½ cups granulated sugar
¾ cup (about 3½ ounces) macadamia nuts, preferably unsalted

Chocolate Glaze
2 ounces bittersweet (not unsweetened) or semisweet chocolate, coarsely chopped
1½ tablespoons unsalted butter
1 teaspoon light corn syrup
1 tablespoon unsweetened cocoa powder
¼ cup heavy (whipping) cream
1½ tablespoons cognac or good brandy

remove pie weights and foil and continue baking shell until golden, 12 to 16 minutes longer. Transfer pan to wire rack and let stand until shell is completely cooled. Use immediately or store, wrapped airtight, for up to 24 hours.

To prepare caramel filling and nuts: In a medium-sized, heavy saucepan bring cream, butter, and vanilla bean (if used) just to a boil over medium heat; immediately remove from heat and set aside. (If substituting vanilla extract, do not add at this point.) In a 2-quart or larger heavy saucepan over medium-high heat, stir together corn syrup, 2 teaspoons water, and ¾ cup sugar until blended. When sugar is incorporated and starts to liquify, stir in half of remaining sugar until evenly incorporated. Repeat with remaining sugar. Cook, stirring and scraping down pan sides, about 4 to 6 minutes longer, until sugar dissolves, bubbles, and turns a pale tan color. Immediately remove from heat. Working carefully to avoid splatters and steam, pour hot cream mixture into caramel, stirring with a clean *very long-handled wooden spoon,* until caramel completely dissolves. Return mixture to burner and heat over medium heat, stirring. (If using a candy thermometer to gauge doneness, clip it to pan side, inserting so tip is completely submerged but not touching pan bottom.) Continue cooking, stirring, until mixture turns a rich caramel color and almost reaches the soft-ball stage, about 2 to 3 minutes longer. To test for doneness drop a teaspoon of caramel in a cup of ice water, let stand for 30 seconds, and then squeeze mixture between fingers; it should almost be stiff enough to press into a very soft, sticky ball. (Alternatively, cook until thermometer registers 234° to 235°F.) Remove pan from heat. Remove vanilla bean and discard. If vanilla bean was not used, stir in vanilla extract. Avoiding scraping any undissolved sugar from pan sides, pour caramel through a very fine sieve into a heat-proof bowl. Cover and set aside at room temperature for up to 6 hours. Halve macadamia nuts and set aside.

To prepare chocolate glaze: Combine chocolate, butter, and corn syrup in a small, heavy saucepan over low heat. Warm, stirring frequently, until mixture is completely melted and smooth. Put cocoa powder in a small saucepan. Gradually stir in cream, then cognac, until mixture is smooth and well blended. Bring mixture to a simmer, stirring; then remove from heat. Gradually add cream mixture to chocolate mixture, stirring until completely blended and smooth. Set glaze aside at room temperature, covered, for up to 6 hours. Refrigerate for longer storage.

To assemble tart: Pour caramel into tart shell. Sprinkle nuts evenly over caramel. Press down nuts to imbed them in caramel. Refrigerate until caramel is firm, at least 1½ hours. Pour chocolate glaze over caramel, tipping tart from side to side to even surface. Return to refrigerator until glaze sets, at least 30 minutes and up to 24 hours, before serving. Serve tart, chilled, cut into wedges. *Makes about 8 servings*

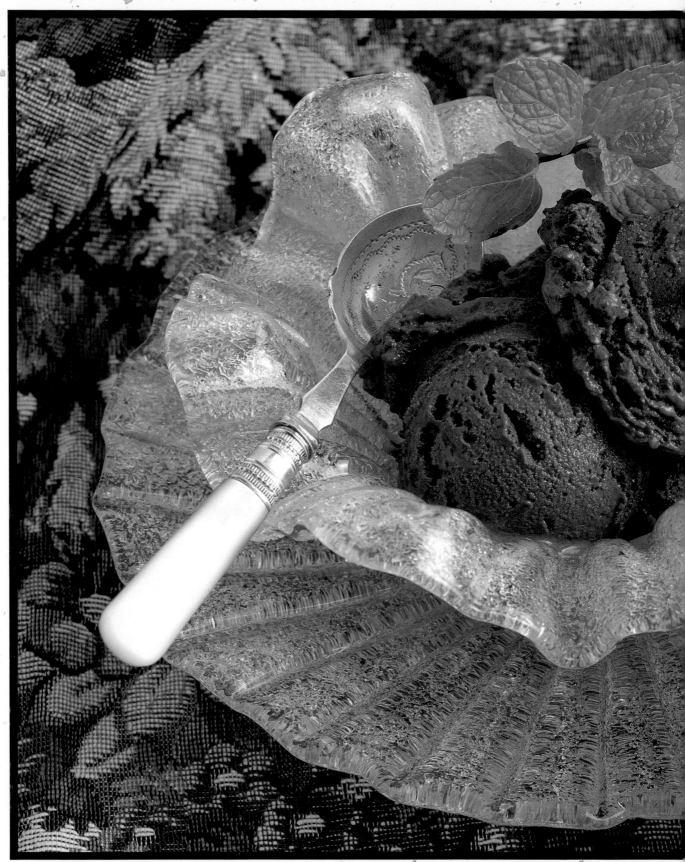

Chocolate Mint Sorbet

ICE CREAMS
AND FROZEN DESSERTS

As the creator of the original recipe for chocolate-mint sorbet led me through her mint patch, she snipped some peppermint sprigs to use in her summer chocolate sorbet. The resulting flavor of dark chocolate infused with cool menthol made for an incredibly refreshing ending to our meal.

CHOCOLATE-MINT SORBET

Sprinkle gelatin over 1 tablespoon cold water in a small cup; set aside for about 5 minutes, until gelatin softens. Place chocolate in a small, deep bowl and set aside. Thoroughly stir together sugar and cocoa powder in a large saucepan. Stir in cream and gelatin, until well blended. Bring to a boil, stirring frequently, over medium-high heat. Boil, stirring and scraping pan bottom, for one minute or until sugar and gelatin completely dissolve. Remove pan from heat. Immediately stir ¾ cup of cocoa mixture into chopped chocolate. Continue stirring until chocolate partially melts and mixture is smooth. Stir in ¾ cup more cocoa mixture. Continue stirring until chocolate completely melts and mixture is smooth. Return chocolate mixture to saucepan, stirring to blend. Stir 2 cups hot tap water and the schnapps into saucepan. Bruise (crush between fingers a bit) peppermint sprigs (if used) and stir into saucepan. Cover and refrigerate for one to two hours. Strain mixture through a fine sieve into a storage container. Cover and refrigerate mixture until very cold, at least six hours and preferably overnight. (If kitchen is warmer than 75°F., put the mixture in the freezer for an hour to chill it even further before processing.)

Pour chilled mixture into an ice-cream maker and process according to manufacturer's directions, except use a little extra salt. (Due to the alcohol in the schnapps, this sorbet will freeze more slowly and require longer processing than most ice creams.) When sorbet finishes processing, turn out into chilled storage container. Freeze at least four hours, or until firm. Garnish with mint sprigs, if desired.

Makes about 1½ quarts sorbet

1 teaspoon unflavored gelatin

4 ounces bittersweet or semisweet chocolate, chopped into ¼-inch pieces

1¼ cups granulated sugar

Generous ½ cup unsweetened, non-alkalized, American-style cocoa powder

2 cups light cream

¼ cup peppermint schnapps (see Note)

10 to 15 large sprigs of fresh peppermint, washed and patted dry (optional)

Fresh mint sprigs, for garnish (optional)

Note: If fresh variegated or plain peppermint is unavailable, the recipe can be prepared using only the peppermint schnapps, although the sorbet will of course have a less pronounced mint flavor and fragrance. (Don't substitute other varieties of mint for peppermint as they will not have the right taste.)

Not too bitter, sweet, or bold, but not bland either, this is the choice when you yearn for really good chocolate ice cream. The custard base not only lends the ice cream mellow flavor, but assures its smoothness as well.

CHOCOLATE CUSTARD ICE CREAM

Glace au Chocolat

Thoroughly stir together cocoa powder and ½ cup sugar in a large saucepan. Gradually whisk in milk, then cream, until blended. Bring mixture to a full boil over medium-high heat. Boil, stirring continuously, for 2 minutes; remove pan from heat. In a medium-sized, non-aluminum bowl, whisk together remaining sugar, eggs, and egg yolks, until smooth and well blended. Whisking continuously, gradually add about 1 cup cocoa mixture to egg mixture. Pour ⅓ cup cocoa mixture over chocolate in a small deep bowl, stirring until chocolate almost completely melts. Stir ½ cup more cocoa mixture into chocolate, stirring until chocolate is completely melted and smooth. Set aside.

Add egg mixture back to saucepan. Return saucepan to stove, continuously stirring and scraping pan bottom and adjusting burner so mixture heats efficiently but gently enough that it *does not near the boiling point* or eggs may curdle. (If using a candy thermometer, clip to pan side, adjusting so tip is completely submerged but does not touch pan bottom.) Watch carefully and if mixture begins to heat rapidly, immediately lift pan from heat and stir vigorously, as overheating may cause it to curdle. Continue cooking until mixture is very hot to the touch and leaves a film on a spoon (or until the thermometer registers 160°F.). Immediately remove pan from heat, continuing to stir for 30 seconds. Stir about 1 cup hot mixture into chocolate mixture, until well blended and smooth. Add chocolate mixture, then vanilla, back to egg mixture, stirring until well blended and smooth. Pour mixture through a fine sieve into a storage container. Cover and refrigerate until very cold, at least 6 hours.

Process mixture in an ice-cream maker according to manufacturer's directions. When ice cream finishes processing, turn out into a chilled storage container. Freeze until firm, at least 5 hours and preferably overnight, before serving. *Makes about 2 quarts ice cream*

⅓ cup unsweetened cocoa powder, preferably Dutch-process
1 cup granulated sugar, divided
2 cups whole milk
2⅓ cups heavy (whipping) cream
2 large eggs, plus 4 large egg yolks
4 ounces bittersweet (not unsweetened) or semisweet chocolate, coarsely chopped
2 teaspoons vanilla extract

Most ice creams called "fudge chunk" are noticeably dark and chocolatey, but they are not necessarily made from real fudge. The following version lives up to its name: a delicious fudge base is studded with succulent chunks of dark chocolate fudge.

FUDGE CHUNK ICE CREAM

To prepare fudge: Using a large wooden spoon, stir together sugar, corn syrup, ¾ cup cream, milk, and salt in a 4-quart or larger enameled cast-iron or other heavy saucepan. Stirring, bring mixture to a boil over medium-high heat; initially, it will boil up pan sides, then gradually subside. Carefully wash all sugar from stirring spoon. Continue to cook, uncovered and stirring frequently but gently, for 3 or 4 minutes, or until mixture begins to boil down and thicken slightly.

Lower heat to medium and continue to cook, stirring constantly and watching carefully to prevent scorching, until mixture turns a pale caramel color. Immediately remove pan from heat and add chocolate, gently stirring until completely melted. Stir in remaining ¼ cup cream and vanilla until evenly incorporated. Measure out ¾ cup fudge mixture in a heat-proof measuring cup. Pour measured amount into center of a large square of aluminum foil; let stand until thoroughly cooled. Wrap fudge in foil and refrigerate until thoroughly chilled.

To prepare ice cream base: Return pan with remaining fudge to burner. Stir cream and 2 cups milk into fudge until well blended. Heat mixture to hot, but not simmering, over medium-high heat. Remove from heat. In a small non-aluminum bowl, beat eggs, remaining ¼ cup milk, and sugar with a fork, until smooth and well blended. Using a fork, gradually beat about ½ cup fudge mixture into eggs until well blended. Stir egg mixture back into fudge mixture. Return pan to stove, continuously stirring and scraping pan bottom and adjusting burner so mixture heats efficiently, but gently enough that it *does not near the boiling point.* (If using a candy thermometer, clip to pan side, adjusting so tip is submerged but does not touch pan bottom.) Watch carefully and if mixture begins to heat rapidly, immediately lift pan from heat and stir

Fudge

1⅔ cup granulated sugar

⅓ cup light corn syrup

1 cup heavy (whipping) cream, divided

½ cup whole milk

⅛ teaspoon salt

7½ ounces unsweetened chocolate, broken or coarsely chopped

2 teaspoons vanilla extract

Ice Cream Base

Previously prepared fudge

2 cups heavy (whipping) cream

2¼ cups whole milk, divided

3 large eggs

3 tablespoons granulated sugar

Ice Cream Sandwich, Mocha Almond Ripple Ice Cream and Fudge Chunk Ice Cream

vigorously, as overheating may cause it to curdle. Continue cooking several minutes longer until mixture leaves a film on the spoon and is very hot to the touch, but not boiling (or until the thermometer registers 160°F.). Immediately remove pan from heat, continuing to stir for 15 seconds. Pour mixture through a fine sieve into a storage container. Cover and refrigerate until very cold, at least 6 hours and preferably overnight.

Meanwhile, prepare fudge chunks by peeling cold fudge from foil. Transfer to a cutting board. Chop fudge into about ⅛-inch or smaller chunks using a large sharp knife. Return chopped fudge, covered, to refrigerator.

Process chilled ice-cream mixture in an ice-cream maker according to manufacturer's directions. When finished processing, turn out about half of ice cream into a chilled storage container. Fold in half of cold fudge chunks. Repeat procedure, folding until ice cream and fudge chunks are blended. Freeze at least 5 hours before serving.

Makes about 2 quarts ice cream

Similar to a popular flavor at Baskin-Robbins ice cream shops, this ice cream features a mild mocha-flavored base enriched with ripples of chocolate and bits of toasted almonds. The almonds and ripple sauce can be made well in advance of the ice cream base, if desired. (They may also be omitted, as indicated in the note at the end of the recipe.)

MOCHA ALMOND RIPPLE ICE CREAM

In a heavy, 2-quart non-aluminum saucepan over high heat, combine half-and-half, cream, and coffee powder. Heat, stirring until coffee dissolves and mixture just comes to a boil; remove pan from heat. Pour ¼ cup hot cream mixture over chocolate in a small, deep bowl, stirring until chocolate almost completely melts. Stir in ¼ cup more hot liquid, stirring until chocolate is completely melted and smooth.

In a medium non-aluminum bowl, whisk together sugar and eggs until well blended. Whisking, gradually add about 1 cup of hot cream mixture to egg mixture until thoroughly incorporated. Then stir egg mixture back into saucepan. Return saucepan to stove, continuously stirring and scraping pan bottom and adjusting burner so mixture heats efficiently but gently enough that it *does not near the boiling point* or eggs may curdle. (If using a cooking thermometer to gauge doneness, clip it to pan side, inserting so tip is completely submerged but does not touch pan bottom.) Watch carefully and if mixture begins to heat rapidly, immediately lift pan from heat and stir vigorously, as overheating may cause it to curdle. Continue cooking until mixture is very hot to the touch and leaves a film on the spoon (or until it registers 160°F.

2 cups half-and-half

1½ cups heavy (whipping) cream

1½ teaspoons instant coffee powder or granules

2½ ounces bittersweet (not unsweetened) or semisweet chocolate, chopped moderately fine

¾ cup granulated sugar

4 large eggs

1½ teaspoons vanilla extract

¾ cup blanched sliced almonds, coarsely chopped

1 cup Chocolate Ripple Sauce (see page 235)

on a cooking thermometer). Immediately remove pan from heat, continuing to stir for 15 seconds. Stir about 1 cup hot mixture into chocolate mixture until well blended and smooth. Add chocolate mixture, then vanilla, back to cream mixture, stirring until well blended and smooth. Pour mixture through a fine sieve into a storage container. Cover and refrigerate until very cold, at least 6 hours and preferably overnight.

Preheat oven to 350°F. and spread almonds in a large roasting pan. Toast, stirring occasionally, for 5 to 6 minutes, or until nicely browned but not at all burned. Let stand until cooled. Refrigerate almonds until thoroughly chilled. (Almonds may be prepared ahead and refrigerated, in an airtight container, for up to 2 weeks.)

Refrigerate Chocolate Ripple Sauce, tightly covered, until very cold (or for up to 1 week, if desired).

Pour chilled mocha mixture into an ice-cream maker and proceed according to manufacturer's directions. When ice cream has finished processing, turn out a third of it into a chilled 2-quart storage container. Immediately fold in a third of the almonds and a third of the *chilled* ripple sauce until ice cream is rippled but not overmixed. Fold in remaining almonds and sauce in thirds, until all almonds and sauce are incorporated. Freeze at least 4 hours or until completely firm before serving. *Makes about 2 quarts ice cream*

Variations: Omit almonds for a good mocha-ripple ice cream. Or omit both the ripple sauce and the almonds for plain mocha ice cream.

RICH SWISS DOUBLE CHOCOLATE CHUNK ICE CREAM

Hans Geller's Eis

White Chocolate Ice Cream with Chocolate Truffle Chunks and Rich Swiss Double Chocolate Chunk Ice Cream

SWITZERLAND

Coarsely chop 7 ounces bittersweet chocolate; set aside in a medium bowl. Using a large, sharp knife, finely chop remaining 5 ounces bittersweet chocolate and the white chocolate. Cover and refrigerate.

In a heavy, 4-quart non-aluminum saucepan over high heat, combine half-and-half and heavy cream. Heat until mixture just comes to a boil; immediately remove from heat. Pour ½ cup hot mixture over the 7 ounces chopped bittersweet chocolate; stir until *very well blended* and smooth. Add ½ cup more hot mixture to chocolate, stirring until chocolate melts completely.

> 12 ounces Lindt Surfin or Excellence bittersweet chocolate, divided
> 6 ounces Lindt Blancor white chocolate
> 2¼ cups half-and-half
> 2 cups heavy (whipping) cream
> ½ cup granulated sugar
> 8 large egg yolks
> 2 teaspoons vanilla extract
> 2½ tablespoons light rum (see Note)

In a medium, non-aluminum bowl whisk together sugar and egg yolks, until smooth and well blended. Whisking, gradually add about 1 cup of hot cream mixture to egg mixture. Mix until well blended. Stir yolk mixture back into saucepan. Return saucepan to stove, continuously stirring and scraping pan bottom and adjusting burner so mixture heats efficiently but *does not near the boiling point.* (If using a candy thermometer to gauge doneness, clip it to pan side, inserting so tip is completely submerged but not touching pan bottom.) Watch carefully and if mixture begins to heat rapidly, immediately lift pan from heat and stir vigorously. Continue cooking until mixture just begins to thicken slightly and leaves a film on spoon (or until thermometer registers 160° to 161°F.). Immediately remove pan from heat, continuing to stir for 15 seconds. Stir about 1 cup hot mixture into chocolate-cream mixture until well blended. Stir chocolate mixture, vanilla, and rum back into yolk mixture until well blended. Pour mixture through a fine sieve into a storage container. Cover and refrigerate until very cold, at least 6 hours and preferably overnight.

Pour chilled mixture into an ice-cream maker and proceed according to manufacturer's directions. When ice cream finishes processing, turn out half of it into a chilled 2-quart storage container. Immediately fold in half of the chopped bittersweet and white chocolates. Add remaining ice cream and chocolate, folding until blended. Freeze at least 4½ hours, or until firm, and up to 8 hours before serving.

Makes about 1⅔ quarts ice cream

Note: The alcohol in the rum helps prevent this ice cream from firming up completely during storage. If rum must be omitted, serve ice cream within 8 hours of preparation, or allow it to soften prior to serving.

This is good! Some people even find it addictive. Inspired by one of the most popular flavors of the Ben & Jerry's ice cream company, it contains delicious, crunchy bits of chocolate-coated toffee in a light chocolate-coffee base. Ben & Jerry's version features Heath bars, which may be used here if you do not want to make the toffee crunch in the recipe.

TOFFEE CRUNCH ICE CREAM

Stir together cocoa powder, coffee powder, ½ cup sugar, and salt in 4-quart or larger saucepan, until thoroughly blended. Gradually stir in half-and-half and cream until evenly incorporated. Bring mixture just to a boil over high heat; immediately remove pan from burner. In a medium, non-aluminum bowl, whisk eggs and remaining ¼ cup sugar until smooth and well blended. Whisking continuously, gradually add about a third of cream mixture to eggs. Whisk until well blended. Stir egg mixture back into cream mixture. Return saucepan to stove, continuously stirring and scraping pan bottom and adjusting burner so mixture heats efficiently but gently enough that it *does not near the boiling point.* (If using a cooking thermometer to gauge doneness, clip it to pan side, inserting so tip is fully submerged but not touching pan bottom.) Watch carefully and if mixture begins to heat rapidly, immediately lift pan from heat and stir vigorously, as overheating may cause it to curdle. Continue cooking several minutes until mixture leaves a film on spoon and is very hot to the touch but not boiling. (Alternatively, cook mixture, stirring constantly and scraping pan bottom, until the thermometer registers 160° to

1½ tablespoons unsweetened, non-alkalized, American-style cocoa powder (such as Hershey's)

1 teaspoon instant coffee powder or granules

¾ cup granulated sugar, divided

⅛ teaspoon salt

2 cups half-and-half

2¼ cups heavy (whipping) cream

4 large eggs

2 teaspoons vanilla extract

7 ounces (about 1½ cups) Toffee Crunch, or chopped Heath bars

Toffee Crunch

1 tablespoon unsalted butter

1 tablespoon light corn syrup

½ cup granulated sugar

⅛ teaspoon salt

2 tablespoons chopped blanched slivered almonds

3 ounces (½ cup) semisweet chocolate chips or mini-chips

161°F.) Immediately remove pan from heat, continuing to stir for 15 seconds. Stir in vanilla. Pour mixture through a fine sieve into storage container. Cover and refrigerate until very cold, at least six hours and preferably overnight.

Refrigerate Heath bars or prepare Toffee Crunch as follows: Grease a heat-proof plate and set next to stove. Combine 1½ tablespoons water, butter, corn syrup, sugar, salt, and almonds in a 2-quart heavy sauce-pan. Stir with large wooden spoon until blended and sugar starts to dissolve; *do not stir mixture again.* Wipe any sugar crystals from pan sides using a damp paper towel. Heat pan over medium-high heat until mixture just comes to a boil. Cover tightly and boil 2 minutes. Uncover saucepan, lower heat, and continue boiling gently, occasionally lifting pan and swirling mixture to redistribute contents, until it *turns a me-dium-caramel color.* Immediately lift pan from heat and quickly pour mixture onto greased plate; do not scrape out excess from bottom. Spread out mixture slightly using lightly greased table knife. Let stand for 5 minutes or until slightly firm and very warm but not hot. Sprinkle chocolate chips over toffee. When chips have partially melted, spread them over toffee surface using table knife. Immediately refrigerate until toffee is completely cooled and chocolate is hard. Place toffee slab in heavy plastic bag. Pound into small bite-sized pieces using a mallet or heavy spoon. Refrigerate pieces in an airtight container until needed.

Pour chilled cream mixture into an ice-cream maker and proceed according to manufacturer's directions. When ice cream finishes processing, turn out about half of it into a chilled storage container. Fold in half of toffee. Add remaining ice cream and toffee, folding until blended. Freeze at least 5 hours before serving. *Makes about 2 quarts ice cream*

The appealing interplay of flavors and textures—mild, custardy white chocolate ice cream, smooth chunks of creamy chocolate ganache, and crisp shards of bittersweet chocolate—make this gourmet ice cream exceptional. ❖ *For a good white chocolate ice cream simply omit the chopped chocolate and truffle mixture.*

WHITE CHOCOLATE ICE CREAM WITH CHOCOLATE TRUFFLE CHUNKS

Trüffeleis

To prepare ice cream: In a heavy, 2-quart or larger non-aluminum saucepan over high heat, combine half-and-half and 1½ cups heavy cream. Heat until mixture just comes to a simmer; immediately remove pan from heat. Pour 1 cup hot cream mixture over chopped white chocolate in a medium bowl, stirring until *very well blended* and smooth. Add ½ cup more hot cream mixture to chocolate, stirring until chocolate completely melts.

In a medium-sized non-aluminum bowl whisk together sugar, eggs, and remaining ½ cup cream, until smooth and well blended. Whisking, gradually add about 1 cup of hot cream mixture to egg mixture. Mix until well blended. Then stir egg mixture back into cream in saucepan. Return saucepan to burner, continuously stirring and scraping pan bottom and adjusting burner so mixture heats efficiently but *does not near the boiling point.* (If using a candy thermometer to gauge doneness, clip to pan side, adjusting so tip is submerged but does not touch pan bottom.) Watch carefully and if mixture begins to heat rapidly, immediately lift pan from heat and stir vigorously, as overheating may cause it to curdle. Continue cooking for 2 to 3 minutes or until mixture is very hot to the touch and leaves a film on the spoon (or until the thermom-

Ice Cream

2 cups half-and-half or light cream

2 cups heavy (whipping) cream, divided

12 ounces Swiss white chocolate, coarsely chopped

¼ cup granulated sugar

4 large eggs

2 teaspoons vanilla extract

2 tablespoons white crème de cacao or light rum

Truffle Mixture

6 ounces Swiss bittersweet chocolate, very finely chopped (divided)

3 ounces top-quality Swiss milk chocolate, chopped into ¼-inch pieces

¼ cup heavy (whipping) cream

1½ tablespoons unsalted butter, cut into small pieces

¼ teaspoon instant coffee powder or granules

¼ teaspoon vanilla extract

eter registers 160°F.). Immediately remove pan from heat, continuing to stir for 15 seconds. Stir about 1 cup hot egg mixture into white chocolate–cream mixture, until well blended. Then stir chocolate mixture, vanilla, and crème de cacao back into egg mixture, until well blended. Pour mixture through a fine sieve into a storage container. Cover and refrigerate until very cold, at least 6 hours.

To prepare truffle mixture: Refrigerate half of chopped bittersweet chocolate in a medium bowl. Line an 8-inch baking pan with aluminum foil, allowing foil to overhang 2 opposite ends slightly. Set milk chocolate and remaining bittersweet chocolate in a small, deep bowl. In a small saucepan over medium-high heat, bring cream, butter, and coffee powder to a boil. Continue boiling until butter completely melts. Remove pan from heat and strain mixture through a fine sieve into chocolate, stirring. Continue stirring until chocolate completely melts and mixture is smooth. (If mixture has cooled and unmelted bits of chocolate remain, set bowl in a shallow bowl of very hot water and stir until chocolate melts.) Stir in vanilla. Pour truffle mixture into pan, spreading to even surface. Cover and freeze for at least 2 hours and up to 48 hours, if desired. Lift truffle mixture from pan using foil as handles. Gently peel off foil. Transfer slab to cutting board. Cut truffle slab into thirds. Return two portions to freezer to stay cold while working with remaining third. Chop mixture into 1/8-inch pieces using a sharp knife. As truffle pieces are chopped, stir them into bowl of reserved finely chopped bittersweet chocolate until coated (to keep them from clumping together). Repeat chopping procedure with remaining two portions of truffle mixture. Cover bowl of chopped chocolate and truffle pieces and return to freezer.

Pour chilled ice cream mixture into an ice-cream maker and proceed according to manufacturer's directions. When ice cream finishes processing, turn out about half of it into a *chilled* storage container. Fold in half of frozen truffle chunks and chilled chopped bittersweet chocolate. Repeat procedure, folding until ice cream and bits are blended. Freeze at least 5 hours before serving. (If liqueur or rum is omitted, allow ice cream to soften slightly before serving.)

Makes about 2 quarts ice cream.

White Chocolate–Bittersweet Chip Ice Cream Variation: Omit the chocolate truffle mixture and fold 6 ounces finely chopped bittersweet chocolate into finished ice cream.

Described in simplest terms, this is an ice cream cake. But, oh what an ice cream cake! Pinwheel slices of whipped cream–filled chocolate cake are arranged around the bottom and sides of a dome-shaped bowl; then the interior is filled with ice cream. The frozen cake is unmolded and served garnished with whipped cream, candied cherries, and chocolate sauce. ❖ *Though dramatic and festive to look at, frozen charlotte royale is not really difficult to make and can be assembled and decorated entirely in advance.*

FROZEN CHOCOLATE-CHERRY CHARLOTTE ROYALE

Charlotte Royale Glacée au Chocolat et aux Cerises

To prepare cake roll: Position a rack in center of oven and preheat to 375°F. Generously grease a 10-by-15-inch (or similar) jelly-roll pan. Line pan with wax paper or baking parchment, allowing paper to overhang pan ends slightly. Generously grease paper or spray with nonstick vegetable cooking spray.

Sift together flour and cocoa powder; set aside. Combine yolks in a large mixer bowl with ½ cup sugar, salt, and 1 tablespoon hot tap water. Beat on medium speed until foamy. Raise speed to high and continue beating 3 to 4 minutes or until mixture is lightened, increased in volume, and drops from beaters in thick ribbons. Beat in vanilla and almond extract. Working quickly and gently (so as not to deflate), sprinkle flour-cocoa mixture over beaten yolks and lightly fold five or six times with a rubber spatula to partially incorporate. Set aside.

Continuing to work quickly, in a grease-free mixer bowl with grease-free beaters, beat egg

Sponge Cake Roll
⅓ cup all-purpose flour
¼ cup unsweetened cocoa powder, preferably Dutch-process (European-style)
4 large eggs, plus 1 large egg yolk, separated (whites completely free of yolk)
¾ cup granulated sugar, divided
⅛ teaspoon salt
1½ teaspoons vanilla extract
¼ teaspoon almond extract
Additional cocoa powder for dusting cake roll

whites with mixer on medium speed, until frothy. Raise speed to high and beat until soft peaks just begin to form. Gradually add remaining sugar. Continue beating until whites stand in slightly firm peaks. Using a wire whisk, mix about a third of whites into yolk mixture. Add remaining whites and continue mixing until ingredients are evenly incorporated but not overmixed. Immediately turn out batter into prepared pan, spreading to edges to form a layer of even thickness.

Quickly transfer to oven. Bake for 10 to 14 minutes or until cake is just slightly darker at the edges and springs back when lightly pressed in center. Transfer pan to a wire rack. Very loosely drape a slightly damp tea towel over cake and let stand for about 5 minutes. Remove towel. Run a knife around pan edges to loosen cake and paper. Very lightly dust a long sheet of wax paper with cocoa powder. Loosen cake and attached paper from pan and invert onto cocoa-dusted wax paper. Gently peel off attached wax paper and discard. Trim off any dry edges of cake. Cover cake with another fresh sheet of wax paper. Let cake stand for about 10 minutes longer, until cooled to warm; discard top sheet of wax paper.

Working from a longer side, carefully and *tightly* roll up sponge cake in wax paper to form an even 15-inch log; don't worry about any cracks in cake. Secure log in the wax paper by folding or twisting ends. Tighten wrap-

Fillings

1½ tablespoons kirsch (cherry brandy), or substitute 1 tablespoon water and 3 drops almond extract, if preferred

⅔ cup sour-cherry preserves, heated, strained, and cooled to barely warm

¾ cup heavy (whipping) cream

2 tablespoons powdered sugar

¼ teaspoon vanilla extract

1½ to 2 quarts vanilla, French vanilla, or cherry-vanilla ice cream, slightly soft but not at all melted

Garnishes

About ½ cup red candied cherries, cut in half (optional)

1 cup lightly sweetened whipped cream, for garnish (optional)

10 to 15 red candied cherries, halved, for garnish (optional)

Warm Chocolate Sauce (page 233) or, Hot Fudge Sauce (page 232)

ping to compress log and keep it from unrolling. Store log refrigerated for up to 2 days, or wrapped airtight and frozen for up to 2 weeks. (If frozen, thaw before using.)

To fill cake-roll: Carefully unroll cake-roll. Stir together kirsch and strained cherry preserves. Cover cake surface evenly with preserves, brushing with pastry brush or spreading with long-bladed spatula. In a large mixer bowl on high speed, beat cream, powdered sugar, and vanilla until cream stands in firm but not stiff peaks. Using a long-bladed spatula or table knife, spread whipped cream evenly over surface of cake roll, stopping about ½ inch before reaching outside long edge (to prevent filling from squeezing out along length of rolled-up cake). Working from opposite long side, roll up cake-roll neatly (but not so tightly that cream is squeezed out from ends). Wrap in a clean sheet of wax paper, folding or twisting ends. Transfer roll to tray and freeze until roll is completely frozen, at least 3 hours.

Assemble charlotte as follows: Line interior of a 2-quart or larger kitchen bowl with tapered bottom with plastic wrap, smoothing wrap as much as possible and leaving several inches of wrap overhanging on all sides. Slice frozen cake-roll crosswise into scant ¼-inch slices using a large serrated knife and cutting with a sawing motion. Arrange slices attractively in bottom of bowl. Then add two rows around bowl sides, spacing as close together as possible. Press down on slices to fill any gaps. Spoon ice cream into bowl. Lay a sheet of wax paper over ice cream and press down firmly to eliminate air pockets and fill spaces around cake slices. Remove wax paper. Working in concentric circles, beginning just inside side layers, arrange remaining slices attractively over ice cream to cover bottom. (If there aren't enough slices to fully cover interior, just leave center plain.) Lay a sheet of wax paper over slices and press down all over to even surface; discard paper. Cover bowl with plastic wrap and freeze at least 8 hours and preferably 24 hours until charlotte is completely frozen.

To garnish and serve charlotte: Loosen and lift dessert from bowl using overlapping plastic wrap as handles. Invert and center dessert on serving plate and lift off plastic wrap. If desired, press cherry halves, domed side out, in spaces between the slices. If desired, pipe a crown of whipped-cream rosettes or shells around top of charlotte and a ring of shells around bottom edge. Garnish whipped cream with candied cherry halves, if desired. (Cake may be returned to freezer until serving time or served immediately.) Serve cake frozen, cut into wedges using a large, sharp knife. Pass chocolate sauce separately.

Makes about 12 servings

FRANCE

This incredibly smooth and mellow ice cream–like dessert is enriched with bits of hazelnut praline and topped with a bittersweet mocha glaze. It does not require an ice-cream freezer.

CHOCOLATE-HAZELNUT PARFAIT

Parfait au Chocolat et aux Noisettes

Position a rack in center of oven and preheat to 350°F. Lightly grease an 8- or 8½-inch springform pan. Grease a piece of aluminum foil. Lay, greased-side up, on a heat-proof plate.

Place hazelnuts in a roasting pan and toast, stirring occasionally, for 12 to 15 minutes, or until hulls loosen and nuts are tinged with brown. Using hands or kitchen towel, rub off and discard loose bits of hull. Chop nuts moderately fine.

Melt chocolate in the top of a double boiler over about 1 inch hot but not simmering water, stirring occasionally, until chocolate melts. Set aside with top of double boiler still over bottom to keep chocolate warm.

Beat yolks and 1 tablespoon hot tap water in a large mixer bowl, until smooth and well blended. With mixer on high speed, beat mixture about 3 minutes longer, until very light and fluffy.

Meanwhile, combine ⅔ cup sugar and corn syrup in a medium-sized, heavy saucepan, stirring with a large wooden spoon until well mixed and sugar begins to dissolve. Wipe sugar from pan sides using a damp paper towel. Bring mixture just to a boil over medium-high heat, stirring. Cover mixture and boil, without stirring, for exactly 1 minute.

Immediately remove saucepan from heat. Measure out ½ cup syrup into a heat-proof cup. With mixer on high speed, begin pouring a thin stream of measured syrup down bowl side into yolk mixture, avoiding pouring on beaters or directly on yolks as

¾ cup hazelnuts

4½ ounces bittersweet (not unsweetened) or semisweet chocolate, coarsely chopped or broken into pieces

7 large egg yolks

⅔ cup plus 3 tablespoons granulated sugar, divided

½ cup light corn syrup

2 tablespoons sifted unsweetened cocoa powder, preferably Dutch-process (European-style)

2½ cups heavy (whipping) cream

2 teaspoons vanilla extract

1 tablespoon light or dark rum (optional)
Glaze

2 tablespoons unsweetened cocoa powder, preferably Dutch-process (European-style)

3 tablespoons granulated sugar

2 tablespoons light corn syrup

¾ teaspoon instant coffee powder or granules

1½ ounces bittersweet (not unsweetened) or semisweet chocolate, chopped into ¼-inch pieces

syrup will stick to beaters and may curdle yolks. Add syrup in a thin continuous stream, pouring so all is incorporated in about 10 seconds. Beat on high speed for about 2 minutes. Add cocoa powder and continue beating until the mixture cools to warm and is very light and fluffy, about 3 minutes. Using a rubber spatula, fold melted chocolate into the beaten mixture until well blended

Return syrup remaining in saucepan to burner over medium-high heat. Continue heating, lifting pan and swirling mixture occasionally, until it turns golden but not brown. Immediately remove from heat and stir in hazelnuts until evenly incorporated. Turn out mixture onto foil-lined plate, spreading into a layer with a spoon. Carefully lift foil and wrap around mixture. Transfer to freezer until cooled and firm, about 8 to 10 minutes. Transfer mixture to heavy plastic bag and break into ¼-inch or smaller pieces using kitchen mallet or back of a heavy metal spoon.

In a large mixer bowl, beat heavy cream to soft peaks. Beat in remaining 3 tablespoons sugar and continue beating until firm but not dry peaks form. Fold vanilla and rum (if used) into cream. Fold in chocolate mixture and hazelnuts until thoroughly blended.

Turn out the mixture into springform pan, smoothing surface, then rapping on counter until even. Freeze in a very cold freezer until surface is firm (at least 2 hours) before adding glaze.

To prepare glaze: Stir together cocoa and sugar in a small saucepan until well blended. Stir in ¼ cup hot tap water until evenly incorporated. Stir in corn syrup. Bring mixture just to a boil over medium-high heat. Boil for 30 seconds, stirring, and remove from heat. Stir in coffee powder and chocolate. Continue stirring until chocolate completely melts and mixture is smooth. Refrigerate glaze until cool but *not stiff,* about 15 minutes. Pour over surface of frozen parfait. Immediately spread evenly to edges using a table knife. Cover parfait and return to freezer for at least 4 hours longer and up to 48 hours prior to serving.

Serve parfait cut into wedges. *Makes 9 to 12 servings*

FROZEN PRALINE CHOCOLATE TERRINE

Semifreddo al Torrone

ITALY

A number of different Italian desserts are called semifreddo—iced mousses, whipped frozen custards, and layered frozen terrines, such as the following. Most are rich and airy and studded with nuts, cookie crumbs, and/or chocolate. ❖ *This recipe features light, creamy layers accented with bits of crushed caramelized almonds and bittersweet chocolate.*

Position a rack in center of oven and preheat to 350°F. Line a 4½-by-8-inch loaf pan with plastic wrap, allowing wrap to overhang by at least 2 inches on all sides. Chill pan in freezer. Line a heat-proof plate with aluminum foil; grease foil. Spread almonds in a roasting pan. Toast, stirring occasionally, for 6 to 7 minutes until tinged with brown. Set aside to cool.

In a large bowl with stand mixer set on medium speed, beat eggs until blended. Raise speed to high and beat in cocoa and coffee powder. Allow mixture to continue beating and prepare caramel syrup. To prepare syrup, combine sugar, corn syrup, and ¼ cup water in a medium saucepan, stirring until well blended. Wipe sugar from pan sides with a damp paper towel. Bring to a simmer over medium-high heat. Cover and boil for 2 minutes to allow steam to wash any remaining sugar crystals from pan sides. Uncover and continue simmering, lifting pan and swirling occasionally but never stirring, for about 2 minutes longer, until syrup thickens, bubbles vigorously, and just begins to turn pale amber. Immediately remove pan from heat. Working carefully as mixture is very hot, measure ¾ cup syrup into a heat-proof cup. Raise mixer speed to high and immediately add syrup to egg mixture by pouring measured ¾ cup syrup in a thin but steady stream down bowl side (avoid beaters or whip as syrup will stick), adjusting flow so that all syrup is incorporated in about 15 seconds. Continue beating on high speed until mixture cools to lukewarm, about 4 to 5 minutes. Beat in vanilla.

1 cup coarsely chopped blanched slivered almonds

3 large eggs

1 tablespoon unsweetened, non-alkalized, American-style cocoa powder

½ teaspoon instant coffee powder or granules

1⅓ cups granulated sugar

¼ cup light corn syrup

1 teaspoon vanilla extract

2 cups heavy (whipping) cream

2 ounces bittersweet (not unsweetened) or semisweet chocolate, coarsely grated or very finely chopped

Chocolate curls or shavings, for garnish (optional)

Caramel-Chocolate Sauce (page 234), for serving (optional)

Meanwhile, return pan with remaining caramel syrup to stove and heat until fluid. Quickly add nuts, stirring with a clean wooden spoon until well coated with syrup. Immediately spread praline on greased foil. Let stand until cooled slightly. Then wrap foil around mixture and place in freezer until completely cold, about 10 minutes. Peel mixture from foil. Transfer to a heavy plastic bag and crack into ⅛-inch or smaller pieces using kitchen mallet or back of a heavy spoon.

In a large mixing bowl, beat heavy cream to firm but not stiff peaks. Using a wire whisk, whisk cream into egg mixture until completely blended and smooth. Turn out about a scant third of mixture into prepared loaf pan, smoothing surface with table knife. Sprinkle *half* of grated chocolate and a *third* of reserved praline down center of layer. Carefully add another third of cream mixture, gently smoothing surface. Sprinkle over remainder of grated chocolate and another third of praline. Top with remaining cream mixture, smoothing surface. Rap pan sharply on counter several times to remove air pockets. Lay plastic wrap over surface, pressing down firmly. Cover and freeze in *very cold* freezer for at least 8 hours and preferably 24 hours. Reserve remaining praline to garnish terrine just before serving.

To garnish and serve, discard top sheet of plastic. Lift terrine from pan using plastic for handles. Invert on serving plate; discard plastic. Smooth terrine sides and top slightly using table knife or long-bladed spatula. Sprinkle reserved praline over top and sides of terrine, pressing firmly to imbed just slightly. Garnish top with a few chocolate curls, if desired. Serve terrine whole or cut into slices using a large knife. Slices should be served immediately accompanied by Caramel-Chocolate Sauce (page 234), if desired.   *Makes 8 to 10 servings*

Chocolate-covered banana pops are a favorite summer treat among children (and a lot of grownups), and make a fun and easy dessert project for teenagers, or for younger children supervised by an adult. Since some folks like banana pops studded with peanut chunks and others like them plain, directions are included for preparing them both ways.

❖ *Wooden sticks, which can often be found in craft shops, are needed for this recipe. If necessary, substitute lengths of small, sturdy dowels or balsa wood strips. Never use thin skewers or pointed sticks as these can splinter and jab the skin.*

FROZEN BANANA-CHOCOLATE POPS

Peel bananas; discard any stringy fibers. Cut each banana in half crosswise to yield 2 pops. Push a stick about 1½ inches into each banana half to form a holder. Wrap banana halves individually in plastic wrap or plastic sandwich bags. Freeze at least 5 hours and up to 48 hours, if desired.

In a small, heavy saucepan over *lowest heat,* slowly melt chocolate and oil, stirring frequently. Pour melted chocolate into a jar or sturdy drinking glass that is tall enough to hold chocolate and wide enough for bananas to be conveniently dipped into it. Refrigerate, stirring occasionally, about 10 minutes, until cooled slightly but not stiff. Meanwhile, line a metal tray or pan with wax paper and place in freezer until very cold. If preparing peanut-coated pops, spread peanuts on a plate.

3 to 4 unbruised, fully ripe or slightly over-ripe small or medium-sized bananas

8 ounces bittersweet or semisweet chocolate, coarsely chopped

3½ tablespoons corn oil, sunflower oil, or safflower oil

¼ to ⅓ cup finely chopped unsalted roasted peanuts (optional)

Working one at a time, hold banana by the stick and dip into chocolate, tipping jar to one side and quickly rotating banana until covered all over. Hold banana upright so excess chocolate drips toward stick. For peanut-topped pops immediately roll banana in nuts or spoon nuts over top, turning until lightly coated. For plain pops, hold banana upright for about a minute, until chocolate begins to chill and harden. Immediately transfer pop to chilled tray. Continue until all pops are formed. Freeze at least 20 minutes and preferably 1 hour until chocolate is completely chilled. Store pops airtight, for up to a week.

Makes 6 to 8 banana pops

White Chocolate Drop Cookies and Thick and Chewy Chocolate Chip Cookies

COOKIES AND BARS

Both the current American passion for white chocolate and our enduring love for chocolate chip cookies are satisfied in these buttery, tender-crisp drop cookies.

WHITE CHOCOLATE DROP COOKIES

Melt butter in a medium saucepan over medium heat. Adjust heat so butter boils very gently, but steadily. Cook, uncovered, stirring frequently, for 4 to 6 minutes, until foaming subsides and butter turns golden but not brown; watch carefully to avoid burning on the bottom. Immediately remove pan from heat, stirring for 30 seconds. Refrigerate 45 to 55 minutes, until butter resolidifies but is not hard. (Alternatively, to hasten chilling, freeze mixture, stirring occasionally, for about 30 minutes; be careful butter doesn't become too cold and hard.) Very finely grate about a third of the chocolate. If white chocolate bars or large chips are used, chop remaining two thirds into ¼-inch pieces.

Position rack in center of oven and preheat to 350°F. Grease several baking sheets. Thoroughly stir together flour, cornstarch, baking soda, and salt; set aside. In a large mixer bowl, with mixer set at medium speed, beat butter until softened and light. Add brown sugar and beat 3 or 4 minutes, until very light and smooth. Beat in egg and vanilla until well blended. Beat in dry ingredients just until incorporated. Stir in grated and chopped chocolate and macadamia nuts (if used) until distributed throughout. Drop dough by scant, rounded teaspoonfuls, spacing about 2½ inches apart. (Don't crowd, as cookies may spread.)

Bake for 6 to 9 minutes or until cookies are rimmed with brown, puffy, and tinged with light brown in center. (The cookies will fall slightly as they cool.) Remove pan from oven and let stand for 2 minutes, until cookies firm up slightly. Using a thin, wide-bladed spatula immediately remove cookies to wire racks. (If they are too cool and brittle to remove without breaking, return pan to oven for a few seconds to soften cookies just slightly.) Let cookies stand on racks until thoroughly cooled.

Since cookies are fragile, pack them flat, with wax paper between layers. Store in an airtight container for up to a week. Freeze for longer storage.

Makes about 35 2½-inch cookies

⅔ cup (1 stick plus 2⅔ tablespoons) unsalted butter

8 ounces top-quality white chocolate or white chocolate chips

¾ cup plus 2 tablespoons all-purpose flour

1 tablespoon cornstarch

¼ teaspoon baking soda

Generous ⅛ teaspoon salt

¼ cup packed light brown sugar

1 large egg

1½ teaspoons vanilla extract

⅓ cup chopped macadamia nuts (optional)

Both kids and grownups like these plump, chewy cookies studded with semisweet chocolate chips and flecks of milk chocolate.

THICK AND CHEWY CHOCOLATE CHIP COOKIES

Position a rack in center third of oven and preheat to 375°F. Grease several baking sheets and set aside.

Place rolled oats in a food processor fitted with a steel blade and process until ground to a *very fine powder.* (Or grind in a blender, stopping and stirring to redistribute contents several times.) Add milk chocolate and process until chopped fairly fine. (If blender is used, coarsely grate milk chocolate by hand; do not blend.) In a large bowl, thoroughly stir together ground oats, milk chocolate, flour, baking powder, baking soda, and salt; set aside.

In a large mixer bowl with mixer set on medium speed, beat butter until lightened. Add sugars and beat until fluffy and smooth. Beat in egg and yolk, vanilla, and milk, until well-blended. Beat in two-thirds of flour-oat mixture just until incorporated. Stir in remaining flour-oat mixture, chocolate chips, and walnuts (if used), just until evenly incorporated. Set mixture aside for 5 to 10 minutes to stiffen just slightly. Using lightly greased hands, shape dough into 1½-inch balls (it will be soft but manageable). Space cookies about 2½ inches apart on baking sheets.

Bake cookies for 8 to 11 minutes or until lightly tinged with brown on top and just barely darker at the edges, reversing pans from front to back halfway through baking to ensure even browning. (Cookies will not be completely firm on top; be very careful not to overbake.) Remove pans from oven and let stand for 1 minute. Using a spatula, transfer cookies to wire racks and let stand until thoroughly cooled.

Store in an airtight container for up to a week. Freeze for longer storage.

Makes 45 to 50 2¾- to 3-inch cookies

Note: If milk chocolate is unavailable, ½ cup extra semisweet chocolate chips may be substituted and finely chopped instead. The flavor of the cookies will be different, however.

---

1 cup old-fashioned or quick-cooking rolled oats

3 ounces high-quality milk chocolate, broken into small pieces (see Note)

2¼ cups all-purpose flour

1 teaspoon baking powder

1 teaspoon baking soda

Generous ¼ teaspoon salt

1¼ cups (2½ sticks) unsalted butter, slightly softened

1 cup packed light brown sugar

Scant ½ cup granulated sugar

1 large egg, plus 1 large egg yolk

1 tablespoon vanilla extract

2 teaspoons whole milk

2 cups (12 ounces) regular or mini-size semisweet chocolate chips

1½ cups chopped walnuts (optional)

Crinkles are named for their dramatic, crinkly-cracked tops. The fudgy, brownie-like balls of dough are coated with powdered sugar prior to baking; later when dark cracks form they stand out in bold contrast to the powdery white surface.

Melt butter and chocolate in a large, heavy saucepan over lowest heat, stirring constantly, until well blended and smooth. Remove pan from heat. Stir in sugar until mixture is well blended. One at a time, beat in eggs with a fork. Stir in vanilla. Set mixture aside, stirring occasionally, for 6 to 8 minutes to allow sugar to dissolve. Thoroughly stir together flour, cocoa powder, salt, and baking powder. Add dry ingredients to chocolate mixture, stirring just until well blended. Cover and refrigerate mixture until firm enough to shape into balls, at least 1½ hours and up to 8 hours, if desired.

Position a rack in center of oven and preheat to 325°F. Generously grease several baking sheets and set aside. Set out about half of powdered sugar in a deep, medium-sized bowl; reserve remainder. Roll chilled dough between lightly greased palms to form a 1¼-inch-diameter ball. Then drop ball into powdered sugar and rotate bowl until ball is heavily coated and no chocolate shows through. Lift with slotted spoon, tapping off excess sugar against bowl side. Transfer to baking sheet. Continue forming cookies, spacing about 1½ inches apart on sheets. Frequently wipe chocolate from hands with paper towels. Replenish bowl of powdered sugar as needed. Clean and regrease sheets after each sheet of cookies is baked.

Bake cookies for 11 to 14 minutes or until just beginning to feel firm when pressed in center top. (For moist, chewy cookies don't over-bake.) Transfer pan to a wire rack. Let stand several minutes. Remove cookies from pan and let stand on racks until thoroughly cooled.

Pack cookies, airtight, in a single layer. They are best fresh, but can be stored for several days.

Makes 35 to 40 1½-inch cookies

Note: To make superfine sugar, grind in a food processor until very fine.

6½ tablespoons unsalted butter

7 ounces semisweet or bittersweet (not unsweetened) chocolate, coarsely chopped or broken into small pieces

⅔ cup granulated sugar, preferably superfine (see Note)

3 large eggs

2½ teaspoons vanilla extract

1½ cups all-purpose flour

3 tablespoons unsweetened, non-alkalized, American-style cocoa powder (such as Hershey's)

¼ teaspoon salt

½ teaspoon baking powder

About 1 to 1¼ cups sifted powdered sugar, for coating cookies

CHOCOLATE CRINKLES

The following is adapted from a recipe shared with me by one of my recipe testers, Trish Trahan. She says these are her family's all-time favorite chocolate chip cookies. Fairly thin, very crisp, buttery, and chock-full of flavor, they may become a favorite at your house as well.

CRISPY CHOCOLATE CHIP COOKIES

Bring butter to a boil in a small, heavy saucepan over medium-high heat. Adjust heat so butter simmers gently (it will foam up at first, then gradually foaming will subside). Stirring frequently and watching carefully to prevent burning, cook for about 4 minutes, until butter turns a rich golden color *but not brown*. Immediately remove from heat, stirring for 30 seconds. Transfer butter to a mixer bowl and refrigerate for about 1 hour until resolidified but not hard. (Or speed up cooling by placing butter in freezer for 20 to 30 minutes; be careful it doesn't get too hard.)

Position a rack in center third of oven and preheat to 375°F. Grease several baking sheets and set aside. Thoroughly stir together flour, baking powder, baking soda, and salt; set aside.

In a large mixer bowl with mixer set on medium speed, beat butter several minutes until lightened and smooth. Add sugars, egg, and vanilla and beat until very well blended and smooth. Gently beat in half of flour mixture just until incorporated. Beat or stir in remaining flour mixture until evenly incorporated but not overmixed. Stir in chocolate chips and walnuts just until evenly distributed. Drop cookies by teaspoonfuls, 2 inches apart, on baking sheets.

Bake cookies for 8 to 10 minutes or until tinged with brown on top and just slightly darker on the edges, reversing pans from front to back halfway through baking to ensure even browning. (For the most tender cookies be careful not to overbake.) Remove pans from oven and let stand for 1 minute. Using a spatula, transfer cookies to wire racks and let stand until thoroughly cooled.

Store in an airtight container for up to 1 week. Freeze for longer storage.

Makes about 35 2¾-inch cookies

---

1 cup (2 sticks) unsalted butter
1¾ cups plus 1 tablespoon all-purpose flour
¾ teaspoon baking powder
½ teaspoon baking soda
Generous ¼ teaspoon salt
1 cup packed light brown sugar
¼ cup granulated sugar
1 large egg
2½ teaspoons vanilla extract
1 cup (6 ounces) regular or mini-size semisweet chocolate chips
1 cup chopped walnuts (optional)

A crispy-chewy texture and flavorful mix of coconut, peanut butter, and chocolate chips make these cookies distinctive and appealing. ❖ The cookies are soft and crumbly when warm, so be sure to let them firm up a few minutes before transferring to cooling racks.

PEANUT BUTTER COCONUT CHIPPERS

Position rack in center third of oven and preheat to 325°F. Generously grease several baking sheets and set aside. In a large bowl, thoroughly stir together coconut, oats, and milk until well blended; set aside. In a medium saucepan over medium heat, stir together butter, peanut butter, sugars, and corn syrup just until butter melts. Immediately remove pan from heat. Stir peanut butter mixture and vanilla into oat mixture. In a medium bowl, thoroughly stir together flour, baking soda, baking powder, and salt. Stir flour mixture into oat mixture just until incorporated. Refrigerate for about 15 to 20 minutes, until mixture is cool to the touch. Stir in chocolate chips and peanuts (if used) just until distributed throughout. Using lightly greased hands, shape dough into 1¼-inch balls. Space on baking sheets about 2½ inches apart. Using heel of hand, flatten tops of cookies just slightly.

Bake cookies for 13 to 16 minutes, or until lightly tinged with brown all over and just barely darker at the edges, reversing pans from front to back halfway through baking to ensure even browning. (Cookies will still be very soft in center.) Remove pans from oven and let stand for 4 to 5 minutes, or until cookies firm up. Using a spatula, carefully transfer cookies to wire racks. Let stand until thoroughly cooled.

Store in an airtight container for up to 3 or 4 days. Freeze for longer storage.

> 1⅓ cups (about 3½ ounces) lightly packed flaked or shredded sweetened coconut
> 1 cup old-fashioned or quick-cooking rolled oats
> 2½ tablespoons whole or lowfat milk
> ½ cup (1 stick) unsalted butter, slightly softened
> ½ cup smooth or chunky-style peanut butter
> ¾ cup packed light or dark brown sugar
> ¼ cup granulated sugar
> 3½ tablespoons light or dark corn syrup
> 2 teaspoons vanilla extract
> 1¼ cups all-purpose flour
> ¾ teaspoon baking soda
> ¼ teaspoon baking powder
> ⅛ teaspoon salt
> 2 cups (12 ounces) semisweet chocolate chips
> ⅔ cup roasted peanuts (preferably unsalted), chopped moderately fine (optional)

Makes 30 to 35 2½- to 2¾-inch cookies

These mild, pleasantly crisp chocolate sugar cookies are cut out in teddy-bear shapes.

❖ *Although the cookies are nice undecorated, they can be dressed up with a thin, shiny "brown bear" icing and even finished with colorful contrasting piping, if desired. A fun family baking project and thoughtful children's gift, they also make charming edible ornaments for a Christmas tree. (To prepare cookies for stringing and hanging, push a short length of spaghetti through dough at the point where the hole is desired just prior to baking. Remove the spaghetti pieces while cookies are still warm.)*

CHOCOLATE SUGAR BEARS

Thoroughly stir together flour, baking powder, and salt; set aside. Combine chocolate and powdered sugar in a food processor. Process in on/off pulses until chocolate is *very finely ground*. (Alternatively, finely grate chocolate. Stir together with powdered sugar.)

In a large mixer bowl with mixer set on medium speed, beat butter until light and fluffy. Beat in brown sugar and powdered sugar mixture until well blended and smooth. Lower speed and add oil, egg, and vanilla, beating until well blended. Gradually beat in about half of dry ingredients. Stir in remainder using a large wooden spoon.

Divide dough into thirds. Lay each portion between two large sheets of wax paper and roll out to a generous ⅛-inch thickness, checking underside of dough frequently and smoothing out any wrinkles that form. Stack dough sheets on a tray or baking sheet and place in freezer for 15 to 20 minutes, until cold and slightly stiffened. (Dough may be left in the freezer longer but must be allowed to warm up just slightly before cookies can be cut out).

2⅓ cups all-purpose flour
¾ teaspoon baking powder
Scant ¼ teaspoon salt
3 ounces semisweet chocolate, finely chopped
Generous ½ cup powdered sugar
½ cup (1 stick) unsalted butter, slightly softened
½ cup packed dark brown sugar
⅓ cup corn oil or other flavorless vegetable oil
1 large egg
2½ teaspoons vanilla extract
Shiny Chocolate Glaze (optional)
2 cups powdered sugar, sifted after measuring if lumpy
2 teaspoons light or dark corn syrup
½ teaspoon vanilla extract
1 to 2 teaspoons unsweetened cocoa powder, to taste

Position a rack in center of oven and preheat to 350°F. Grease several baking sheets; set aside. Working with one dough sheet at a time (keep others frozen), peel off one sheet of wax paper, then replace it. Turn over dough and peel off and discard second layer of paper. Cut out cookies with desired cutter. Using a spatula, lift cookies from paper to baking sheets, spacing about 1 inch apart. (If cookies become too soft to lift easily, transfer wax paper and cookies to tray or baking sheet and chill in freezer briefly.) Recombine scraps and roll out between sheets of wax paper. Repeat chilling and cutting-out process.

Bake for 6 to 8 minutes or until cookies are just barely dark at the edges. Remove from oven and allow cookies to firm up for a minute or two. Using a spatula, transfer them to wire racks to cool.

To prepare optional glaze: Stir together powdered sugar, $2\frac{1}{2}$ teaspoons hot water, corn syrup, and vanilla, until thoroughly blended and smooth. If planning to decorate with a contrasting piping, spoon out about $\frac{1}{4}$ cup icing and reserve, tightly covered, in a small bowl. Sift cocoa powder into remaining icing, adding minimum for milder taste and maximum for stronger flavor. Gradually add a little more water, stirring until well blended and smooth. If mixture is still too thick to spread into a very thin, smooth layer, add a bit more water until desired consistency is obtained. Lightly glaze cooled cookies using a table knife or small pastry brush. If the icing begins to stiffen, stir in a few more drops of water. Let cookies stand on racks for at least 1 hour, or until glaze is set. If piping is desired, stir reserved icing until blended, adding a drop or two of water if mixture is too stiff to pipe. Outline or accent cookies with piping using a paper cone or pastry bag fitted with a fine-line tip. Let stand an additional hour until piping sets.

Store cookies in an airtight container (with wax paper between layers if glazed), for up to 1 week. Freeze for longer storage.

Makes about 40 to 45 $3\frac{1}{2}$-inch sugar bears

These thin, dark rounds are crisp and faintly bittersweet. They can be crumbled and folded into ice cream or used to make the ice-cream sandwiches shown on page 131.

❖ *Although this dough is soft, the rolling, chilling, and cutting-out method provided here makes it quite manageable. Work with rolled dough sheets taken straight from the freezer and promptly cut out and transfer wafers to baking sheets. If the kitchen is warm, lay the dough on a well-chilled metal tray or baking sheet to keep it from thawing too rapidly while you work.*

DARK CHOCOLATE WAFERS

Thoroughly stir together cocoa powder, coffee, and vanilla in a small bowl until very well blended; mixture will form a stiff paste. Combine 1 cup flour, baking powder, salt, and cinnamon in a food processor. Chop chocolate into ¼-inch pieces. Add to processor. Process until chocolate is *very finely ground.* Stir remaining flour into dry ingredients. (Alternatively, if processor is unavailable, finely grate chocolate by hand. Then stir together with dry ingredients until well blended.)

In a large mixer bowl with mixer set on medium speed, beat butter until very light and fluffy. Beat in sugar until well blended and smooth. Add eggs and cocoa mixture, beating until very well blended and smooth. Gradually beat in dry ingredients until thoroughly incorporated, but not overmixed. Refrigerate dough, covered, for 35 to 45 minutes, until fairly firm but not hard.

Divide dough into fourths. Place each dough portion between two large sheets of wax paper and roll out to a generous ⅛-inch thickness, checking underside of dough frequently and smoothing out any wrinkles that form. Stack dough sheets on a tray or baking sheet and freeze for at least 25 to 30 minutes, until

Scant ¼ cup unsweetened cocoa powder, preferably Dutch-process
3 tablespoons boiling hot coffee (or boiling water)
2½ teaspoons vanilla extract
2 cups plus 2 tablespoons all-purpose flour, divided
¾ teaspoon baking powder
Scant ¼ teaspoon salt
Pinch of ground cinnamon
5½ ounces bittersweet or semisweet chocolate
1 cup (2 sticks) unsalted butter, slightly softened
Generous 1 cup granulated sugar
2 large eggs

frozen and somewhat stiff. (Dough may be frozen for up to 24 hours, if desired.)

Position rack in center of oven and preheat to 325°F. Grease several baking sheets. Working with one dough sheet at a time (keep others frozen), carefully peel off one sheet of wax paper (since dough tends to stick, peel firmly and steadily to keep paper from tearing). Replace wax-paper sheet, then turn over dough with second paper sheet facing up. Working carefully, peel off and discard second layer of paper. (If necessary, to keep dough cold, lay wax paper and dough on a thoroughly chilled metal tray or baking sheet.) Cut out cookies using a 2- to 2¼-inch scalloped, fluted, or plain round cutter or drinking glass. As cookies are cut out, immediately transfer from wax paper to baking sheets, spacing about 1½ inches apart. If dough becomes soft, return to freezer to firm up again. Prick each wafer decoratively three or four times with tines of fork, dipping fork in cocoa powder if needed to prevent dough from sticking. Combine scraps and roll out between sheets of wax paper. Repeat chilling and cutting-out process.

Bake for 6 to 9 minutes or until cookies are almost firm in the center (see Note). Remove from oven and let stand on pans for a minute or two. Using a spatula, transfer to wire racks until cooled. Store in an airtight container for up to a week.   *Makes 85 to 95 2½- to 2¾-inch wafers*

Note: The dark color makes it difficult to tell when these wafers are done, but it's important to bake them just the right length of time. If underdone, they will not be as crisp as they should be; if overdone, they will have a slightly burnt taste. Usually, my solution is to bake a test pan, timing the baking period carefully, allowing the cookies to cool, and then checking for proper texture and taste before proceeding. It's also possible to remedy underbaking by returning cooled wafers to the oven and baking a few minutes longer.

Ice Cream Sandwiches: Roll out the dough to a generous ¼-inch thickness. Cut dough into about 2½-by-3¼-inch rectangles using a sharp knife (or into 2¾ to 3-inch rounds using a large cutter or drinking glass). Decoratively prick cookies with a fork as shown in photograph on page 131 or as desired. Baking time will be about 10 to 15 minutes, depending on size.

To prepare cookies for filling, freeze for at least an hour, or until very cold. Working with one sandwich at a time, spread underside of one cookie with ice cream. Top with second cookie, pressing into place. Immediately return to freezer until ice cream firms up again. Pack sandwiches airtight. Sandwiches are best eaten within 36 hours of assembly, as ice cream causes cookies to gradually lose their crispness.

CHECKERBOARD COOKIES

COOKIES

Schachbrettplätzchen

Checkerboard cookies are a standard in the repertoire of most European pastry chefs, and many home cooks enjoy making them, too. In this unusually flavorful German version, the light-colored dough is accented with orange, and the dark with orange, cocoa, coffee, and hazelnuts—a slightly exotic but very enticing combination. ❖ *Though these cookies take time, they are not at all difficult to prepare. The key to success is in keeping the doughs quite cold as portions are stacked, cut, and reassembled. (If time is short, the doughs can also be used to make pinwheel cookies; see variation at end of recipe.)*

Stir together flour and salt; set aside. Combine hazelnuts and cocoa in food processor. Process in on/off pulses until hazelnuts are powder fine but not oily; set aside.

In a large mixer bowl with mixer on medium speed, beat butter and sugar for about 2 minutes, or until light and fluffy. Add egg, vanilla, and orange zest, and continue to beat until very well blended and smooth. Lower speed and gradually beat in about half of flour mixture just until incorporated. Using a large spoon, stir in remaining flour mixture, until evenly incorporated.

Divide dough in half; return one portion to mixer bowl to use for chocolate dough. Lay other portion between large sheets of wax paper and roll out into a 6½-by-10½-inch rectangle; check underside of dough frequently and smooth out any wrinkles that form. Place dough sheet on a tray or baking sheet. Freeze for 15 to 20 minutes until very cold.

Add dissolved coffee and hazelnut-cocoa mixture to mixer bowl. Stir dough with a wooden spoon or knead with hands, until ingredients are evenly incorporated and dough is smooth. Measure out generous ½ cup chocolate dough; cover and set aside. Lay remainder between large sheets of wax paper and roll out into a 6½-by-10½-inch rectangle; check underside of dough frequently and smooth out any wrinkles that

2½ cups all-purpose flour
⅛ teaspoon salt
⅓ cup toasted, hulled, and chopped hazelnuts (see Note)
2½ tablespoons unsweetened cocoa powder, preferably Dutch-process (European-style)
1 cup (2 sticks) unsalted butter, slightly softened
¾ cup granulated sugar
1 large egg
1 teaspoon vanilla extract
Finely grated zest (orange part of skin) of 1 medium orange
½ teaspoon coffee powder or granules dissolved in 1½ teaspoons hot water

form. Place dough sheet on a tray or baking sheet. Freeze for 15 minutes or until very cold.

Peel wax paper from one dough portion. Lay dough on cutting board. Peel paper from second portion. Lay dough directly on first portion. Using a large sharp knife, trim away edges so dough measures about 6 by 10 inches. Reserve the chocolate trimmings along with the ½ cup already reserved; discard light-colored dough trimmings. Working lengthwise, cut rectangle into thirds, to yield three 2-by-10-inch stripes. Working on a sheet of wax paper, stack portions on top of one another (with dark and light layers alternating), pressing down lightly all over to form a 2-inch-wide-by-10-inch-long block. Wrap wax paper around dough.

Freeze for at least 15 minutes, until dough block is very cold and firm. If sides of block are uneven; use a sharp knife to trim so they are straight. Cut combined layer lengthwise at ¼-inch intervals into 10-inch-long strips. Turn every other strip so top faces down and bottom faces up, then neatly replace strips in the block (to produce checkerboard effect on ends of block). Return block to freezer until very cold and firm.

Meanwhile, knead together reserved dark dough and scraps. Roll out dough between wax paper sheets into a 9½-by-10½-inch rectangle, checking undersides frequently and smoothing out any wrinkles that form; chocolate layer will be thin. Place dough sheet on a tray or baking sheet. Refrigerate for about five minutes to firm up slightly.

Carefully peel one sheet of wax paper from chocolate layer and replace it. Turn over dough and peel off second sheet of paper. Center checkerboard dough block on chocolate rectangle and wrap and smooth chocolate dough around block to enclose it; trim off excess chocolate dough. Press chocolate dough into place around block. Wrap chocolate-covered block in plastic wrap. Freeze for at least 30 minutes and up to 2 weeks, if desired.

To prepare for baking: Position a rack in center of oven and preheat to 350°F. Very generously grease several baking sheets; set aside. Working on a cutting board and using a large sharp knife, cut frozen block crosswise into generous ⅛-inch-thick slices. Immediately transfer to baking sheets, spacing about 1 inch apart.

Bake on center oven rack for five to eight minutes or until cookies just begin to brown at the edges. Remove from oven and allow cookies to firm up for one minute. Using a spatula, immediately transfer cookies to wire racks before they cool and become brittle. Let stand until thoroughly cooled. Regrease baking sheets before reusing.

Store cookies, airtight, for up to one week. Freeze for longer storage.

Makes about 60 1½-by-2¼-inch cookies.

Note: To prepare hazelnuts: Toast in a preheated 350°F. oven for 12 to 15 minutes, until nuts brown and hulls loosen. Rub cooled nuts in a kitchen towel or between your fingers, discarding loose bits of hull. Chop nuts.

Pinwheel Cookies: Make two doughs as directed above, except do not reserve ½ cup chocolate dough. Roll light and dark doughs into about 8-by-11-inch rectangles. Chill until cool and slightly firm but still flexible. Stack rectangles on a cutting board and trim away uneven edges. Working from a longer side, neatly roll up dough jelly-roll style. Wrap in wax paper. Place on a tray and freeze until very firm, at least one hour. Cut frozen log crosswise into generous ⅛-inch slices and bake as directed for checkerboard cookies.

GERMANY

The fragile, curled wafers known as tuiles (tiles in English) got their name from the curved tiles that cover so many of the roofs in southern France. Extraordinarily light, thin, and crisp, tuiles go particularly well with ice cream, sorbet, or fruit compote. Although plain almond tile cookies are more traditional, chocolate versions such as the following are also popular. ❖ For a professional touch, this same recipe can be varied to create eye-catching, leaf-shaped wafers that are accented with lines of light-colored batter to suggest natural leaf-veining, and slightly furled to look like real autumn leaves. The basic leaf shapes can be formed with either a commercial metal leaf stencil or a homemade stencil cut from cardboard (for which I have provided instructions). This variation was inspired by a recipe from Roland Mesnier, the Executive Pastry Chef at the White House. ❖ Tuiles and leaf wafers must be quickly lifted from baking sheets and bent while still hot and flexible, so bake only one pan at a time.

Set butter in a warm spot (or microwave with oven on lowest power for several seconds) until very soft, but *not thin and melted.* Position a rack in center of oven and preheat to 350°F. Very generously grease several baking sheets. If preparing tuiles, set out several rolling pins, wine bottles, or similarly curved objects for draping cookies as they cool. If making leaf wafers, prepare a stencil by tracing a 3- to 4-inch oak or other leaf onto the center of a sturdy cardboard square, and then cutting away interior of leaf shape from cardboard. Alternatively, use a purchased metal leaf stencil.

Using a wire whisk, beat together egg whites, salt, vanilla, and almond extract until frothy. Sift powdered sugar over mixture, whisking until blended and smooth. Sift flour over mixture. Add softened butter, whisking until mixture is smooth. If preparing leaf wafers, remove ¼ cup batter and set aside in a small, deep bowl (to be used for adding leaf-

5 tablespoons unsalted butter
¼ cup (about 2 large) egg whites
Generous pinch of salt
¾ teaspoon vanilla extract
½ teaspoon almond extract
¾ cup plus 1 tablespoon powdered sugar
⅓ cup all-purpose flour
2 tablespoons sifted unsweetened cocoa powder, preferably Dutch-process (European-style)
⅓ cup unblanched almonds (omit if making leaf wafers), sliced

CHOCOLATE TILE WAFERS (OR LEAF WAFERS)

Tuiles au Chocolat

veining). Stir cocoa powder into large bowl of batter until well blended.

Prepare a test wafer by dropping a small rounded teaspoonful of batter onto baking sheet, spreading with a table knife into a 2¾-inch round. Bake 5 to 7 minutes, until slightly darker on edges, monitoring baking time carefully. (If wafers are underbaked they will not be crisp; if overbaked they may taste burned.) Also, if wafer spreads to more than 3¾ inches, batter is too thin; stir in a teaspoon or two flour until smoothly incorporated. If wafer does not spread at all batter is too thick; stir in a teaspoon of tap water until incorporated.

To prepare tile wafers: Drop batter by small rounded teaspoonfuls, spacing at least 3¼ inches apart on a baking sheet. (Don't crowd, as cookies spread a great deal.) Using tip of a table knife and working in a circular motion, spread each portion into about a 2¾-inch round. Sprinkle each round generously with almonds.

To prepare chocolate leaf wafers: Lay stencil on baking sheet and spoon in a teaspoon of batter. Then holding stencil in place with one hand, smooth batter into entire leaf form using long-bladed offset spatula or knife. Scrape off any excess batter and return to bowl. Carefully lift up stencil from sheet. Repeat, spacing wafers about 3 inches apart. Add veining with reserved light-colored batter as follows: Using a paper cone or a small pastry bag fitted with a fine writing tip, pipe lines suggesting leaf veins on each wafer. (Alternatively, drizzle light batter back and forth across wafers in a random pattern using a piping cone or a spoon.)

One sheet at a time, bake wafers for 5 to 7 minutes; they will be slightly darker on edges (and veins will be just tinged with brown). Remove pan from oven and let stand for about 20 seconds or until wafers are firm enough to lift without tearing; quickly loosen them from sheet using a thin-edged, wide-bladed spatula. For tuiles, immediately drape cookies, bottom-side down, over rolling pins until cool enough to hold shape. For leaves, randomly bend cookies by hand to suggest natural furling of autumn leaves. (If some wafers cool too much while others are being removed, return pan to oven for a minute or two.) Transfer cool, firm cookies to wire racks. Cool, clean off, and thoroughly re-grease baking sheets before reusing.

As soon as cookies are thoroughly cooled, pack *completely airtight*. Store airtight, with no extra space in container, for up to a week. Freeze for longer storage. Handle cookies gently as they are extremely fragile.

Makes about 30 4-inch tile or leaf wafers

This recipe is an adaptation of one I collected during a trip to Orkney, an island chain off the northern coast of Scotland. As there are not a lot of chocolate cookie recipes in Britain, I consider it a great find. ❖ A chocolate and walnut-flavored batter is piped into shell shapes, baked, and then sandwiched together around a chocolate buttercream filling. When put together, the cookie pairs actually look a bit like whole walnuts.

CHOCOLATE WALNUT MELTAWAY CREAMS

Position a rack in center third of oven and preheat to 350°F. Grease several baking sheets and set aside. Sift together flour, cornstarch, cocoa powder, baking powder, and salt. Combine powdered sugar and walnuts in a food processor fitted with a steel blade. Process until nuts are *very finely ground,* but not oily. (Alternatively, combine sugar and walnuts in a blender and grind until very fine. Stop blender and stir to redistribute contents several times.)

In a large mixer bowl with mixer set on medium speed, beat butter and powdered sugar-nut mixture for about 3 minutes, until very light. Add egg yolk and vanilla and continue beating until very fluffy and smooth. Beat in dry ingredients just until thoroughly incorporated. Let stand for 2 to 3 minutes while cornstarch absorbs moisture and batter becomes firmer. If mixture seems too stiff to pipe, beat in a teaspoon or two of water to soften it just slightly.

Spoon mixture into a pastry bag fitted with a ⅓-inch or slightly larger open-star tip. (For convenience, stand bag in a tall glass and turn cuff about 3½ inches before filling. Turn cuff up again and twist top tightly

1¼ cups all-purpose flour

2 tablespoons cornstarch

3 tablespoons unsweetened cocoa powder, preferably Dutch-process

¼ teaspoon baking powder

Generous ⅛ teaspoon salt

⅔ cup powdered sugar

⅓ cup chopped walnuts

¾ cup (1½ sticks) unsalted butter, slightly softened

1 large egg yolk

1½ teaspoons vanilla extract

Buttercream

6 tablespoons unsalted butter, slightly softened

Scant 1¼ cups powdered sugar

2 ounces unsweetened chocolate, melted and cooled

½ teaspoon vanilla extract

CHOCOLATE
WALNUT MELTAWAY
CREAMS

to close.) Pipe scant 1¼-inch-long and 1-inch-wide shells onto baking sheets, spacing about 1½ inches apart. Rap baking sheet against counter to flatten shells just slightly. (Although the shells will seem quite small when piped, remember that two are used to form one cookie.)

Bake cookies for 8 to 11 minutes or until edges are just barely tinged with brown. Remove baking sheets to cooling racks and let cookies stand for about 2 minutes. Transfer cookies to wire racks until completely cooled. Shells may be made ahead and stored before assembling, or cooled, sandwiched together with buttercream, and then stored.

To prepare buttercream: Beat together butter and powdered sugar until very light and fluffy. Beat in chocolate and vanilla until mixture is smooth and well blended. To assemble cookies, pipe ½-inch wide mounds of buttercream over flat side of half the thoroughly cooled shells, using a ⅓-inch diameter plain or open-star tip. Top cookies with remaining shells, flat side down. Gently press down on shells so filling just extends to edges.

Store meltaway creams in an airtight container in the refrigerator for up to 4 days. Allow them to warm to room temperature before serving. If desired, freeze for up to 10 days. Thaw before serving.

Makes 40 to 50 1½-inch-long sandwich cookies

In this fine Austrian recipe, tender oblong butter wafers are paired with a silky mocha buttercream and, if desired, dipped in a chocolate glaze. These are just the sort of elegant little sweets Austrians enjoy along with coffee in their fancier cafés and pastry shops. ❖ *You will need a pastry bag and tip for this recipe.*

MOCHA-FILLED BUTTER COOKIES

Gefüllte Butterstangerl

Position a rack in upper third of oven and preheat to 375°F. Lightly grease several baking sheets. Thoroughly stir together flour and baking powder.

In a small mixer bowl with mixer set on medium speed, beat butter, salt, and sugar for about 3 minutes, until very light and smooth. Add vanilla and 2 teaspoons milk and beat a few seconds longer. Gradually beat in the dry ingredients just until thoroughly incorporated. If mixture seems too stiff to pipe smoothly through a pastry tube, stir in enough additional milk to soften dough to piping consistency.

Put dough in a pastry bag fitted with a ⅜-inch (or similar) plain tip or open-star tip. Pipe dough into thin 2-inch long strips, spacing about 2 inches apart. Using a table knife gently smooth down any points at ends of strips. Sharply rap pan on counter a few times to flatten strips just slightly.

Bake one sheet at a time for 6 to 8 minutes or until cookies are just barely tinged with brown at edges. About halfway through baking reverse sheet from front to back to ensure even browning. Remove pan from oven and let cookies firm up for 1 minute. Using a

1¼ cups all-purpose flour
¼ teaspoon baking powder
¾ cup (1½ sticks) unsalted butter, slightly softened
Pinch of salt
⅓ cup powdered sugar
1¼ teaspoons vanilla extract
2 to 4 teaspoons milk
Mocha Buttercream
⅔ cup powdered sugar
½ teaspoon unsweetened cocoa powder, preferably Dutch-process
¼ cup (½ stick) unsalted butter, slightly softened
¾ teaspoon instant coffee powder or granules dissolved in ¾ teaspoon hot water
Chocolate Glaze (optional)
3½ ounces bittersweet or semisweet chocolate, coarsely chopped
1 tablespoon solid white vegetable shortening
1 tablespoon light corn syrup

spatula, loosen and transfer cookies to racks. (Work carefully as cookies are fragile.) Let stand until thoroughly cooled. Scrape off any crumbs from sheets and then cool and regrease before using again.

To prepare buttercream: Sift powdered sugar and cocoa powder into a mixer bowl. Add butter and coffee mixture to sugar mixture. With mixer on medium speed, beat until buttercream is thoroughly blended and smooth.

Put buttercream in a pastry bag fitted with a small (¼-inch or similar) plain or open star tip. Pipe a line of buttercream along flat side of half the cookies. (Alternatively, using a table knife, spread a ⅛-inch thick layer of buttercream over flat side of half the cookies.) Top each iced cookie with flat side of a remaining cookie, pressing down very gently as cookies are fragile.

To prepare optional glaze: Melt chocolate and shortening together in a small saucepan over *lowest heat*, stirring frequently, until completely melted. Stir in corn syrup until thoroughly incorporated. One at a time, dip ends of each cookie into glaze only until about ¼ inch is covered. (If necessary, tip pan to facilitate dipping.) Lightly scrape ends against pan edge to remove excess glaze. Return cookies to cooling racks until glaze is completely set, about 1 hour. (Or speed setting process by laying cookies on wax paper-lined baking sheets and refrigerating for about 20 minutes.)

Store cookies flat, with wax paper between the layers, in an airtight container. They will keep for 4 or 5 days. Unassembled cookies can be frozen for up to 10 days and assembled and glazed shortly before serving time, if desired.   *Makes about 30 to 35 2½-inch long sandwich cookies*

Most linzer cookies are made with a light almond dough sandwiched around raspberry preserves, but in this unusual *Viennese* version the dough also contains hazelnuts and chocolate. ❖ *For best results, use a very good-quality, flavorful seedless raspberry jam or jelly. For a romantic touch, use heart-shaped cutters.*

CHOCOLATE LINZER COOKIES

Schokoladen Linzer Tortchen

Position a rack in the center of the oven and preheat to 350°F. Spread hazelnuts in a roasting pan. Spread almonds in a separate pan. Toast almonds in oven, stirring occasionally, for 8 to 10 minutes, or until tinged with brown. Toast hazelnuts, stirring occasionally, for 13 to 15 minutes or until hulls loosen and nuts are lightly browned. Set toasted nuts aside until cooled. Remove loose hulls from hazelnuts by rubbing between hands or in a clean tea towel, discarding bits of hull as you work. (Nuts should be fairly clean, but don't worry about removing every bit of hull.)

Combine hazelnuts, almonds, chocolate, and 1 cup flour in a food processor fitted with a steel blade. Process until nuts are *very finely ground* but not oily.

In a large mixer bowl with mixer set on medium speed beat butter until lightened. Add sugar and beat until light and fluffy. Beat in vanilla. Gradually add ground nut mixture, then remaining ¾ cup flour, stirring or kneading until thoroughly incorporated but not overworked; mixture will be crumbly. Divide dough in half. Between 2 sheets of wax paper, roll out each portion to a ⅛-inch thickness, occasionally checking underside and smoothing out any wrinkles that form. Stack dough portions on a large tray or baking sheet and refrigerate for 15 to 20 minutes, or until dough is cold but not hard.

⅔ cup (about 3 ounces) hazelnuts

1 cup (about 3 ounces) blanched or unblanched sliced almonds

5½ ounces semisweet chocolate, finely chopped

1¾ cups all-purpose flour, divided

⅔ cup (1 stick plus 2⅔ tablespoons) unsalted butter, slightly softened

⅓ cup granulated sugar

1 teaspoon vanilla extract

Approximately ½ to ⅓ cup seedless red-raspberry jam or jelly

Approximately ¼ cup confectioners sugar, for garnish

Working with one dough portion at a time (leave the other one refrigerated), peel off a sheet of wax paper. Replace it loosely. Turn dough over and peel off and discard second sheet of paper. To prepare cookie bottoms, cut out half the cookies using a 2¾-inch plain round cutter or doughnut cutter with hole cutter removed (or use a heart-shaped cutter). To prepare cookie tops, cut out remaining dough using doughnut cutter with center hole inserted, or use a 2¾-inch cutter (or a heart-shaped cutter) and then cut away centers using a 1-inch small round cutter, liqueur glass, or thimble (or use a heart-shaped mini-cutter). Lift out center dough portions with point of paring knife. Using a wide-bladed metal spatula, transfer cookie tops and bottoms from paper to separate ungreased baking sheets. (If dough warms and cookies are difficult to lift from paper, transfer entire sheet to a tray and refrigerate for a few minutes to firm up dough again.) Combine dough scraps. Then roll out between wax paper, chill, and cut out, continuing until all dough is used.

Bake cookies in preheated 350°F oven until just barely darker at edges, about 6 to 8 minutes for tops and 7 to 9 minutes for bottoms. Remove from oven and let cookies stand on baking sheets for 2 minutes. Transfer to wire racks until cooled. Store cookie tops and bottoms in an airtight container. To retain crispness, do not assemble until shortly before serving time.

To assemble cookies: Melt preserves in small saucepan over low heat until syrupy (or in a microwave-safe cup in microwave oven for 20 to 30 seconds on 100-percent power), stirring occasionally. Remove from heat and let stand until cooled and slightly thickened. Lightly sift powdered sugar over cookie tops. Spread about ½ teaspoon jelly onto center of each cookie bottom, then gently press down top (work carefully, as cookies are tender). Plain, unassembled cookies may be stored in an airtight container for up to 5 or 6 days; assembled cookies are best eaten within a few hours as jelly filling causes them to lose their crispness.   *Makes about 30 to 35 2¾-inch sandwich cookies*

BUTTERCREAM-FILLED MERINGUE SANDWICH COOKIES

Luxembourgerli

Position two racks in center third of oven and preheat to 325°F. Line two 12-by-15-inch or larger baking sheets with baking parchment.

Spread almonds in a roasting pan. Transfer to oven and toast, stirring occasionally, for 6 to 8 minutes or until tinged with brown. Let stand until cool. Lower oven temperature to 300°F.

In a food processor fitted with a steel blade, process almonds and about half of powdered sugar until very fine but not oily. Thoroughly stir remaining powdered sugar into almond mixture.

Combine granulated sugar and 3½ tablespoons hot tap water in a small, heavy saucepan. Over medium-high heat, stir mixture until sugar dissolves and syrup comes to a boil. Cover pan and boil for 1½ minutes to allow steam to wash sugar crystals from pan sides. Uncover pan. Continue boiling, lifting pan and swirling contents occasionally but never stirring, for about one minute longer, until syrup thickens, bubbles vigorously, and reaches firm-ball stage (242° to 243°F. on a candy thermometer). To test for doneness without a thermometer, remove pan from heat, drop a small amount of syrup in a cup of ice water and let stand for 15 seconds; syrup should form an almost firm, brittle ball when squeezed between fingers. Set aside.

In a large grease-free mixer bowl with mixer on medium speed, beat egg whites until frothy. Add cream of tartar and raise mixer speed to high. Continue beating just to soft peaks; turn off mixer. Quickly return

Meringue

1¼ cups (about 3½ ounces) sliced almonds, blanched

1 cup plus 3 tablespoons powdered sugar, divided

½ cup granulated sugar

½ cup (4 to 5 large) egg whites, completely free of yolk

½ teaspoon cream of tartar

¼ teaspoon vanilla extract

⅛ teaspoon almond extract

Chocolate Buttercream

½ cup (1 stick) unsalted butter, slightly softened

2½ tablespoons unsweetened cocoa powder, preferably Dutch-process

½ cup powdered sugar

3 ounces bittersweet (not unsweetened) or semisweet chocolate, melted and cooled to barely warm

½ teaspoon vanilla extract

syrup to burner and heat just until simmering. With mixer on high speed, immediately pour a thin, steady stream of syrup down bowl side (avoid beaters or whip as syrup will stick), until all syrup is added. Add vanilla and almond extract. Continue beating until mixture cools to lukewarm.

Using a rubber spatula, stir almond mixture into whites just until evenly incorporated. Cover and set aside for 10 minutes. Spoon batter into pastry bag fitted with a plain or open-star ⅜-inch diameter tip. A plain tip is traditionally used, but a star tip produces more decorative cookies and does not require advanced piping skills. Pipe scant 1-inch rounds onto parchment, spacing about ¾ inch apart. If plain round tip is used, pat down any peaks on meringues using a finger very lightly dipped in cold water.

Place pans, staggered, on two racks in center third of oven. Bake cookies for 17 to 22 minutes, reversing pans from front to back and switching racks about halfway through, until barely tinged with brown and just firm on top (but still slightly soft inside). Transfer parchment to flat surface and let meringues stand until cooled. Peel from paper. Store airtight until assembled.

To prepare buttercream: In a mixer bowl, beat together butter, cocoa powder, and powdered sugar until very light and fluffy. Beat in chocolate and vanilla until mixture is smooth and well blended.

Not more than 12 hours before serving, assemble cookies (do not store longer as filling will cause meringues to soften). Pipe small mounds (scant ¾ teaspoonfuls) of buttercream over flat side of half the cookies using a ⅓-inch diameter or smaller plain or open-star tip. (Use the same bag and tip, washed and dried, as for meringues, if desired.) Top cookies with remaining meringues, flat side down, pressing down lightly.

Store cookies airtight and refrigerated. (If desired, wrap plain meringues and store in freezer for up to a week; thaw and add buttercream before serving.) Allow to warm almost to room temperature before serving.

Makes 40 to 45 1¼-inch round sandwich cookies

CHOCOLATE-GLAZED NUT BRITTLE BARS

Biscotti Croccanti

Chocolate-Glazed Nut Brittle Bars, Chocolate Sugar Bears, Chocolate-Caramel Pecan Clusters and Chocolate Fudge

Many fruits and nuts flourish in the warm, sunny climate of Italy, and resourceful cooks routinely incorporate them into a host of desserts and sweets. In these toothsome bar cookies, almonds, walnuts, or hazelnuts, candied orange, and honey are folded together, poured over a short crust, and baked to a bubbly, chewy-crisp caramelized consistency. The shiny, golden brittle layer (called croccanti in Italian) is finished with a drizzling of chocolate. ❖ Although chopped candied orange peel is traditional and delicious in this recipe, it is not always easy to find, and excellent nut bars can be prepared without it.

To prepare pastry layer: Generously grease a 7½-by-11½-inch rectangular flat baking dish. Thoroughly stir together flour, sugar, and salt in a small bowl. Add butter and cut in with a pastry blender or forks until mixture resembles coarse meal. Lightly stir 1 tablespoon milk into dry ingredients until distributed and particles begin to hold together when pressed. If necessary, gradually add a bit more milk, but do not overmoisten. (Alternatively, process dry ingredients and butter in on/off pulses in a food processor fitted with a steel blade until mixture resembles coarse meal; be careful not to overprocess. Add 1 tablespoon milk and process in on/off bursts until mixture begins to hold together; add a bit more if needed to lightly bind particles, but do not overmoisten.) Press dough into bottom of pan, forming a smooth, even layer. Refrigerate, covered, for at least 20 minutes and up to 24 hours.

Position a rack in center of oven and preheat to 375°F. Bake pastry for 10 minutes. Remove to wire rack and let stand while nut layer is prepared. Reset oven to 350°F.

To prepare nut layer: Stirring constantly, bring butter, sugar, and honey to a boil in a heavy, medium-sized saucepan over medium heat. Boil for 3 minutes, stirring

Pastry Layer

1 cup all-purpose flour
2 tablespoons granulated sugar
⅛ teaspoon salt
5 tablespoons cold unsalted butter, cut into small chunks
Approximately 1 to 2 tablespoons whole milk or light cream

Nut Layer

¾ cup (1½ sticks) unsalted butter
1 cup granulated sugar
¼ cup clover honey
1¼ cups chopped slivered almonds
1¼ cups chopped walnuts or toasted, hulled, and chopped hazelnuts (see Note)
⅓ cup chopped candied orange peel (optional)
2 tablespoons whole milk or light cream

Chocolate Glaze

2 ounces bittersweet (not unsweetened) or semisweet chocolate, coarsely chopped
2 teaspoons solid white vegetable shortening
2 teaspoons clover honey

frequently; then remove pan from burner. Stir in nuts, candied orange peel (if used), and milk, until thoroughly combined. Spread mixture evenly over pastry layer. Bake for 23 to 27 minutes or until mixture is bubbly and deep golden brown. Remove baking pan to a rack and let stand about 1 hour or until cool and fairly firm, but not completely cold. Meanwhile, prepare glaze by combining chocolate, shortening, and honey in a small, heavy saucepan. Warm over *lowest* heat, stirring frequently, until completely melted and fluid; be careful not to burn. Set aside to cool just slightly.

Run a knife around dish to loosen layer from sides. Cut rectangle into 1½- to 2-inch bars (or as desired), using a large sharp knife. Piping glaze through a paper piping cone (see directions on page 267) or dropping it from a spoon, drizzle surface to form vertical, then horizontal lines. Refrigerate pan for about 30 minutes until chocolate sets. Lift bars from dish using a wide-bladed spatula.

Store, airtight, in a cool place, with wax paper between the layers, for up to 4 or 5 days. Or freeze for up to 2 weeks.

Makes about 36 1½-by-2-inch bars

Note: To toast and hull hazelnuts: Spread in a roasting pan and toast, stirring occasionally, in a preheated 350°F. oven for 11 to 13 minutes or until hulls loosen and nuts are tinged with brown. Rub cooled nuts between palms or in a clean kitchen towel to remove loose bits of hull.

These brownies are dense, fudgy-moist, and have a rich chocolate flavor. Though quick and easy to make, they always win accolades.

FUDGY BROWNIES

Position a rack in center of oven and preheat to 350°F. Line an 8-inch square baking pan with aluminum foil, overlapping foil on two sides by about 2 inches. (To easily shape foil, turn pan upside down and mold foil to fit around bottom. Turn pan upright and insert shaped foil in pan, folding overlapping ends outside.) Grease foil.

Combine butter and chocolates in a medium-sized, heavy saucepan over low heat, stirring until melted and smooth. Remove from heat and let cool to lukewarm. Sift together flour, baking powder, and salt; set aside.

Stir sugar into chocolate mixture until blended. Stir eggs and vanilla into chocolate until evenly incorporated. Using a large wooden spoon, stir flour mixture into saucepan until evenly incorporated but not overmixed. Fold in chopped walnuts (if used).

Turn batter into prepared pan, spreading to edges. Bake for 15 minutes. Lower heat to 325°F. and continue baking for 9 to 14 minutes longer or until center top is almost firm when lightly pressed and a toothpick inserted in center comes out clean. Transfer pan to a wire rack and let stand for about 20 minutes. Using overlapping foil as handles, lift brownie from pan and return it to rack until thoroughly cooled. (Or speed up cooling process by refrigerating brownie until cooled and firm.) Peel off foil.

Transfer brownie to a cutting board and cut into 2-inch squares, or as desired, using a large sharp knife. (For neatest appearance, use a ruler to measure and mark squares before cutting, and clean knife blade with a damp towel after each cut.)

Store brownies in an airtight container with wax paper between layers. Or wrap squares individually in plastic wrap. Store for up to 3 days. Freeze for longer storage.

Makes 16 2-inch squares

½ cup (1 stick) unsalted butter

4½ ounces bittersweet (not unsweetened) or semisweet chocolate

1½ ounces unsweetened chocolate

¾ cup plus 1 tablespoon all-purpose flour

½ teaspoon baking powder

⅛ teaspoon salt

1 cup granulated sugar

2 large eggs

2 teaspoons vanilla extract

¾ cup chopped walnuts (optional)

Position a rack in center of oven and preheat to 325°F. Line an 8-inch square baking pan with aluminum foil, overlapping foil on two sides of pan by about 2 inches. (To fit foil, invert pan and mold foil around bottom. Turn pan right side up and place foil neatly inside, folding overlapping edges outside.) Grease foil.

Melt butter and chocolate in a medium-sized, heavy saucepan over medium-low heat, stirring constantly, until well blended and smooth. Remove pan from heat. Stir in sugar until mixture is well blended. One at a time, beat in eggs with a fork. Stir in vanilla. Set mixture aside, stirring occasionally, for 6 to 8 minutes, to allow sugar to dissolve. Thoroughly stir together flour, cocoa powder, salt, baking soda, and baking powder. Add to chocolate mixture, stirring just until well blended; batter will be thick. Fold in nuts (if used).

Turn out batter into pan, spreading evenly to edges. Bake for 28 to 33 minutes or until center top is almost firm when tapped. Transfer pan to a wire rack and let stand for 1 hour.

To prepare glaze: Bring cream and powdered sugar just to a boil in a small saucepan over medium-high heat. Remove pan from burner and immediately stir in chopped chocolate. Continue stirring until completely melted and smooth. Stir in corn syrup and vanilla until evenly incorporated. Pour glaze over cooled brownie top, spreading evenly out to edges. Refrigerate for about 30 minutes or until glaze sets. Using overlapping foil as handles, carefully lift brownie from pan and peel foil from bottom.

Transfer brownie to cutting board and cut into 2-inch squares using a large sharp knife.

Pack in a single layer in an airtight container and store for up to 3 days. Freeze unglazed brownies, tightly wrapped, for up to 10 days. Let brownies return to room temperature before glazing.

Makes 16 2¼-inch squares

⅓ cup unsalted butter

5½ ounces semisweet or bittersweet (not unsweetened) chocolate, coarsely chopped or broken into small pieces

¾ cup plus 2 tablespoons granulated sugar

2 large eggs

2½ teaspoons vanilla extract

1 cup plus 1 tablespoon all-purpose flour

2½ tablespoons unsweetened, non-alkalized, American-style cocoa powder (such as Hershey's)

¼ teaspoon salt

¼ teaspoon baking soda

¼ teaspoon baking powder

½ cup chopped walnuts (optional)

Glaze

¼ cup heavy (whipping) cream

1½ tablespoons powdered sugar

4½ ounces bittersweet (not unsweetened) or semisweet chocolate, chopped into about ¼-inch pieces

1 tablespoon light corn syrup

½ teaspoon vanilla

CHEWY
BROWNIES

UNITED STATES

CREAM CHEESE SWIRL BROWNIES

Position a rack in center of oven and preheat to 325°F. Line an 8-inch square baking pan with aluminum foil, overlapping foil on two sides by about 2 inches. (To fit foil, invert pan and mold foil around bottom. Turn pan right side up and place foil neatly inside, folding overlapping ends outside.) Grease foil.

To prepare chocolate batter: Melt butter and chocolates in a medium-sized, heavy saucepan over very low heat, stirring until melted and smooth. Remove from heat and set aside to cool to lukewarm. Sift together flour, baking powder, and salt; set aside.

Combine egg and yolk, sugar, and vanilla in a small bowl. Beat with a fork until blended. Using a large wooden spoon, beat egg mixture into melted chocolate mixture until well blended. Stir in flour mixture until thoroughly incorporated but not overmixed.

To prepare cream cheese mixture: In a mixer bowl with mixer set on medium speed, beat together cream cheese and sugar until well blended. Beat in egg white and vanilla until creamy and smooth.

Working with about half of chocolate batter, spoon dollops, slightly separated, into prepared pan. Spoon dollops of cream cheese batter in spaces between chocolate batter. Spoon dollops of remaining chocolate batter over top. Using a table knife held vertically, swirl mixtures together until *very well marbled and intermingled* but not completely blended together. Rap pan on counter and shake several times to even surface.

Chocolate Mixture
5 tablespoons unsalted butter
2 1/2 ounces bittersweet (not unsweetened) or semisweet chocolate
1 1/2 ounces unsweetened chocolate
1/2 cup all-purpose flour
1/4 teaspoon baking powder
1/8 teaspoon salt
1 large egg, plus 1 large egg yolk
2/3 cup granulated sugar
1 teaspoon vanilla extract

Cream Cheese Mixture
6 ounces cream cheese, slightly softened
1/4 cup granulated sugar
1 large egg white
1 teaspoon vanilla extract

Bake for 28 to 33 minutes or until center top is almost firm when lightly pressed and a toothpick inserted in center comes out clean. Transfer pan to a wire rack and let stand for at least 20 minutes. Using overlapping foil as handles, lift brownie from pan and return it to rack until thoroughly cooled. (Or speed up process by refrigerating.)

Peel off foil, transfer brownie to a cutting board, and cut into 2-inch squares using a large sharp knife. (For neatest appearance, use a ruler to measure and mark squares before cutting, and clean knife blade with a damp paper towel after each cut.)

Store brownies in an airtight container, preferably in a single layer. Or wrap squares individually in plastic wrap. Store for up to 2 or 3 days. Freeze for longer storage.   *Makes 16 2-inch squares*

CANDIES

Simple Bittersweet Truffles, Classic Bittersweet Chocolate-Cognac Truffles, Grand Marnier-Chocolate Truffles and White Chocolate-Mocha Hazelnut Truffles

CHAPTER

Chocolate-Coated Dried Fruit and Nuts

EIGHT

Although there are numerous perfectly round, elegantly decorated chocolates called truffles on the market nowadays, they are modern elaborations on the original classic theme: chocolate-cream (ganache) centers encased in crisp chocolate and rolled in cocoa powder. ❖ *If the traditional cocoa powder finish is too bitter for your taste, try substituting the sweeter coating mixture suggested at the end of the recipe.*

CLASSIC BITTERSWEET CHOCOLATE-COGNAC TRUFFLES

Truffes au Chocolat et au Cognac

To prepare ganache: Put chocolate in a medium-sized, deep bowl set in a warm place. In a medium saucepan bring cream to a simmer over medium-high heat. Lower heat until mixture just barely simmers and cook, uncovered and stirring occasionally, three to four minutes, or until liquid is reduced to ⅔ cup. Immediately strain cream through a fine sieve into chocolate, stirring until chocolate completely melts. (If any chocolate pieces remain unmelted, set bowl in a slightly larger bowl of hot water and stir until melted.) Stir cognac into ganache until well blended. Cover and refrigerate for at least four hours (or freeze, stirring frequently, for about one hour), until mixture is very cold and stiff.

To form truffle centers: Using a melon baller or teaspoon, scoop up ganache and roll between palms into ¾-inch balls. (They don't have to be perfectly round.) Transfer to wax paper–lined baking sheet, slightly separated. (As chocolate builds up on hands, wipe it off with a paper towel and continue.) If ganache becomes too soft to shape, return to refrigerator briefly; then proceed. Lightly cover balls with plastic wrap and return to refrigerator until portions are cool and firm.

Meanwhile, set out a wax paper–lined tray and a long-tined dipping fork

Ganache
8½ ounces finely chopped bittersweet (not unsweetened) chocolate

¾ cup heavy (whipping) cream

1½ tablespoons cognac (or very good brandy)

Coating
About ⅔ cup sifted unsweetened cocoa powder, preferably Dutch-process (European-style), for dusting truffles (see Note)

About 1¼ pounds coarsely chopped bittersweet (not unsweetened) chocolate

2 tablespoons solid white vegetable shortening (no substitutes)

(or a meat fork, fondue fork, or dinner fork). Put cocoa powder in a medium-sized, deep bowl. When ready to dip truffles, quick-temper coating chocolate following Master Recipe on page 220. To hold tempered chocolate at the proper temperature, place a heating pad (inserted in a heavy plastic bag to protect it from drips) under bowl of tempered chocolate. Turn pad to lowest setting. Lay a kitchen towel over plastic bag and, as you work, adjust the thickness of the towel as needed to keep bottom of bowl just barely warm.

To chocolate-coat and dust truffles: Tip bowl so chocolate pools on one side. Dip a chilled ball of ganache into chocolate, turning with fork until completely submerged. Immediately lift truffle, tapping fork against pan side and then scraping it against side to remove excess chocolate. Quickly drop truffle into bowl of cocoa powder, shaking and swirling bowl, until ball is completely coated. Push to one side and let rest a few seconds until chocolate layer begins to set. Shake off excess cocoa powder, reshape truffle into a ball with fingers if necessary, and lay on wax paper–lined tray. Repeat procedure, *gently stirring chocolate about every two minutes* to maintain even temperature, until all truffles are prepared. Wipe off dipping fork with dry paper towel as chocolate builds up. If chocolate begins to stiffen and set before all the truffles have been dipped, remove towel from heating pad and turn up heat, stirring just until chocolate melts and thins out again but is not warm. Immediately lower heat and replace towel. Recheck for tempered state by inserting a knife in chocolate and timing to see if it sets within 1½ minutes. If not, add about ½ ounce more chocolate; gently stir to cool mixture slightly and try again. When all truffles are formed, immediately cover tray with plastic wrap and refrigerate for *five minutes only*. Immediately remove from refrigerator. Pack airtight and keep in a cool place (but preferably not refrigerated) for up to a week.

Makes about 1⅓ pounds, about 35 1¼-inch truffles

Note: For a sweeter coating that lends the same dusty look as cocoa powder, combine ¼ cup unsweetened cocoa powder and ⅔ cup chopped bittersweet (not unsweetened) chocolate in a food processor fitted with a steel blade. Process in on/off pulses until chocolate is finely chopped. Continue processing until mixture is powder fine. Then proceed to chocolate-coat and dust truffles exactly as instructed.

*Because these truffles are finished with a
smooth layer of melted chocolate rather than
a powdery coating, they are a bit more
challenging to make than the other kinds
presented in this book. The truffle centers must
be dipped properly and the chocolate must be
in very good temper since there is no
additional coating to camouflage mistakes.*

GRAND MARNIER–CHOCOLATE TRUFFLES

Truffes au Chocolat et au Grand Marnier

To prepare ganache: Put chocolate in a medium-sized, deep bowl set in a warm place. In a medium saucepan, bring cream and orange zest to a simmer over medium-high heat. Lower heat until mixture just barely simmers and cook, uncovered and stirring occasionally, for about 4 minutes or until liquid is reduced to ⅔ cup. Immediately strain cream through a fine sieve into chocolate, stirring until chocolate completely melts. (If any chocolate remains unmelted, set bowl in a slightly larger bowl of hot water and stir until melted.) Stir Grand Marnier into ganache until well blended. Cover and refrigerate for at least four hours (or freeze, stirring frequently, for about one hour), until mixture is very cold and stiff.

To form truffle centers: Using a melon baller or teaspoon, scoop out about ¾-inch portions of ganache. Shape truffles by lightly rolling each portion into a ball between palms. Lay on a wax paper-lined, rimmed baking sheet. As chocolate builds up on hands, wipe off with paper towels. If ganache becomes too soft to shape, return to refrigerator briefly; then proceed. Lightly cover baking sheet with plastic wrap and place in refrigerator until balls are cool and firm.

Meanwhile, set out a wax paper-lined tray and a long-tined dipping fork (or a meat fork, fondue fork, or dinner fork).

When ready to dip truffles, quick-temper coating chocolate following

Ganache

8 ounces bittersweet (not unsweetened) or semisweet chocolate, finely chopped

¾ cup heavy (whipping) cream

⅛ teaspoon grated orange zest (orange part of skin)

1½ tablespoons Grand Marnier

Coating and Garnish

About 1½ pounds bittersweet (not unsweetened) or semisweet chocolate, preferably couverture, coarsely chopped or broken into pieces (see Note)

2 tablespoons solid white vegetable shortening

Melted and partially cooled white chocolate, for garnishing tops of truffles (optional)

Master Recipe on page 220. To hold tempered chocolate at the proper temperature, place a heating pad (inserted in a heavy plastic bag to protect it from drips) under bowl of chocolate. Turn pad to lowest setting. Lay a kitchen towel over plastic bag and, as you work, adjust the thickness of the towel as needed to keep bottom of bowl just barely warm.

To add first coating to truffles: Working quickly, put several tablespoons tempered chocolate in one hand and rub palms together. Place truffles in palms and lightly and quickly rub together palms until truffles are thinly coated with chocolate. Return truffles to wax paper-lined tray. Repeat process until all truffles are thinly coated. Refrigerate truffles for about 10 minutes until chocolate sets.

To dip truffles: Tip bowl so chocolate pools on one side. Place a truffle on fork and submerge in chocolate. Lift truffle, tapping fork against pan side and then scraping it against side several times to thoroughly remove excess chocolate. Tap truffle again to remove excess chocolate and to slide it down to end of fork. Slide truffle off onto wax paper, using tip of a knife to push off truffle, if necessary. Repeat until all truffles are completely coated, *stirring chocolate about every two minutes* to maintain even temperature and tempered state. After dipping about a dozen truffles, transfer them to the refrigerator for about 5 minutes. If chocolate begins to set before all truffles are dipped, remove towel from heating pad and turn up heat, stirring just until chocolate melts but is not warm. Immediately lower heat and replace towel. Recheck for tempered state by inserting a knife in chocolate and timing to see whether chocolate sets in 1½ minutes. If not, add another ½ ounce chocolate; gently stir to cool mixture slightly and then try again.

If desired, using a paper piping cone, pipe a zig-zag line of white chocolate over truffles. The white chocolate should be melted and cool, but still fluid when it is piped. See page 267 for directions on preparing cone. Pack airtight and keep in a very cool place (but preferably not refrigerated or surfaces will be marred by condensation) for up to a week. *Makes about 1¼ pounds or 30 to 35 truffles*

Note: Couverture is the French term for covering, or dipping, chocolate. Due to a high percentage of cocoa butter, couverture is very fluid when it melts. This makes dipping easier and yields very thin, crisp coatings.

As these mellow, richly flavored truffles demonstrate, white chocolate, coffee, and hazelnuts have a great affinity for one another. In the ganache, creamy white chocolate smooths and enriches the coffee flavor while the coffee offsets the sweetness of the chocolate. When the ganache centers are dipped, the sweetness of the white chocolate is again balanced, this time with a finishing coat of chopped hazelnuts.

WHITE CHOCOLATE MOCHA-HAZELNUT TRUFFLES

Truffes Ivoire au Moka et aux Noisettes

To prepare ganache: Place chocolate in a medium-sized, deep bowl and set aside in a warm place. Combine cream and coffee in a medium saucepan and bring just to a boil over medium-high heat. Immediately strain hot cream mixture through a fine sieve into chocolate, stirring until chocolate completely melts. (If any chocolate remains unmelted, set bowl in a pan of hot water for a minute or two and stir until melted.) Stir liqueur into mixture until blended. Cover and refrigerate for at least four hours (or freeze, stirring frequently, for about one hour), or until cold and firm.

To form truffle centers: Using a melon baller or teaspoon, scoop out scant ¾-inch portions of ganache; keep portions small, as nut coating builds up and enlarges truffles considerably. Quickly and lightly roll each portion into a ball between palms. Wipe off hands with paper towels as necessary. If portions become too soft to shape, return tray to refrigerator briefly and then proceed. Lightly cover baking sheet with plastic wrap and refrigerate portions until cool and firm.

To prepare coating mixture: Position a rack in center of oven and preheat to 350°F. Spread hazelnuts and almonds in separate baking pans. Toast almonds for six to seven minutes, or until lightly browned, stirring once or twice; set aside. Toast hazelnuts, stirring occasionally, for 12 to 16 minutes, or until hulls loosen and nuts are tinged with brown. Set aside until

Ganache
8 ounces top-quality white chocolate, finely chopped
¼ cup heavy (whipping) cream
½ teaspoon instant coffee powder or crystals
1½ tablespoons white crème de cacao or coffee-flavored liqueur (or coffee, if preferred)

Coating
1¼ pounds top-quality white chocolate, coarsely chopped or broken into pieces
2 tablespoons solid white vegetable shortening
¾ cup hazelnuts
⅔ cup blanched almond slices

cooled. Remove hazelnut hulls by vigorously rubbing nuts between your fingers or in a clean kitchen towel, discarding bits of hull as you work. (Nuts do not have to be completely free of hull, but should be relatively clean.) Coarsely chop hazelnuts. In a food processor fitted with a steel blade, process hazelnuts and almonds until chopped moderately fine. Transfer nut mixture to a medium-sized, deep bowl. Set out a wax paper-lined tray and a long-tined chocolate dipping fork or other suitable fork (a meat fork, fondue fork, or dinner fork).

When ready to dip truffles, quick-temper white chocolate following Master Recipe on page 220. To hold tempered chocolate at the proper temperature, place a heating pad (inserted in a heavy plastic bag to protect it from drips) under bowl of chocolate. Turn pad to lowest setting. Lay a kitchen towel over plastic bag and, as you work, adjust the thickness of the towel as needed to keep bottom of bowl just barely warm.

To dip and coat truffles: Tip bowl so white chocolate mixture pools on one side. Place a chilled ganache ball on fork and dip in chocolate, turning until submerged. Lift truffle with fork, tapping fork and then scraping it against pan side to remove excess chocolate. Immediately drop truffle into nuts, shaking and swirling bowl until ball is completely coated. Push truffle to one side for a few seconds, until chocolate starts to set. Shake off excess nuts, reshape truffle into round with fingers, if necessary, and lay on clean wax paper-lined tray. Repeat procedure, gently stirring chocolate about every two or three minutes to maintain tempered state, until all truffles have been prepared. Wipe off fork with paper towel if chocolate builds up. If chocolate begins to set before all truffles have been dipped, remove towel from heating pad and turn up heat, stirring just until chocolate melts and thins out again, but is not warm. Immediately lower heat and replace towel. Recheck for tempered state by inserting a knife in chocolate and timing to see whether it sets in 1½ minutes. If not, add another ½ ounce chocolate; gently stir to cool mixture slightly and then try again. When all truffles are formed, refrigerate for about five minutes, until coating is firm. Pack airtight and store in refrigerator for up to a week. Allow to return to room temperature before serving.

Makes about 1½ pounds or 30 truffles

As part of their traditional Christmas festivities, many Swiss families enjoy turning out simple but delectable chocolate truffles. These are finished with a coating of chopped chocolate rather than a thin layer of tempered chocolate, which eliminates the need for special confectionery skills.

SIMPLE BITTERSWEET TRUFFLES

Bitterschokolade Trüffeln

To prepare truffle mixture: Combine chocolate and clarified butter in a medium-sized, heavy saucepan over lowest heat. Warm, stirring, until chocolate completely melts and mixture is smooth. Refrigerate, stirring occasionally, until mixture thickens but is *not completely stiff or hard,* about 50 to 60 minutes

Spoon scant teaspoonfuls of chocolate mixture onto a wax paper-lined baking sheet, separating them slightly. (Keep portions small as finished truffles are very rich.) Roll portions between palms into rough balls, frequently wiping off hands with paper towels as chocolate builds up. (If mixture is too soft to handle, refrigerate until mixture firms enough to shape into balls, about 5 minutes.) After shaping, return balls to refrigerator for a minute or two so surfaces can firm up just slightly.

To coat truffles: Finely and evenly chop chocolate using a large, sharp knife; pieces should be very fine but not powdery or they will lose their crisp texture. (Do not use food processor as some pieces will be chopped too fine.) Stir together cocoa powder and chopped chocolate in a small bowl until well blended. One at a time, roll truffles in coating mixture, turning with a teaspoon. Press coating into truffle surface using two spoons. Store truffles, airtight, in a cool place for up to 10 days. Or refrigerate for up to 3 weeks; allow to warm to room temperature before serving.

Makes about 1 pound, or 30 1-inch truffles

> **Truffle Mixture**
> 12 ounces coarsely chopped top-quality bittersweet (not unsweetened) chocolate, preferably Swiss
> 6½ tablespoons clarified butter (see Note)
>
> **Coating**
> 3 ounces top-quality bittersweet (not unsweetened) chocolate, chopped into ¼-inch pieces
> 1½ tablespoons unsweetened cocoa powder, preferably Dutch-process (European-style)

Note: To clarify butter, bring ½ cup (1 stick) to a simmer in a small saucepan. Simmer for about 4 minutes or until foaming subsides and solids begin to drop to pan bottom. Strain through a fine sieve into a 1 cup measure. Let stand until any remaining solids begin to drop to cup bottom. Measure out and reserve 6½ tablespoons of clarified butter from top; discard remainder or use for another purpose. Clarified butter may be made ahead and refrigerated, tightly covered.

With a set or two of candy molds, a little tempered chocolate, and a few drops of peppermint oil or crème de menthe oil (not mint extract, which can cause chocolate to seize), delicious professional-looking mints can be turned out quickly and easily. ❖ This recipe requires plastic or metal molds designed for candymaking, specifically the very shallow or flat molds that yield wafers, leaves, or other thin shapes. (Thick, solid portions of tempered chocolate are too hard and chunky to eat.)

MOLDED CHOCOLATE MINTS

Set out clean, thoroughly dry molds (see Note). Add to chocolate a drop or two of mint oil and (for pastel white chocolate mints) desired food color paste, stirring until very evenly incorporated; start with very small amounts of oil and color and add more as needed.

Immediately pipe (using a large paper piping cone) or spoon tempered chocolate into molds, underfilling them just slightly and avoiding dripping chocolate over edges. Rap molds on counter several times to spread chocolate and release air bubbles. Carefully wipe away drips around edges using a soft, dry cloth. Immediately transfer molds to refrigerator and let chill for about 15 minutes, or until chocolate sets. Candies may be unmolded immediately but are easier to unmold if chilled for up to 2 hours longer.

To unmold, invert mold. Rap on counter or flex to release candies onto work surface. If candies stick to mold, either chocolate is not completely set or mold is scratched. If reusing molds, allow them to return to room temperature before filling again.

Store candies airtight and in a cool place for up to a month.

Tempered bittersweet, semisweet, or white chocolate (use any leftover amount, or prepare a batch following the Master Recipe on page 220); see Note

Oil of peppermint or oil of crème de menthe (optional); see Note

Paste food color, for pastel white chocolate mints (optional)

Yield will vary depending on the amount of chocolate and the size of molds

Note: Any amount of chocolate may be used, but it must be tempered. Untempered chocolate will not have a smooth, satiny finish, nor will it set up and unmold properly. Mint oils can be purchased in confectioners' supply shops. (For mail-order sources, see page 278.)

It's a good idea to have several sets of molds so all the tempered chocolate can be placed in molds and chilled at once. The alternative is to fill a single mold set, and then try to keep the rest of the tempered chocolate from setting before the molds can be emptied and used again.

I tested dozens of modern (unbeaten) fudge recipes before coming up with this one. It has been carefully devised to avoid graining problems and ensure good results, so measure accurately and don't leave out ingredients or make alterations. Also, avoid the temptation to stir the mixture any more than necessary during cooking; excessive agitation encourages the sugar to form large crystals and thus yield a grainier fudge. Although a candy thermometer is helpful in gauging doneness, the recipe can be made without one. Simply follow the cooking times carefully and test for proper consistency as directed. ❖ For an unusual "gourmet" twist, try the mocha variation at the end of the recipe.

CHOCOLATE FUDGE

In the top of a double boiler, over about 1 inch hot but not simmering water, heat chocolates, stirring occasionally, until melted and smooth. Set aside with boiler top still over bottom to keep chocolate warm. Line an 8- or 9-inch square baking pan with aluminum foil, keeping foil as smooth as possible and overlapping foil on two sides by at least 1 inch. (To easily fit foil, invert pan and mold foil around bottom. Turn pan upright and insert foil in pan, folding overlapping ends outside.)

4 ounces semisweet or bittersweet (not unsweetened) chocolate, coarsely chopped

3 ounces unsweetened chocolate, coarsely chopped

½ cup (1 stick) unsalted butter, cut into chunks

¾ cup heavy (whipping) cream

2 tablespoons light or dark corn syrup

2⅓ cups granulated sugar

1 cup commercial marshmallow creme

2½ teaspoons vanilla extract

1½ cups (about 6 ounces) chopped walnuts or pecans (optional)

In a 4-quart or larger enameled cast-iron saucepan or other large heavy pan, stir together butter, cream, corn syrup, and sugar. Heat over medium heat, stirring with a long-handled wooden spoon, until butter melts and mixture just comes to a boil. Wipe sugar from pan sides with damp paper towel. Cover pan with a tight-fitting lid, and *boil for 2 minutes* to allow steam to wash any remaining sugar crystals from side of pan. Meanwhile, thoroughly wash and dry stirring spoon.

Remove lid and adjust heat so mixture boils steadily but not hard. If using a candy thermometer to gauge doneness, clip it to pan side, inserting so tip is completely submerged but not touching pan bottom. *Boil mixture for 2 minutes, occasionally slowly stirring and scraping pan bottom* in a figure-eight motion. (Stir mixture just enough to prevent sticking but not vigorously as this can cause graininess.) Begin testing for doneness by dropping a teaspoonful of mixture into a cup of very cold water, allowing it to cool for about 15 seconds. If the cooling mixture forms a firm, but flexible ball that holds its shape upon removal from the water (or the mixture reaches 239° to 244°F. on thermometer), it is done. Immediately remove pan from heat and quickly but *gently stir* in melted chocolates, marshmallow creme, and vanilla until completely melted and distributed throughout. Gently fold in nuts (if used). *Immediately* turn out fudge into prepared pan. Quickly shake pan and rap it on counter several times to level mixture. (Don't try to spread with knife as the fudge will already be setting up.) Transfer pan to wire rack and let stand until set and completely cooled, about 2 hours. (To speed cooling let stand 20 minutes, then refrigerate for an hour.)

Using overlapping foil as handles remove slab from pan. Peel foil from slab. For best appearance, refrigerate fudge for a few minutes to firm up before cutting. Working on a cutting board and using a large, sharp knife, trim off and discard uneven edges of slab, if desired. Wiping off knife between cuts, cut slab into 1- to 2-inch square or rectangular pieces as desired.

Pack fudge in an airtight container with wax paper between layers. Store in a cool place. Keeps for up to a week.

Makes about 2 pounds plain or 2⅓ pounds nut fudge

Mocha-Hazelnut Fudge: Increase butter to ¾ cup (1½ sticks). Add 2 teaspoons instant coffee powder or granules to saucepan along with butter and cream, stirring until granules dissolve. Use 3½ ounces unsweetened chocolate and omit semisweet chocolate. Fold in 1½ cups toasted, hulled, and chopped hazelnuts. If desired, hazelnuts may be omitted for a good plain mocha fudge.

This fast-and-easy modern fudge combines the all-American flavors of peanut butter and chocolate. It sets up quickly with no beating, and is moist, fairly firm, and flavorful.

❖ *For smoothest consistency, stir the fudge only as directed. The contents of the saucepan need to be mixed and gently redistributed during cooking to prevent scorching, but any extra agitation will simply increase the graininess of the fudge.*

CHOCOLATE-PEANUT BUTTER FUDGE

Line an 8-inch square baking pan with aluminum foil, keeping foil as smooth as possible and overlapping it at ends by at least 1 inch. (To easily fit foil, invert pan and mold foil around bottom. Turn pan upright and insert shaped foil in pan, folding overlapping edges outside.)

In a 3-quart or larger enameled cast-iron or other *heavy suacepan* over medium-low heat, stir together butter and chocolate until completely melted. Gradually stir in corn syrup and sugar until mixture is well blended and warm. Gradually stir in cream until well blended. Heat over medium heat, stirring with a long-handled wooden spoon, until mixture just comes to a full boil. Cover pan with a tight-fitting lid, and *boil for 2 minutes* to allow steam to wash sugar crystals from pan sides. Meanwhile, thoroughly wash and dry stirring spoon.

Remove lid and adjust heat so mixture boils steadily but not hard. If using a candy thermometer to gauge doneness, clip it to pan side, inserting so tip is completely submerged but not touching pan bottom. Boil

2/3 cup (1 stick plus 2²/3 tablespoons) unsalted butter, cut into chunks

2 ounces unsweetened chocolate, cut into chunks

2 tablespoons light or dark corn syrup

2¹/4 cups granulated sugar

2/3 cup heavy (whipping) cream

1 cup (about 4¹/2 ounces) commercial marshmallow creme

¹/4 cup smooth-style peanut butter, at room temperature

1 teaspoon vanilla extract

mixture for *3 minutes longer, occasionally slowly stirring and scraping pan bottom* in a figure-eight motion. Immediately begin testing for doneness by dropping a teaspoonful of mixture in a cup of very cold water and allowing it to cool for about 15 seconds. If the mixture forms a slightly firm but flexible ball that holds its shape upon removal from water (or mixture reaches 243° to 246°F. on thermometer), it is done. Immediately remove pan from heat. *Gently stir* in marshmallow creme, peanut butter, and vanilla until completely distributed throughout. *Immediately* turn out fudge into prepared pan. Quickly shake pan several times and rap on counter to level mixture. (Do not try to spread out with a knife as fudge will already be setting up.) Transfer pan to wire rack and let stand until thoroughly cooled and set, about 2 hours. (To speed cooling, let stand 20 minutes, then refrigerate for one hour.) If fudge is still soft, refrigerate for 4 to 5 more hours or overnight.

Using overlapping foil as handles, remove slab from pan. Peel foil from slab. For best appearance, refrigerate fudge a few minutes until firmed up before cutting. Working on a cutting board and using a large sharp knife, trim off and discard uneven edges of slab, if desired. Wiping off knife between cuts, cut slab into 1- to 2-inch square or rectangular pieces as desired.

Pack peanut butter fudge in an airtight container with wax paper between layers. Store in a cool place or, if firmer texture is preferred, in the refrigerator. Keeps for up to a week.   *Makes about 2 pounds fudge*

It is important to follow the directions for this recipe carefully, as success with old-fashioned fudge depends on controlling the graining of the sugar. During the cooking and cooling (don't skip this latter step), sugar crystallization must be discouraged through careful handling. Then during beating, it is encouraged so extremely small crystals will form and the fudge will set up with a silky texture.

OLD-FASHIONED BROWN SUGAR CHOCOLATE FUDGE

Line an 8-inch square pan with a sheet of aluminum foil, overlapping pan on two sides by at least 2 inches. (To easily shape foil, turn pan upside down and mold foil to fit around bottom. Turn pan upright and insert shaped foil in pan, folding overlapping ends outside.)

Stir together sugars, salt, and ½ cup cream in a 3- to 4-quart heavy saucepan or Dutch oven until well blended. Place over medium-low heat, stirring until sugar begins to dissolve and mixture is warm. Add butter and chocolate, stirring until completely melted and smooth. Heat mixture almost to boiling point. A bit at a time, add remaining cream, stirring until mixture is completely blended. Scrape down as much residue as possible from pan sides into mixture. Carefully wipe pan sides with a damp cloth or paper towel to remove all grains of sugar. Thoroughly wash all sugar from stirring spoon. If using a candy thermometer to gauge doneness, clip it to pan side, adjusting so tip is completely submerged but not touching pan bottom.

1 pound (2⅓ cups packed) light or dark brown sugar
1 cup granulated sugar
Pinch of salt
1 cup heavy (whipping) cream, divided
½ cup (1 stick) unsalted butter, cut into chunks
2 ounces unsweetened chocolate, broken or coarsely chopped
2½ teaspoons vanilla extract
1¼ cups (about 5 ounces) chopped pecans (optional)

Bring mixture to a boil over medium heat. Adjust heat so mixture boils steadily but not hard. *Slowly stirring and scraping pan bottom in a figure-eight motion, but never scraping down pan sides,* cook for about 10 minutes longer or until mixture reaches 238° to 240°F. (or forms a slightly soft ball when a small amount is dropped in a cup of ice water, cooled slightly, and then pressed between fingers).

Immediately remove pot from heat and set aside *without stirring or jarring.* Let fudge cool, without stirring, to very warm but not hot to touch (115°F.); for smoothest fudge do not begin beating early. (To hasten chilling, gently and carefully set pan in a bowl of cold water, changing the water several times as it warms up.) Add vanilla.

Beat mixture with a clean metal spoon, frequently scraping down pan sides, until fudge begins to lose its gloss and thicken, about 8 to 12 minutes. (Alternatively, if a heavy-duty mixer is available, fudge may be beaten by machine. Scrape down sides of bowl frequently and watch carefully for signs of setting.) Immediately stir in nuts (if used) and turn out into pan, spreading with a greased table knife to even surface. Let stand until cool. Refrigerate until cold and firm. Carefully peel off aluminum foil and discard. Cut fudge into 1-inch squares (or as desired); for very neat cuts, use a sharp knife and wipe clean between each cut. Allow fudge to warm up slightly before serving. Store pieces in an airtight container between sheets of wax paper.

Makes about 1¾ pounds plain fudge or 2¼ pounds pecan fudge

A wonderful combination of toasted almonds, chocolate and crunchy caramelized sugar, this delicious candy always wins high marks from tasters. ❖ *Since this recipe calls for quick-tempering and setting of chocolate, it is best not to work in an overheated kitchen or on excessively warm days.*

Very generously butter a 10½-by-15-inch jelly-roll pan or similar rimmed, heat-proof baking pan; set aside. Position a rack in center of oven and preheat to 325°F. Spread almonds in a large baking pan. Toast, stirring occasionally, for 8 to 10 minutes, or until lightly browned. Immediately remove from oven. Remove ⅔ cup toasted almonds from pan and set aside to cool. Reduce oven setting to barely warm; when oven cools, return remaining sliced almonds to oven to keep them warm while candy is prepared.

Stir together corn syrup, butter, sugar, and salt in a 3½- to 4-quart heavy saucepan or Dutch oven. Add 2½ tablespoons hot tap water, stirring until blended. Heat over medium heat, stirring with a long-handled wooden spoon, until mixture comes to a boil. Cover saucepan with a tight-fitting lid, and boil for 2½ minutes to allow steam to wash all sugar crystals from pan sides. Meanwhile, thoroughly wash and dry stirring spoon. Remove lid and cook for about 5 to 6 minutes longer, gently and slowly stirring occasionally in a figure-eight motion, until mixture thickens slightly and turns a light-caramel color. Stir in almonds and continue cooking, stirring until mixture turns a rich, medium-dark caramel color. Immediately remove pan from heat and continue stirring gently for 30 seconds. Fold in vanilla. Working quickly but carefully (mixture is very hot), turn out into prepared greased pan. Using a greased table knife, immediately spread mixture so it forms an even layer over entire pan bottom.

Transfer pan to wire rack and let stand until toffee is firm and cool enough to touch. Using a knife, loosen toffee slab from pan and remove. (If toffee sticks to pan, place it over a burner turned on low for a few seconds to melt butter, then remove slab.) Line pan with aluminum foil, overlapping pan on two sides by at least 2 inches. Return

3 cups (about 9½ ounces) blanched or unblanched sliced almonds

¼ cup light corn syrup

1 cup (2 sticks) unsalted butter, cut into chunks

1¾ cups granulated sugar

¼ teaspoon salt

1½ teaspoons vanilla extract

12 ounces bittersweet (not unsweetened) or semisweet chocolate

1½ tablespoons solid white vegetable shortening (no substitutes)

ALMOND BUTTERCRUNCH

toffee, smooth side up, to pan. Wipe excess butter from slab with a paper towel. Let toffee cool completely. Using a kitchen mallet or large heavy spoon, crack toffee into bite-sized pieces, *being careful to leave pieces in place in pan.*

Chop reserved ⅔ cup almonds. Quick-temper chocolate following Master Recipe on page 220: When chocolate sets on knife within 1½ minutes, remove any unmelted chocolate chunks from mixture. Quickly pour chocolate onto *cooled* toffee. (It must be cooled or chocolate may discolor as it sets.) Using a long-bladed metal spatula or a knife, working quickly, spread chocolate evenly and lightly over surface, taking care not to dislodge pieces. Immediately sprinkle reserved finely chopped almonds over chocolate. Transfer pan to refrigerator *for 5 minutes.* Immediately remove from refrigerator and let stand until chocolate completely sets. Break toffee pieces apart with fingers.

Pack toffee pieces in an airtight container, and store in a cool place (not in refrigerator). Toffee will keep well for 2 to 3 weeks.

Makes about 2¼ pounds toffee

Chocolate-caramel pecan clusters, or turtles as they are otherwise known, take some time, but they are not difficult to make. ❖ *Cook the caramel mixture in an enameled cast-iron or other heavy saucepan that will distribute the heat evenly; this reduces the chance of scorching once the mixture has boiled down and thickened. Also, use a very large pan or the caramel may boil over during the first stage of cooking.*

CHOCOLATE-CARAMEL PECAN CLUSTERS (TURTLETTES)

Line a 10-by-15-inch jelly-roll pan with aluminum foil. Lightly grease foil, or lightly spray with nonstick vegetable cooking spray. Line a second tray or large pan with foil; leave ungreased.

To prepare caramel: Using a large wooden spoon, stir together sugars, corn syrup, cream, milk, butter, and salt in a *4-quart or larger* heavy saucepan or Dutch oven. Bring mixture to a boil over medium-high heat, stirring until sugar dissolves. Wash off any sugar crystals from stirring spoon. Carefully dry spoon. (If using a candy thermometer to gauge doneness, clip it to side of pan after foaming has subsided, inserting so tip is completely submerged but not touching pan bottom.) Continue to cook, uncovered, over medium-high heat, occasionally stirring and scraping pan bottom in a figure-eight motion. Gradually, as mixture boils down, it will be more likely to scorch, so stir more frequently.

When mixture boils down enough to thicken slightly, about 5 minutes, lower heat to medium and continue cooking, stirring gently but continuously. When mixture thickens further and bubbles loudly, begin testing for doneness as follows: Remove pan from burner. Drop about ½ teaspoon mixture into ice

Caramel

1 cup packed light or dark brown sugar
½ cup granulated sugar
⅔ cup light corn syrup
1 cup heavy (whipping) cream
½ cup whole milk
1 tablespoon unsalted butter
Generous ⅛ teaspoon salt
2½ teaspoons vanilla extract

Nuts and Chocolate

3 cups (about 10 ounces) pecan halves or pieces, preferably lightly toasted (see Note)
12 ounces semisweet chocolate, broken or coarsely chopped
2 tablespoons solid white vegetable shortening

water, let cool for about 20 seconds, and then press between fingers; caramel is done when a flexible, almost firm ball is formed. (Alternatively, if using a candy thermometer, cook until mixture registers 254° to 256°F.; immediately remove from heat.) Gently stir in vanilla. Let caramel stand for 10 to 15 minutes, until slightly stiffened but still somewhat gooey in consistency.

Form caramel mounds as follows: Spread pecans in pan lined with greased foil. Using two teaspoons, drop small spoonfuls of caramel onto pecans, spacing about 1½ inches apart. If mixture cools and stiffens too much before all is used, reheat for a few minutes over a burner set on low and then continue forming candies. As caramel mounds cool and firm up, gently remove from foil to a clean, foil-lined tray or baking sheet, spacing about 1 inch apart. Rearrange unused pecans to form a solid layer on greased foil and continue forming candy mounds until all caramel is used. (Some pecans will be left over.) To ready mounds for topping with chocolate, place in refrigerator for about 10 minutes.

Quick-temper chocolate following Master Recipe on page 220. When chocolate sets on knife within 1½ minutes, remove any unmelted chocolate chunks from mixture. Place top of double boiler on a heating pad turned on to very low setting, to maintain desired temperature of chocolate. (Slip heating pad into a large plastic bag to protect it from chocolate drips.) Lay kitchen towel over protected heating pad to insulate pan bottom from direct heat of pad.

Cover caramel mounds with chocolate as follows: Using a table knife and working quickly, spread thin layer of chocolate over bottom of mound. Then very generously spread chocolate over top of each caramel mound. Place clusters on foil, slightly separated. Continue forming clusters, gently *stirring the chocolate every 2 or 3 minutes to maintain tempered state.* If chocolate cools too much and begins to set, return top of double boiler to bottom and warm, stirring gently, just briefly until remelted. (If mixture inadvertently warms too much, add 1 ounce additional unmelted chocolate and stir until tempered state is reached again.) Transfer clusters to refrigerator for 5 minutes to firm up chocolate. Let stand at room temperature until completely set.

Pack clusters, flat and with foil between layers, in an airtight container. Store in a cool place but not in refrigerator.

Makes about 2 pounds, about 35 clusters

Note: Spread pecans in roasting pan and toast in a preheated 350°F. oven, stirring occasionally, for 7 to 10 minutes or until nuts are tinged with brown. Set aside until cooled.

The old-fashioned poured candy called toffee has long been a favorite in Great Britain. In the past, cooks would keep a small toffee hammer in the kitchen for cracking the cooled candy slab into bite-sized pieces. But, nowadays, many recipes call for scoring the warm slab into uniform rectangular portions and then separating them when the candy sets. Though most early recipes were for treacle (or molasses) toffee, today chocolate, coffee, and butterscotch flavors are popular as well. ❖ The following toffee is chewy-firm, with a good chocolate taste. For a chewier toffee cook to the minimum temperature given; for firmer toffee cook to the maximum indicated. It is best to use a candy thermometer for this recipe.

CHOCOLATE TOFFEE

Line a 10-by-15-inch jelly-roll pan with aluminum foil, keeping foil as smooth as possible and overhanging it at ends by at least 1 inch. Very generously grease foil (or spray with nonstick vegetable cooking spray). In a 4-quart or larger heavy saucepan or Dutch oven, stir together corn syrup, coffee powder, lemon juice, butter, sugar, and salt until well mixed. Heat over medium heat, stirring with a long-handled wooden spoon, until mixture comes to a boil. Cover pan with a tight-fitting lid, and boil for 4 minutes to allow steam to wash all sugar crystals from pan sides. Meanwhile, thoroughly wash and dry stirring spoon.

Remove lid and adjust heat so mixture boils vigorously. If using a candy thermometer to gauge doneness, clip it to side of pan, adjusting so tip is completely immersed but not touching pan bottom. Boil mixture for about 3 minutes, stirring occasionally in a figure-eight motion, until mixture thickens slightly. Lower heat slightly and continue boiling, stirring frequently but gently, a few minutes longer or until mixture reaches 276° to 279°F. on a candy thermometer (or forms very firm ropes when a small amount is dropped in a cup of ice water,

1½ cups light corn syrup

¾ teaspoon instant coffee powder or granules

1 teaspoon lemon juice

1¼ cups (2½ sticks) unsalted butter, cut into chunks

2¼ cups granulated sugar

¼ teaspoon salt

3 ounces unsweetened chocolate, chopped into small pieces

1½ teaspoons vanilla extract

cooled slightly, and then stretched). (Watch temperature carefully as it may rise rapidly after reaching 270°F.) Immediately remove pan from heat. Gently fold in chocolate just until completely melted. Gently stir in vanilla. Quickly turn out toffee into prepared pan. Immediately rap pan on counter several times and shake to spread out toffee and release air bubbles. Transfer pan to wire rack. If planning to score slab, let stand just until toffee begins to set up, but is still warm enough to cut through easily; start checking at about 15 minutes.

To cut toffee: Using a greased table knife, score surface lengthwise at 1-inch intervals and crosswise at ½-inch intervals or as desired to form toffee pieces. Keep pieces small (under 1 inch) or they will be difficult to eat. Let toffee cool 15 to 25 minutes longer, or until almost set up. Retrace scoring, cutting deeply into toffee surface. Cover and refrigerate for at least 35 to 40 minutes, or until thoroughly chilled. Using overhanging foil as handles, lift toffee from pan. Carefully peel foil from toffee. By hand, break toffee pieces apart along score lines. Alternatively, omit scoring of toffee surface and let toffee stand until thoroughly cooled. Carefully peel off foil. Break toffee into bite-sized pieces using kitchen mallet or back of a heavy spoon.

Toffee pieces must be wrapped individually in wax paper or packed in a shallow container with wax paper between layers and refrigerated to prevent them from sticking together. Allow pieces to warm up slightly before serving. Toffee keeps for up to two months.

Makes about 2½ pounds toffee

A dense, dark fruit-and-nut confection that looks like a thin cake, panforte is a traditional Italian Christmas specialty that originated in the town of Siena. ❖ The following panforte may be garnished in the traditional manner with cocoa powder or, for a fancy finish, it can be glazed with melted, quick-tempered chocolate and "tied" with a festive white- and dark-chocolate ribbon, as shown.

FRUIT, NUT, AND CHOCOLATE CHRISTMAS CONFECTION

Panforte Scuro

Position a rack in center of oven and preheat to 350°F. Line an 8- or 8½-inch springform pan with heavy-duty aluminum foil, placing foil with dull side visible and letting it extend up pan sides at least 2 inches all the way around. (To easily shape foil, invert pan and mold foil around pan bottom. Remove shaped foil from bottom and insert into pan.) Generously grease foil or spray with nonstick vegetable cooking spray.

Spread hazelnuts in a roasting pan and toast in the oven, stirring occasionally, for 12 to 15 minutes, or until hulls begin to loosen and nuts are tinged with brown. Spread almonds in a separate pan and toast, stirring occasionally, for 5 to 6 minutes or until just tinged with brown. Remove nuts from oven and set aside to cool. Reset oven to 300° F.

When hazelnuts are cool enough to handle, remove loose skins as follows: Working with a handful of nuts at a time, vigorously rub them between fingers or in a clean kitchen towel, discarding bits of skin as you work. (It's all right if some bits of skin don't come off completely.) Chop hazelnuts moderately fine. Combine with almonds.

Thoroughly stir together flour, chocolate, cocoa powder, cinnamon, cloves, candied fruit, and nuts in a large bowl. Bring sugar, honey, butter, and 2 teaspoons water just to a *full boil* in a medium-sized, heavy saucepan over medium heat. Boil, uncovered, for exactly 1 minute, stirring frequently; immediately

1 cup hazelnuts
1 cup chopped slivered almonds
⅓ cup all-purpose flour
2½ ounces finely grated or very finely chopped bittersweet (not unsweetened) chocolate
3 tablespoons unsweetened cocoa powder, preferably Dutch-process (European-style)
⅛ teaspoon ground cinnamon
Pinch of ground cloves
⅔ cup chopped candied orange peel
¾ cup granulated sugar
⅓ cup clover honey
2 tablespoons unsalted butter
¼ teaspoon finely grated orange zest (orange part of peel)

Continued on following page

remove pan from burner and stir in orange zest. Working quickly, pour syrup over fruit-nut mixture, stirring vigorously until evenly incorporated. (If mixture stiffens before ingredients are evenly blended, knead with hands until evenly mixed.) Turn out mixture into prepared pan, pressing down with hands to form a very smooth, even layer.

Bake for 27 to 32 minutes or until mixture is just slightly darker and firmer at edges (but still soft in center.) Remove baking pan to a rack and let stand about 1 hour or until cool and hardened on top. Remove pan sides. Lift panforte and foil from pan bottom and transfer to wire rack. Let stand just until *completely cooled.* Peel off and discard foil; turn so the side that was covered with foil becomes the top.

For traditional garnish, process cocoa powder and chopped chocolate in a food processor fitted with a steel blade, until mixture is powder fine. Sprinkle mixture evenly over thoroughly cooled panforte top.

Alternatively, decorate with quick-tempered chocolate as follows: Place panforte on a wire rack. Set rack on a jelly-roll pan. Combine 6 ounces chocolate and the shortening in the top of a double boiler. Proceed with quick-tempering following Master Recipe on page 220, adding remaining chocolate as called for. Remove any unmelted chunks of chocolate from mixture.

> **Garnish**
>
> 1½ teaspoons cocoa powder combined with 1 tablespoon finely chopped bittersweet (not unsweetened) chocolate (omit if glazing top with melted, tempered chocolate)
>
> 8 ounces bittersweet (not unsweetened) chocolate, coarsely broken (omit if decorating top with cocoa powder mixture)
>
> 1 tablespoon solid white vegetable shortening (omit if decorating top with cocoa powder)
>
> Dark- and light-striped chocolate ruffles and chocolate ribbons for decoration, optional (see page 246)

Quickly pour tempered chocolate over panforte. Using a long-bladed spatula or knife, working with only a few quick strokes, spread chocolate evenly out to edges, allowing excess to drip over sides. Quickly smooth and touch up chocolate along sides as necessary. Immediately transfer panforte to refrigerator and let cool for 10 to 15 minutes, until chocolate sets. Remove from refrigerator and let stand at least 30 minutes longer, until chocolate completely firms up.

Add chocolate ribbons and ruffled bow, if desired, arranging on confection as shown in photograph. Serve panforte cut into thin wedges.

Store, airtight, in a cool place for up to 2 weeks. Or wrap airtight and freeze, without cocoa powder or glaze, for up to 2 weeks. Dust with cocoa-powder mixture, or glaze after panforte is completely thawed.

Makes about 16 servings

FRUIT, NUT, AND CHOCOLATE CHRISTMAS CONFECTION

ITALY

Many marzipan figures require considerable practice to produce, but marzipan-chocolate pine cones are an exception: They can be turned out fairly quickly, even on the very first try.

MARZIPAN CHOCOLATE PINE CONES

Schokoladen-Marzipantannenzapfen

Have ready a supply of toothpicks. Make a stand to hold pine cones upright during drying as follows: Invert a lightweight shoe-box bottom or similar box on work surface. Using a metal skewer or very thin, sharp knife-point, poke small holes in box bottom, spacing them at least 1 inch apart. (Holes should be small enough for toothpicks to fit snugly when inserted.)

In a small bowl or cup stir together coffee powder and ¼ teaspoon very hot tap water until well blended. Set aside until coffee dissolves. Combine coffee, marzipan, and cocoa powder in a shallow bowl. Knead with hands until completely blended. Shape mixture into a 12-inch log of even thickness. For 1¾-inch cones, mark and then cut log crosswise into about 18 portions; for 1¼-inch cones mark and cut into 26 portions. Roll each portion between palms into a very smooth ball. Then roll between palms until ball elongates and tapers slightly at one end into a pine cone shape. (Keep cone shapes fairly plump, as they will elongate more during cutting.) Insert a toothpick into bottom of each cone to provide a handle. Insert toothpicks into stand holes.

> ¼ teaspoon instant coffee powder or
>   granules (optional)
> 7 ounces marzipan
> 1 tablespoon unsweetened cocoa powder,
>   preferably Dutch-process (European-
>   style)
> Powdered sugar, for garnish (optional)

Let cones stand and dry on the outside for at least 45 minutes and up to 2 hours, if desired. Holding a cone by the toothpick and working around cone tip with a sharp pair of kitchen shears, snip into surface to create a series of pointed, petal-like protrusions, or scales. For very clean snips, frequently wipe shears with a damp paper towel. Continue until a row of scales has been snipped all the way around cone. Spacing so as to offset scales in first row, snip a second row of scales just below first row. Continue adding rows, each offsetting the preceding row, at even intervals until bottom of cone is reached. As each cone is finished, return to stand. If powdered-sugar garnish is desired, dust comes by lightly sifting powdered sugar over top. Allow cones to dry for 36 to 48 hours, until firm enough to hold their shape. Remove from toothpicks. Pack airtight and store in a cool place for up to 3 weeks. Depending on moisture content in marzipan, cones may need to be redusted with powdered sugar before serving. (For longer storage, freeze plain cones for up to 2 months, allowing them to come to room temperature before dusting with sugar.)

Makes about 18 1¾-inch cones or 26 1¼-inch cones

This recipe calls for tempered chocolate, which means that the chocolate coating will set up smooth and hard and the dipped items can be stored and served at room temperature. A variety of dried fruits can be dipped: Apricots are probably the easiest to obtain and the most popular, but dried pear halves, pineapple slices, and papaya spears (often available at health food and gourmet shops) work well, too. Since pear halves are large, I cut each one lengthwise into strips and discard the center strip, which often contains pithy bits of core. Fresh fruits can be dipped following the same directions, except they must be served within a few hours since they are very perishable. ❖ If dipping nuts, choose large, perfect ones. Pecan and walnut halves, whole almonds, Brazil nuts, and large cashews are all fine. To bring out their flavor, toast the nuts at 350°F., stirring occasionally, until tinged with brown, about seven to 12 minutes, then cool completely before using.

CHOCOLATE-COVERED DRIED FRUIT AND NUTS

Lay fruits or nuts on wax paper–lined trays or baking sheets. Refrigerate for at least 30 minutes until well chilled. Set out several trays or baking sheets lined with wax paper.

Temper chocolate according to Master Recipe, page 220. To hold tempered chocolate at the proper temperature, place a heating pad (inserted in a heavy plastic bag to protect it from drips) under bowl of chocolate. Turn pad to lowest setting. Lay a kitchen towel over plastic bag and, as you work, adjust the thickness of the towel as needed to keep bottom of bowl just barely warm.

Working with one piece at a time and holding with your fingers, dip fruit into chocolate, either at an angle or horizontally, until as much of the

1¹/₂ to 1³/₄ pounds dried fruits or nuts (see Note)
1¹/₄ pounds bittersweet (not unsweetened) or semisweet chocolate, or white chocolate, coarsely chopped or broken into small pieces
2 tablespoons solid white vegetable shortening

surface as desired is coated. Lift piece and scrape off excess chocolate from bottom against pan side. Lay pieces, slightly separated, on wax paper–lined tray. Each time 10 or 12 pieces accumulate, transfer them to the refrigerator before continuing.

Continue until all pieces are dipped, *stirring chocolate about every two minutes* to maintain even temperature and tempered state. If chocolate begins to set before all pieces are dipped, remove towel from heating pad and turn up heat, stirring just until chocolate melts and thins out again, but is not warm. Immediately lower heat and replace towel. Recheck for tempered state by inserting a knife in chocolate and timing to see whether it sets in 1½ minutes. If it does not, add another ½-ounce unmelted chocolate; gently stir to cool mixture slightly and then try again.

Refrigerate dipped pieces for about 10 minutes. Let stand at room temperature for about 30 minutes, until chocolate is completely firm and set. Pack pieces, airtight, with wax paper between the layers. Store in a cool, dry place for up to a month.

Makes 3 pounds chocolate-covered fruit or nuts

Note: This is the quantity of fruits or nuts needed to use up the tempered chocolate produced by following the Master Recipe on page 220. Smaller quantities may be dipped, and the leftover chocolate simply allowed to set so it can be used later for other baking needs.

CHOCOLATE-COVERED FRESH FRUIT

Almost nobody can resist fresh succulent fruits and berries enrobed in white or dark chocolate. Strawberries are particularly popular (see the white and dark chocolate-covered berries presented in Woven Chocolate Baskets, page 243), but I like seedless orange segments and pineapple slices even better. Large sweet cherries are also good, though a bit more trouble to make since they have to be pitted first. ❖ *In the following recipe, the fruit is simply dipped in melted chocolate, then chilled so the chocolate will firm up. Then, if desired, it can be dipped in a second, contrasting coat of chocolate. Since the chocolate isn't tempered, it never fully sets and will melt again unless kept refrigerated. If you want to prepare fruits that can be left out at room temperature for more than about 15 minutes—to use as a table display, for example—follow the Master Recipe for tempering chocolate on page 220.* ❖ *Since even a drop or two of moisture may cause chocolate to seize (become lumpy and hard), only fruits that are firm and dry on the surface can be dipped. Whole, unblemished strawberries and orange segments with unbroken membranes are ideal because the juice is held inside. Cherries may release some juice when pitted, but can be dipped if allowed to dry between layers of paper towels for a few minutes first. Likewise, cut fruits such as pineapple slices can dipped if very carefully blotted dry between several layers and changes of paper towel; let stand for at least 30 minutes before dipping.* ❖ *Chocolate-covered dried fruits and nuts are normally dipped in tempered chocolate (so they can be stored at room temperature), but they may be prepared using the method given here, and stored in an airtight container in the refrigerator for up to a month.*

Thoroughly dry fruit using paper towels. Lay fruit on paper towel-lined trays or baking sheets and let stand at room temperature to air dry for a few minutes. Set out several trays or baking sheets lined with wax paper.

Meanwhile, in the top of a double boiler, over about 1 inch hot but not simmering water, heat chocolate and shortening, stirring occasionally, until completely melted and smooth. Remove top of double boiler from bottom, carefully wiping any moisture from bottom of pan. Let chocolate cool for five minutes, stirring occasionally.

Working one at a time and holding pieces of fruit with your fingers, dip into chocolate, either at an angle or horizontally, until as much of the fruit surface as desired is coated. Lift fruit and scrape off excess chocolate against pan side. Lay fruit pieces, separated, on wax paper-lined tray. Transfer tray to freezer for *five minutes only*, until chocolate is firm and pieces of fruit are chilled *but not frozen*. Immediately transfer to refrigerator and store, lightly covered with plastic wrap, for at least 30 minutes and up to eight hours before serving.

About ¾ pound strawberries, segments of seedless oranges, pitted cherries, large seedless grapes, or firm, completely dry fresh fruit slices, such as pineapple or kiwi fruit

8 ounces bittersweet (not unsweetened) or semisweet chocolate

1 tablespoon solid white vegetable shortening

5 ounces white chocolate, for double-dipping (optional)

2 teaspoons solid white vegetable shortening for double-dipping (optional)

If desired, after 30 minutes fruits may be dipped in second, contrasting coating of chocolate (as shown in photograph, page 242). Prepare chocolate as directed above and let cool slightly. Working with one piece of chilled fruit at a time, dip quickly and lightly into chocolate and remove before first coating begins to melt. Shake off excess chocolate, but do not scrape against pan side. Immediately return to refrigerator, but do not cover with plastic wrap, and continue until all pieces are coated. After 30 minutes re-cover with plastic wrap. Store in refrigerator until serving time.

Makes about 1¼ pounds chocolate-covered fruit, and about 1½ pounds double-dipped fruit

This simple, delicious slab candy is easily prepared by folding together tempered chocolate and toasted nuts. I usually prepare it when I have tempered chocolate left over from another project, but it's certainly worth tempering chocolate just to make bark.

❖ *The following recipe specifies amounts, but any larger quantity can be prepared simply by keeping the ratio of chocolate to nuts the same. For every eight to nine ounces of tempered chocolate (about one fluid cup), add about seven to eight ounces of nuts. (I prefer unsalted, but some people like the taste of salted nuts.) Most nut varieties make tasty bark, but Chocolate-Pecan is especially good. For best flavor, use only very fresh, top-quality nuts.* ❖ *Keep in mind that if you plan to use the last of a batch of tempered chocolate for bark, the nuts must be toasted and cooled in advance. Warm nuts cannot be added to the chocolate as they may wreck its temper, and the chocolate may set if it has to stand until the nuts cool.*

CHOCOLATE-NUT BARK

Position a rack in center of oven and preheat to 350°F. Spread nuts in a baking pan. Toast nuts for six to 12 minutes or until nicely browned, stirring and checking frequently for doneness. (For hazelnuts, toast until hulls loosen and nuts are tinged with brown, about 12 to 15 minutes.) Set aside until cooled. If hazelnuts are used, remove hulls by vigorously rubbing nuts between your fingers or in a clean kitchen towel, discarding bits of hull as you work; they do not have to be completely free of hull, but should be relatively clean. Coarsely chop nuts, preferably by hand, using a large sharp knife. Let nuts stand until cooled to room temperature. (Cooling may be hastened by refrigerating

About 1½ to 1¾ cups (7 to 8 ounces) whole almonds, macadamias, hazelnuts, peanuts, or pecan or walnut halves

8 to 9 ounces tempered bittersweet (not unsweetened) or semisweet chocolate, or white chocolate (use leftover, or prepare a batch following Master Recipe on page 220)

nuts for a few minutes, but they must be at room temperature when added to chocolate.)

For a batch of bark using 8 to 9 ounces chocolate, line an 8-inch square baking pan with aluminum foil; keep foil as smooth and wrinkle-free as possible and allow it to overlap on two sides of the pan by about an inch. (To easily shape foil, turn pan upside down and mold foil to fit around bottom. Turn pan upright and insert shaped foil in pan, folding overlapping ends outside.) For large batches of bark, choose a rectangular pan or dish that will allow bark layer to spread to about a ¼-inch thickness.

Fold a generous three fourths of nuts into chocolate. Turn out mixture into prepared pan. Sprinkle remaining nuts over pan surface. Rap pan on counter several times, then shake it to spread out chocolate and release air bubbles. Lay a completely wrinkle-free sheet of aluminum foil on chocolate, patting down so foil is flat against surface and completely smooth.

Immediately transfer pan to refrigerator for 15 minutes. Remove from refrigerator and let stand in a cool place, with foil still in place, until chocolate completely sets, at least 30 minutes and preferably one hour longer. (The foil gives the bark a shiny, professional-looking finish.) Peel off top and then bottom layers of foil. Crack bark into chunks using a kitchen mallet or back of a heavy spoon (avoid touching bark with fingers as fingerprints will show on surface). Pack airtight and store in a cool place for two to three weeks; storage time will vary depending on the perishability of the nuts used.

Makes about 1 pound of bark

Quick-tempering prepares melted chocolate blocks, bars, or real chocolate chips for coating or dipping (see Note). This process is essential to ensure that the chocolate will set up hard, satiny, and without whitish streaks or flecks (called bloom). The quick-tempering process is not difficult but, because of the particular chemical characteristics of chocolate, must be followed carefully. It is best to quick-temper chocolate in cool weather in a cool room, as heat and humidity can prevent even properly tempered chocolate from setting up as it should. ❖ Couverture, or coating chocolate, is often recommended for dipping and coating because it is quite fluid when melted, but for this particular quick-tempering method you can also use other good bittersweet or semisweet chocolates. This method calls for the addition of a little solid white vegetable shortening (no substitutes), which thins thicker chocolates and also helps retard blooming. The chocolate used must be in a tempered state prior to melting—that is, as purchased, in smooth, hard blocks that have not been previously melted. ❖ The following is a master recipe that should be used when individual recipes in this book do not specify a procedure or indicate exactly how much chocolate should be tempered for a particular task (or when you wish to temper chocolate for your own purposes). When recipes indicate quantities, use the amount they specify and follow any alternate directions they include. The master recipe yields about 1½ pounds of tempered chocolate, but the same method may be used for a larger quantity, and in fact, a larger quantity is recommended if you plan to dip or coat with it over a period of time. (Just keep the proportions in the recipe the same.) It's difficult to work with less than a pound when dipping items because a small amount tends to cool and set rapidly as it stands and is also difficult to dip into. Of course, for chocolate that will be used all at once to glaze a cake or to cover a slab of candy, for example, any quantity can be prepared (see Note). ❖ To help maintain the proper temperature of tempered chocolate while dipping, rest the bowl of chocolate on a kitchen towel laid on a heating pad turned to the lowest setting. Adjust the thickness of the towel as needed to slow or hasten the conduction of heat to the bowl. Stir chocolate every few minutes to maintain the temper. (To keep the heating pad clean, slide it into a plastic bag.) ❖ When using the quick-tempering method, items to be dipped or coated should be at room temperature or chilled, depending on the directions. Also, items to be dipped or coated must be free of surface moisture, which can react with the natural starch in chocolate and cause it to seize (become very stiff and unworkable).

MASTER RECIPE FOR QUICK-TEMPERING CHOCOLATE

Slowly melt generous three quarters of chocolate and solid shortening in a metal bowl (or top of a double boiler) over about 1 inch *hot but not simmering* water, stirring occasionally, until completely melted, fluid, and slightly hot to the touch (120°F.); *be very careful not to allow any steam or water drops into chocolate.* (If melting white chocolate, be sure to melt over low heat, and stir frequently, or it may lump.) Immediately remove bowl from hot water and carefully dry exterior of bowl to *be sure no water can drip into chocolate.* Add all except 2 ounces remaining chocolate (or less, if a very small quantity of chocolate is being tempered) to melted chocolate, stirring. Continue slowly stirring, away from heat, until most chocolate chunks are melted and mixture is cool to the touch (check by dabbing a little on the upper lip). If all bits of chocolate have melted and mixture still does not feel cool to touch, add 1 more ounce chocolate and continue slowly stirring to lower its temperature further.

> 1½ pounds bittersweet (not unsweetened) or semisweet chocolate, or top-quality white chocolate, broken or chopped into chunks
>
> 3 tablespoons solid white vegetable shortening (no substitutes)

When chocolate feels cool or shows signs of setting at the edges, start testing every few minutes to see if it is tempered and ready for use by inserting tip of a knife into the center of the mixture, then tapping off excess. Begin timing to see whether chocolate starts to set (harden and dull) on knife within 1½ minutes. If chocolate has melted and mixture still does not set within 1½ minutes, add about 1 more ounce chocolate and continue slowly stirring, resuming checks, until tempered state is reached. (When chocolate is tempered, simply push any unmelted chunks to one side or remove). If chocolate will be left standing rather than used all at once, set bowl on heating pad (inserted in a heavy plastic bag to protect it from drips) and turn to lowest setting. Cover heating pad with a towel. Begin dipping items (lightly chilled first) or using chocolate as specified in individual recipe. Stir to remix chocolate every three minutes; adjust thickness of towel to provide more or less heat to bowl as necessary. If chocolate begins to stiffen and set as you work, increase heat slightly, stirring until mixture thins out again but is not warm. Immediately lower heat again. (If it inadvertently warms too much, add a fresh ½-ounce chunk of chocolate and gently stir mixture until tempered state has been reached again).

Note: Tempering is required for all "real" chocolate products, because they contain cocoa butter. In some chocolate-like products (variously called summer coating, confectionery coating, or compound chocolate); the cocoa butter is removed and another fat added, making tempering unnecessary. For a detailed explanation, see Working with Chocolate, page 12.

Though having to use fairly large quantities when tempering chocolate might at first seem inconvenient, this does not have to be the case. Leftover tempered chocolate can be put to all sorts of uses—forming piped decorations; dipping cookies, dried fruits, and nuts; combining the chocolate with coconut and raisins and dropping from a spoon into coconut-chocolate clusters; and preparing molded chocolate candies and chocolate bark. And even when time is too short for these preparations, the chocolate never has to be wasted. Simply scrape it out onto an aluminum foil–lined plate; refrigerate until the chocolate sets; then save, wrapped in the foil, until needed for future cooking or baking projects.

Chocolate Fondue

CHAPTER

Swiss-Style Hot Chocolate

Sitting around a fondue pot with friends and dipping skewers of fresh fruit into a luscious pool of chocolate always makes for a relaxing and convivial get-together—especially since the preparation is so simple that you don't have to spend a lot of time in the kitchen.

CHOCOLATE FONDUE

Fondue au Chocolat

In a medium-sized, heavy saucepan over medium-high heat, heat cream and butter, until mixture just simmers and butter melts. Remove from burner. Immediately stir in chocolates. Continue stirring until chocolates melt and mixture is completely smooth. Fondue should be fluid, but have enough thickness and body to evenly coat a piece of fruit (dip a test piece to check). A bit at a time, stir in cognac, until desired consistency and taste is reached.

To serve: Place chocolate in a fondue pot over a heat source that will keep it warm, but *not at all hot*. Serve along with fruit plate and fondue forks for dipping fruit.

Makes 4 to 6 servings

$1/2$ cup heavy (whipping) cream

1 tablespoon unsalted butter, cut into small pieces

6 ounces top-quality bittersweet chocolate, chopped

3 ounces top-quality milk chocolate, chopped

About 1 tablespoon cognac, Grand Marnier, or kirsch (or water, if preferred)

About 8 cups assorted fresh fruit, at least 4 kinds, such as whole, medium strawberries, large seedless orange segments (membranes removed), fresh pineapple chunks, and large, pitted dark sweet cherries

The hot chocolate most Americans drink bears only a faint resemblance to schoggi—a sumptuous blend of melted Swiss chocolate, whole milk, and egg yolk, often topped off with a generous dollop of whipped cream. Schoggi is as widely enjoyed in Switzerland as hot coffee is in some neighboring countries. In fact, the Swiss sometimes refer to it as "hot chocolate–coffee!"

SWISS-STYLE HOT CHOCOLATE

Heiße Schoggi, Schoggoladekafi

Combine chocolate and ¼ cup milk in a small, heavy saucepan over medium-low heat. Heat, stirring occasionally, until chocolate melts and mixture is completely smooth; set aside. In a medium-sized, heavy saucepan over medium-high heat, bring remaining milk just to a boil. Remove from burner. Gradually add ½ cup boiling milk to chocolate, stirring until completely smooth and well-blended. In a cup, beat 2 tablespoons sugar and egg yolk together with a fork, until well blended. Add egg mixture to chocolate, stirring until smooth. Add chocolate mixture to remaining milk mixture, stirring well. Reheat mixture over medium-high heat, stirring constantly, for about 3 minutes or until mixture is steaming hot but *not boiling*; then immediately remove pan from burner. Divide among 3 or 4 preheated cups or mugs.

3½ ounces bittersweet (not unsweetened) chocolate (preferably Swiss), coarsely chopped
3¼ cups whole milk, divided
2½ tablespoons granulated sugar, divided (see Note)
1 large egg yolk
¾ cup heavy (whipping) cream

In a mixer bowl, with mixer set on high speed, beat cream and remaining ½ tablespoon sugar until soft peaks form. Spoon a generous dollop of cream over each serving of hot chocolate. (Alternatively, using a pastry bag fitted with a large open-star tip, pipe a very large rosette of whipped cream over each serving.) Serve immediately.

Makes 3 to 4 servings

Note: Schoggi tends to be less sweet than American hot chocolate, so you may want to increase the sugar to suit your own taste. Correct sweetness during the reheating stage by stirring in a tablespoon or two more sugar, if desired. Keep in mind, however, that the finished drink will be mellowed by the melting cloud of whipped cream.

This frosting has an assertive, but not overpowering, chocolate flavor. Sour cream gives it a slight tang, as well as a pleasing fluffiness and spreadability. Since it is not overly sweet or heavy, it is a good choice for those who like their cake luxuriously slathered with frosting. (I devised it in response to one of my taster's belief that the icing should always be as thick as the cake!)

CHOCOLATE SOUR CREAM FROSTING

Melt chocolates and butter in the top of a double boiler over about 1 inch hot but not simmering water, stirring frequently until completely smooth. Remove top of double boiler from bottom. Stir together sour cream, corn syrup, vanilla, and 1 tablespoon water, until mixture is smooth and well blended. Stir sour cream mixture into chocolate until thoroughly incorporated and smooth.

Cover and refrigerate, stirring occasionally, for 15 to 20 minutes, or until frosting cools and thickens to spreading consistency. Using a table knife or long-bladed spatula, spread frosting over cake layers, then top and sides, swirling attractively. (If the frosting begins to stiffen as you work, dip knife in hot water, shake off excess, and continue spreading.) Let stand until frosting firms slightly before serving, about 30 minutes.

13 ounces bittersweet or semisweet chocolate, broken or coarsely chopped

3 ounces milk chocolate, broken or coarsely chopped

2/3 cup unsalted butter

2/3 cup sour cream

2 tablespoons light or dark corn syrup

2 1/2 teaspoons vanilla extract

Makes enough frosting to generously frost a 9-inch three-layer cake

This frosting has an exceptionally rich, mellow chocolate flavor and appealing smoothness. It spreads beautifully and adds moistness, particularly to American layer cakes.

RICH CHOCOLATE FROSTING

Place chocolate in a medium-sized, heat-proof bowl set over pan of hot but not simmering water. Warm, stirring occasionally and without splashing any moisture into chocolate, until chocolate completely melts. Remove pan from heat. Set aside with bowl still over hot water to keep chocolate warm.

In the top of a double boiler, over about 1 inch hot but not simmering water, whisk together eggs, sugar, salt, and 2 tablespoons hot tap water until well blended. Whisking continuously and scraping pan bottom and edges, cook for about 5 to 6 minutes or until mixture increases in volume, thickens slightly, and is hot to the touch (or reaches 160°F. on a cooking thermometer). Immediately remove top of double boiler from heat. Add chocolate and vanilla, whisking until well blended. A few chunks at a time, whisk in butter until mixture is completely blended and smooth. Cover and refrigerate, stirring occasionally, for 20 to 30 minutes or until cooled and just firm enough to spread. (It will firm up more upon standing on cake.)

To frost a three-layer cake: Using a table knife or long-bladed spatula, spread a scant third of frosting over bottom cake layer. Center a second cake layer, flat side facing up, over frosted layer and add another scant third of frosting. Add final cake layer. Cover cake top and sides with remaining frosting, smoothing or swirling it attractively. (If it stiffens as you work, dip knife in hot water, shake off excess water, and continue spreading.) Let stand until frosting firms slightly before serving, about 30 minutes.

12 ounces bittersweet (not unsweetened) or semisweet chocolate, coarsely chopped
4 large eggs
½ cup granulated sugar
Pinch of salt
1 teaspoon vanilla extract
¾ cup (1½ sticks) cold unsalted butter, cut into chunks

Makes enough frosting to generously frost a 9-inch three-layer cake

FRANCE

FRENCH BUTTERCREAM FROSTING

Crème au Beurre au Chocolat

Place chocolate in top of a double boiler over about 1 inch hot but not simmering water. Do not allow any water into chocolate. Set over lowest heat, stirring frequently, until chocolate melts. (White chocolate must melt very slowly or it may lump.) Remove top of double boiler from bottom and set aside, stirring occasionally, until cooled slightly.

Place eggs in a large mixer bowl. Set bowl in a larger bowl of hot tap water. Let stand for 8 to 10 minutes, stirring occasionally, until eggs are very warm. Using a stand mixer on high speed, beat eggs for 4 to 5 minutes or until lightened and greatly increased in volume.

Meanwhile, combine sugar, ⅓ cup hot tap water, and corn syrup in a medium-sized, heavy saucepan, stirring with a large wooden spoon until well mixed and sugar begins to dissolve. (If using a candy thermometer to gauge doneness, clip it to pan side, inserting so tip is completely submerged but not touching pan bottom.) Bring mixture to a boil over medium-high heat, stirring. Cover mixture and boil for 2 minutes to allow steam to wash sugar crystals from pan sides. Remove lid and continue cooking *without stirring* for about 2 minutes longer, or until mixture thickens slightly, bubbles harder, and reaches soft-ball stage (239° to 240°F. on the thermometer). To test for doneness without a thermometer: Remove pan from heat; drop a teaspoon of syrup in ice water, and let stand for 15 seconds. Syrup should form an almost-stiff, firm ball when squeezed.

6½ ounces bittersweet or semisweet chocolate, or top-quality imported white chocolate, coarsely chopped

3 large eggs

1 cup plus 2 tablespoons granulated sugar

1 tablespoon corn syrup

2 cups (4 sticks) unsalted butter, cool and slightly softened

1 teaspoon vanilla extract

¼ teaspoon very finely grated orange zest (orange part of skin), optional

1½ tablespoons Grand Marnier or crème de cacao (optional)

With mixer on high speed, begin pouring a thin stream of syrup *down bowl sides* into eggs. (Do not pour on beaters or directly into eggs as syrup may stick to beaters or curdle eggs.) Continue adding syrup in a stream, pouring so that all is incorporated in about 10 seconds. Continue beating on medium speed until mixture cools almost to room temperature, about 6 to 8 minutes longer. With mixer on high speed and adding 2 or 3 tablespoons at a time, beat cool, slightly softened butter into mixture. Beat after each addition until well blended and smooth. (If mixture looks curdled, butter is too cold; let it warm slightly before proceeding. If mixture fails to gradually thicken and fluff as more and more butter is added, it is too warm; let it cool a bit before proceeding.) Beat in vanilla, orange zest, and Grand Marnier (if used). A tablespoon at a time, beat *just slightly warm* chocolate into buttercream until well blended and smooth; it should be warm enough not to set but cool enough not to melt the mixture. Buttercream may be used immediately, refrigerated for up to 36 hours, or frozen (tightly covered) for up to a week. If refrigerated or frozen, allow to return to room temperature and beat briefly until fluffy and well blended.

To frost cake: Spread buttercream over thoroughly cooled cake layers and sides using a wide-bladed spatula; since it is very rich keep layer thin, at most a scant ¼ inch. For a professional look, begin with thin buttercream layer (called a crumb coating); chill until buttercream firms up; then use a spatula to smooth and even surface, scraping off any excess. Frost again, smoothing and evening surface as necessary. If desired, pipe decorative shells or other details using a pastry bag fitted with an open-star tip. If room is warm, dip hands in ice water occasionally during piping to prevent them from warming and melting buttercream, which will keep buttercream from holding its piped shape. (Alternatively, frost cake by simply swirling buttercream over layers and top using a wide-bladed spatula or table knife, being sure to keep frosting layers thin. Omit piping.)

Refrigerate cake for a few minutes to allow buttercream layer to set before serving. Store frosted cake in refrigerator; allow to warm up almost to room temperature before serving. Iced cake may be stored, airtight and refrigerated, for up to 3 days. It may also be frozen, airtight, for up to 2 weeks, although there will be some condensation on buttercream surface. Allow frozen cake to thaw completely (6 to 8 hours) before serving.

Makes enough buttercream to frost and decoratively pipe a 9-inch, three-layer cake

Note: To prepare All-Weather French Buttercream, use 1½ cups (3 sticks) unsalted butter and ½ cup room-temperature solid white vegetable shortening in place of 2 cups butter. Beat in butter as directed in recipe, then beat in shortening several tablespoons at a time. Beat in 2 tablespoons powdered sugar until smoothly incorporated. Proceed with recipe as directed above.

This is the type of chocolate glaze generally used on the Viennese Sacher Torte. It is a little more difficult to make than chocolate ganache or powdered sugar glazes, but I feel it is well worth the effort—not only for its smooth, lustrous finish, but for its remarkably clear, clean chocolate taste. ❖ *Before preparing this glaze, be sure your cake is at room temperature and free of crumbs (and coated with preserves, if called for). Place on a supporting cake round set on a rack over a rimmed pan and pour the glaze over the cake top.* ❖ *The recipe is designed so that, if followed carefully, the sugar syrup will automatically cook to the right stage (a very soft soft-ball stage). To ensure success, measure all ingredients carefully; follow cooking times and instructions exactly; and don't make any ingredient substitutions.*

VIENNESE CHOCOLATE-SUGAR GLAZE

Schkolade-Zucker Guß

In the top of a double boiler over about 1 inch of almost simmering water, heat chocolates and butter, until *completely melted and smooth,* stirring occasionally. Reduce heat to very low and let double boiler stand over heat to keep mixture hot; stir occasionally.

In a 2-quart saucepan over medium-high heat, heat sugar, corn syrup, and ⅓ cup hot tap water, stirring with a wooden spoon until sugar dissolves. Wipe sugar crystals from pan sides with a damp paper towel. Without stirring further, bring syrup *just to boiling.* Immediately cover pan with tight-fitting lid and boil over medium-high heat for *exactly 1½ minutes.* Meanwhile, rinse all traces of sugar from stirring spoon. Immediately remove pan from heat. Using cleaned spoon, stir about half of hot syrup into chocolate

5½ ounces bittersweet (not unsweetened) or semisweet chocolate, coarsely chopped

3½ ounces unsweetened chocolate, coarsely chopped

2 tablespoons unsalted butter

1½ cups granulated sugar

¼ cup light corn syrup

1 teaspoon vanilla extract

mixture in double boiler. Continue stirring until syrup is evenly incorporated and mixture is silky smooth, about one minute. Stir in remaining syrup (don't scrape out pan sides), the vanilla, and 1 tablespoon hot tap water, until glaze is well blended and smooth. Remove double boiler top from bottom and continue stirring glaze for about 20 to 30 seconds longer, or until mixture is thick enough not to run off cake rapidly but is still fluid enough to flow over it smoothly. If glaze is too thick to pour and begins to set around edges, stir in a teaspoon or two hot water until a pourable consistency is obtained. Immediately pour glaze over cake top, rapping and jiggling rack so glaze flows evenly over cake top and covers sides; stop as soon as glaze shows any signs of setting and do not try to spread glaze with a knife or to touch up with more glaze or surface will be marred. (Reserve several tablespoons glaze in pan if preparing a Sacher Torte and planning to write on cake top with glaze.) Lift cake and supporting round and gently wipe away excess glaze clinging to bottom edge. Return cake to a clean rack and let stand for 10 minutes.

If writing on cake top, thin reserved glaze by adding a few drops of hot tap water until it is slightly more fluid. Decorate by piping the word Sacher in large flowing letters using a piping cone. (If you are not experienced at writing with a piping cone, practice lettering on a sheet of wax paper.) Let cake stand at least 45 minutes, or refrigerate for about 10 minutes, until firmed up slightly. Transfer cake and supporting round to serving plate. (Do not try to remove cake from round as glaze will develop cracks.)

Makes enough glaze to more than cover a Sacher Torte, or to adequately cover a 9- to 10-inch Bundt or pound cake.

Vivid childhood memories led me to spend weeks experimenting with this recipe. The hot fudge sauce I yearned for was dark, glossy, faintly bittersweet, and tasted of deep, rich chocolate, not cocoa powder. It had body and a certain thickness, yet was somehow light and silky at the same time. Moreover, the consistency changed from flowing and gooey to slightly chewy as the sauce cooled over the ice cream. Finally, after many tests, I devised what I feel qualifies as real *hot fudge sauce.*

❖ *It's important to cook this sauce in a heavy pan that will distribute the heat evenly and is large enough to contain the mixture when it boils up during the early stages of cooking.*

REAL HOT FUDGE SAUCE

Using a large wooden spoon, stir together butter, sugar, corn syrup, cream, and milk in a 4-quart or larger heavy saucepan or cast-iron Dutch oven. Bring mixture to a boil over medium-high heat, stirring; initially, it will boil up pot sides, then gradually subside. Carefully wash all sugar crystals from stirring spoon. Continue to cook, uncovered, occasionally stirring gently, for 3 or 4 minutes or until mixture begins to boil down and thicken slightly.

Lower heat to medium and continue to cook, stirring constantly and watching carefully to prevent scorching, until mixture turns a pale-caramel color. Immediately remove pan from heat and add chocolate, gently stirring until melted. Stir in ⅓ cup hot water and vanilla until evenly incorporated. Set sauce aside to cool to very warm. If sauce is too thick, gradually thin it with more hot water until fluid but still fairly thick and gooey.

¼ cup (½ stick) unsalted butter, cut into chunks
1¼ cups granulated sugar
⅔ cup light corn syrup
1 cup heavy (whipping) cream
⅔ cup whole milk
8 ounces unsweetened chocolate, coarsely chopped (see Note)
2½ teaspoons vanilla extract

Serve sauce immediately, spooned over ice cream. Or store, refrigerated, for up to 3 weeks, and then reheat in top of a double boiler over gently simmering water. If sauce thickens during storage, thin with a bit of warm water *after* it has been reheated to barely hot.

Makes about 3 cups hot fudge

Note: For a slightly sweeter, milder sauce, use 2 ounces semisweet chocolate and 6 ounces unsweetened chocolate.

The simple blending of chocolate and cream gives this European-style chocolate sauce smoothness, body, and depth of flavor. Since the taste depends almost entirely on the kind of chocolate used, choose a brand with a flavor and degree of bittersweetness that you like. The sauce is quite stiff when chilled, so it must be served slightly warm.

WARM CHOCOLATE SAUCE

Sauce au Chocolat Chaud

Place chocolate in a medium-sized, deep bowl. Combine cream and butter in a medium-sized, heavy saucepan. Bring mixture just to a boil over medium-high heat. Remove from burner. Strain ¼ cup cream through a sieve into chocolate, stirring until chocolate partially melts. Strain ¼ cup more cream through sieve into chocolate, stirring until smoothly incorporated. Strain and add remaining cream, stirring until chocolate is completely melted and smooth. Stir in vanilla and cognac (if used). Use immediately or cover and refrigerate.

> 6 ounces top-quality bittersweet chocolate, chopped moderately fine
> Generous ¾ cup heavy (whipping) cream
> 1 tablespoon unsalted butter, cut into pats
> ¼ teaspoon vanilla extract
> 1 tablespoon cognac or good-quality brandy (optional)

Sauce must be reheated to warm and fluid before serving, and may be heated until almost hot. To rewarm, in the top of a double boiler over about an inch of almost simmering water (or in a heavy saucepan over lowest heat), heat, stirring, being careful not to allow sauce to boil. (It can also be microwaved in a microwave-safe container on low power; stop and stir mixture every 15 seconds until desired temperature is reached.) If necessary, thin warmed sauce with a teaspoon or two of hot water.

Sauce will keep, refrigerated, for up to a week. Serve with cake, pastries, fruit, or ice cream.

Makes about 1⅓ cups sauce

Chocolate enhances but does not overpower the caramel in this richly flavored sauce.

❖ *Since the caramel mixture cooks to a high temperature and splatters when the cream is added, work carefully and stir with a very long-handled wooden spoon.*

CARAMEL-CHOCOLATE SAUCE

Sauce Caramel au Chocolat

In a medium-sized, heavy saucepan, over medium-high heat, heat cream and butter until mixture just simmers and butter completely melts. Place over lowest heat to keep warm.

In a medium-sized, heavy saucepan, stir together corn syrup, sugar, and 2 teaspoons hot tap water, until well blended. Heat mixture, stirring with a long-handled wooden spoon, over medium heat until mixture comes to a boil. Wipe sugar from pan sides with a damp paper towel. Cover pan with a tight-fitting lid, lower heat, and simmer for 2 minutes to allow steam to wash remaining sugar crystals from pan sides. Meanwhile, wash all sugar from stirring spoon. Continue cooking, uncovered, stirring gently, until mixture turns a pale tan color, about 3 minutes longer. Remove pan from heat. Being careful to avoid splattering and steam, immediately add all but 3 tablespoons cream mixture to caramel mixture, stirring. Continue stirring until foaming subsides and caramel completely dissolves. Return pan to heat and continue cooking, stirring, a minute or two longer, until mixture turns a rich tan color. Remove from heat.

1 cup heavy (whipping) cream
1½ tablespoons unsalted butter
2½ tablespoons light corn syrup
⅔ cup granulated sugar
1 ounce unsweetened chocolate, chopped into ¼-inch pieces
1 teaspoon vanilla extract

Return saucepan with 3 tablespoons reserved cream to burner and heat just until hot. Remove from heat and stir in chocolate. Continue stirring until chocolate completely melts and mixture is very smooth. Gradually stir about ¼ cup caramel mixture into chocolate, until completely blended and smooth. Stir chocolate, then vanilla back into caramel mixture, until well blended. Strain sauce through a fine sieve into a storage container. Store, refrigerated, for up to 2 weeks. Sauce may be served chilled, at room temperature, or warm; when chilled it will be slightly thick and gooey, at room temperature, slightly thick, and when warm, fairly fluid. (If sauce thickens too much upon standing, thin it with a little hot water.)   *Makes about 1½ cups sauce*

Mocha-Caramel Sauce: Add scant ½ teaspoon instant coffee powder to saucepan when cream and butter are mixed together, and proceed as directed.

Most chocolate sauces become stiff or hard when cold, but this one is specially designed to remain fluid even when well-chilled and swirled into ice creams or other frozen desserts. The secret is in the ratio of sugar to water and butter, so do not alter these proportions. Also, for a perfectly smooth sauce, follow the mixing directions carefully. ❖ This sauce is used in Mocha-Almond Ripple Ice Cream (page 132). It can also be used in the center of an ice cream bombe, providing an instant sauce as slices of bombe are served.

CHOCOLATE RIPPLE SAUCE

Combine sugar, water, corn syrup, and salt in a small, heavy saucepan. Lift pan and swirl mixture until well blended and sugar begins to dissolve. Bring mixture to a boil over medium-high heat, stirring. Add butter, stirring, until mixture returns to a boil. Cover saucepan and boil for 2 minutes so steam can wash any sugar crystals from pan sides. Meanwhile, place chocolate in a small, deep, heatproof bowl. Remove saucepan from heat. Immediately pour about *a fourth* of boiling syrup mixture over chocolate, stirring until chocolate is *completely melted and smooth.*

½ cup granulated sugar
⅓ cup water
1½ tablespoons light corn syrup
  Pinch of salt
½ teaspoon unsalted butter
 2 ounces unsweetened chocolate, chopped moderately fine
¾ teaspoon vanilla extract

Gradually stir another fourth of hot syrup into chocolate, until well blended and smooth. Add remaining syrup, then vanilla, stirring until incorporated and smooth. Cover and refrigerate sauce for at least 2½ hours (and up to a week) before adding to ice cream.

Makes about 1 cup sauce

This simple syrup makes very flavorful chocolate milk or hot chocolate, and can be poured over homemade or store-bought ice cream. It will keep for up to a month in the refrigerator, so make a batch and keep it on hand for unexpected chocolate cravings.

ALL-PURPOSE CHOCOLATE SYRUP

In a medium saucepan over medium-high heat, heat sugar, corn syrup, and ¼ cup hot tap water, stirring with a wooden spoon, until well blended and syrupy. Wipe sugar crystals from pan sides with a damp paper towel. Without stirring further, bring syrup just to boiling. Immediately cover pan with tight-fitting lid; boil over medium heat for 1½ minutes, until all sugar dissolves and mixture is smooth. Immediately remove pan from heat. With a clean long-handled spoon, stir chocolates into syrup mixture. Continue stirring until chocolates *completely melt* and mixture is thickened and very smooth. Slowly stir in ½ cup more hot tap water, about 2 tablespoons at a time, then vanilla, until mixture is completely smooth. Let cool just slightly.

Transfer syrup to a clean storage container. Refrigerate, covered, for up to a month.

For chocolate milk or hot chocolate, vigorously stir 2 to 3 tablespoons syrup (or to taste) into one cup cold or hot milk, until smoothly incorporated.

1 cup granulated sugar
¼ cup light corn syrup
4 ounces bittersweet (not unsweetened) or semisweet chocolate, coarsely chopped
2½ ounces unsweetened chocolate, coarsely chopped
1 teaspoon vanilla extract

Makes about 2 cups chocolate syrup

When preparing Schlemmer Kaffee, try to use Asbach Uralt brandy, as the pronounced flavor and slight bite stand up well against the coffee and lend the drink its distinctive taste. This particular brandy is used so often in Germany that the beverage is sometimes called Rüdesheimer Kaffee, in recognition of the picturesque village of Rüdesheim where Asbach Uralt is distilled. Asbach Uralt is sold at American wine shops, but if you must substitute, choose a brandy with a bold taste and sharp edge; a mild, mellow cognac will not do.

BRANDIED COFFEE WITH WHIPPED CREAM AND CHOCOLATE

Schlemmer Kaffee

In a mixing bowl with mixer on high speed, beat cream and 2½ tablespoons sugar until soft peaks form. Set aside to warm up slightly while other ingredients are prepared.

Preheat 4 large coffee mugs, cider mugs, or large heat-proof punch cups by rinsing in very hot water. Pat mugs dry. Add 2 generous teaspoons of sugar, a heaping tablespoon grated chocolate, and 1½ to 2 tablespoons brandy (or to taste) to each mug. Fill each mug about two-thirds full with hot coffee. Stir briefly. Float several very large dollops of whipped cream in each mug (or pipe whipped cream over coffee using a pastry bag fitted with a large, open-star tip). Divide remaining grated chocolate among mugs, sprinkling it over whipped cream. Serve coffees immediately; do not stir, but serve with spoons so each person can stir in the cream if desired. (Typically, some cream is left floating and the coffee is sipped through it.)   *Makes 4 servings*

> 1½ cups heavy (whipping) cream
>   About 5 tablespoons granulated sugar, divided
> 2 ounces bittersweet (not unsweetened) or semisweet chocolate, finely grated (divided)
> 6 to 8 tablespoons Asbach Uralt (or similar German brandy)
> 4 to 5 cups freshly brewed, strong black coffee

DECORATIONS AND CHOCOLATE ARTISTRY

Chocolate Box with Hearts, Ribbons and Roses

CHAPTER TEN

CHOCOLATE BOX

A hand-crafted chocolate box is perhaps the ultimate edible objet d'art. *Filled with tiny cookies or candies, and adorned with chocolate ribbons, flowers, and leaves (or other appropriate seasonal decorations), it makes a striking presentation piece and an unforgettable gift. Although the box in the photograph was designed with Valentine's Day in mind, equally appealing Christmas or Easter boxes can be created by replacing roses with peppermint-striped or pastel-colored white chocolate ribbons (page 259), carved chocolate pine cones (page 265), or colored bird eggs (page 264).* ❖ *Chocolate boxes of varying sizes and shapes can be created with the following recipe: Four-sided rectangular or square boxes ranging from about 3 to 6 inches across and 1½ to 3 inches high are probably the best choice for a beginner. (Do not plan to make boxes larger than about 6 inches square, as there may not be enough chocolate.) Many-sided, white chocolate–accented boxes are also a possibility, but they involve more pieces and construction time and are, thus, best attempted after plain, four-sided boxes have been successfully completed.*

Select a box to serve as a model; small gift boxes, canisters, or candy boxes all work well. Using selected box as a guide, measure and cut out a pattern for box top, bottom, and side pieces using a manila folder (or other cardboard of similar weight); the side pattern pieces should be exactly the same size as the sides of the model and the bottom and top about ⅛ inch larger on each side than those of the model.

Invert a 10-by-15-inch jelly-roll pan (or similar sturdy baking sheet). Cover pan bottom with a piece of heavy-duty aluminum foil large enough to overhang pan by at least 1½ inches on all sides; wrap overlapping foil securely over pan edges, *working carefully so the foil fits snugly over pan bottom and is completely free of wrinkles.*

> *2 ounces white chocolate, coarsely chopped, for decorative accent lines on chocolate box (optional)*
>
> *1½ pounds bittersweet (not unsweetened) or semisweet chocolate, coarsely broken or chopped*
>
> *2 tablespoons solid white vegetable shortening (no substitutes)*

To accent box with *optional* white chocolate lines: Quick-temper white chocolate in a small bowl set over a small saucepan of hot water following Master Recipe on page 220. Meanwhile, ready a small piping cone or two (see instructions on page 267). Put tempered white chocolate into piping cone. Immediately begin piping chocolate lines or squiggles randomly over surface of foil as desired. Set pan aside.

To prepare box construction pieces from chocolate: Quick-temper dark chocolate following Master Recipe on page 220. Immediately spread tempered chocolate over entire surface of foil (covering white chocolate lines) using a palette knife, offset spatula or long-bladed spatula; work quickly and carefully so chocolate forms a smooth layer of even thickness. If the chocolate around pan edges begins to set, immediately stop spreading and transfer pan, chocolate layer facing up, to refrigerator for three to four minutes, until entire surface of chocolate appears set. Immediately remove from refrigerator and begin testing hardness of chocolate by pressing a finger against surface. When it feels firm and set rather than sticky, arrange box pattern pieces on surface. Using a paring knife and holding pattern pieces in place with free hand, cut cleanly and neatly through chocolate layer following pattern lines, leaving cut pieces of chocolate in place on foil. (If the chocolate seems soft and sticky when cut, wait a minute or two and try again.) For best results, work neatly and carefully; there is no need to rush, and the finished box will fit together better and look more attractive if the pieces are accurately cut. When all pieces have been cut, let them stand, still attached to the foil and resting on the pan bottom, for at least 45 minutes and up to several days (covered lightly with wax paper) if preferred. (Don't attempt to remove them sooner or the shiny exterior surfaces may be marred.)

To construct box: Retrace cutting lines around cut chocolate construction pieces, carefully cutting through foil beneath each box piece so underlying foil can be removed from pan along with each chocolate piece. Carefully transfer each piece *and attached foil* to a clean work surface; the foil will protect pieces from fingerprints during the construction process. Turn over the scraps remaining on pan bottom and peel off foil. Return scraps to a bowl (or top of a double boiler) set over about 1 inch hot but not simmering water and temper following Master Recipe on page 220. (Tempered chocolate will be used to "glue" box pieces together.) Set bowl of chocolate on heating pad as directed in tempering instructions to keep chocolate at proper temperature. Stir chocolate every two or three minutes, watching carefully and adjusting heat as necessary to prevent either excess warming or cooling; the chocolate must be kept tempered throughout the "gluing" process. Ready some piping cones for piping chocolate (see instructions on page 267).

Place box bottom, foil side up, on a wax paper–lined tray or rimmed baking sheet. Gently peel off foil and discard; once foil is removed take care to handle bottom piece only at the edges as the shiny surface will show fingerprints if touched. To determine exact placement, temporarily arrange side panel pieces, *foil side out,* on bottom, propping them up and adjusting positions as necessary so they fit together neatly. Peel back foil *just slightly at the side edges* of side panels so a line of chocolate can be added along seam lines, but don't remove foil completely. Spoon some tempered chocolate into piping cone. Immediately pipe a line of chocolate along bottom edge of a side piece. Put side piece in place on box bottom and hold a few seconds until chocolate begins to set. Add a second side panel, piping chocolate along its bottom edge and along side edges where the two side panels join and then holding the panel in place against first panel until chocolate begins to set; check to make sure no foil catches in seams. Add a reinforcing line of chocolate to the inside seams, gently smoothing chocolate into seams with a finger. Let partially constructed box stand for 3 or 4 minutes, until panels seem sturdy (if room is at all warm or chocolate does not set rapidly, transfer box and tray to refrigerator for three or four minutes instead). Continue construction process, adding side panels until box is complete. Add final reinforcing lines of piped chocolate to all interior seams, smoothing chocolate into seams with a finger. Transfer tray and box to refrigerator for about five minutes, then let stand at room temperature for about 10 minutes, until chocolate is completely set.

Meanwhile, prepare molding strips for finishing box exterior by piping some long, straight ¼-inch-thick lines of chocolate, slightly separated, onto a wax paper-lined baking sheet. (These can vary in length since they will be cut to the exact length needed and used to cover the exterior seams of finished box as shown in photograph on page 238. Pipe some extra strips to accommodate breakage when strips are cut and attached to box.) Transfer piped molding strips to refrigerator for five minutes. Then let stand at room temperature for about five minutes longer until completely set.

Carefully measure height of side seams on outside of box. Using a paring knife, cut piped chocolate strips crosswise into molding strips exactly the same height as box seams. Gently lift cut molding strips from wax paper using a small spatula or knife. Peel foil back about ¼ inch from exterior seams and pipe thick lines of tempered chocolate into each seam. Immediately position a molding strip, flat side against piped chocolate, over each seam to cover gap and form a finished exterior surface. (If box side panels were unevenly cut and gaps are not completely covered by a single molding strip, try arranging pairs of molding strips over seams to finish box.) Gently adjust molding strips and pat into place as necessary. Return box to refrigerator for about three minutes; then let stand for about five minutes longer, until chocolate sets and molding strips are fixed in place. Gently peel foil from all side panels and box top. When handling box, always lift from bottom or edges as shiny surfaces will show fingerprints if touched. Set box lid over bottom, or, if desired, decorate box lid with chocolate ribbons, leaves, or other adornments, following individual directions for these items.

Store box, loosely covered and in a cool place. It will be edible for several months and can be kept for display purposes almost indefinitely.

Makes one box and lid, up to about 6 inches square

"WOVEN" CHOCOLATE BASKETS

Fashioning intricately woven baskets from melted chocolate might seem daunting but, in fact, the task involves only decorative piping and no weaving at all. The illusion of weaving is created by piping chocolate lines vertically over a foil-covered, basket-shaped form to suggest ribs and then horizontally around the form to suggest the woof strands of a weave. (Realistic "ribless" baskets can be created with only horizontally piped lines.) Once the lines of chocolate set, the basket and foil are slipped off the form, and the foil is peeled from the chocolate. ❖ The specific size and shape of chocolate baskets can vary widely depending on the dimensions of the item selected as the underlying form. An assortment of juice glasses, custard cups, or other small containers ranging from about 1¹/₂ to 3¹/₂ inches in diameter can be used so long as they are wider at the top than the bottom. (If the mouth of the basket is narrower than any part of the form that it must be slipped off of, it will break.) Larger baskets can be made, but they require a surprising amount of piping and are best attempted after small baskets have been successfully completed. ❖ Chocolate baskets are created with tempered chocolate, so choose a cool day or work in a well air-conditioned room. Also, since it is difficult to maintain the temper of a small quantity of chocolate, the recipe calls for the same amount regardless of whether one or several baskets will be made.

Select a custard cup, glass, or similar form with a bottom measuring the approximate diameter of the basket to be made. The form may be the same height or taller than the basket planned, and *must be* at least slightly narrower at the bottom than at the mouth. Cut a square of heavy-duty aluminum foil large enough to cover the bottom of the form and extend at least 1 inch higher up its sides than the desired height of the basket. Invert form; smooth foil over bottom and up sides. Slip foil off form, then replace it, to ensure it will slip off easily once chocolate has been piped. Fix foil in place at edge with several small pieces of masking tape. To create a guideline for piping the basket rim, using a ruler and a paring knife, measure and then lightly score foil all the way around basket form. If making a ribbed basket, to indicate placement of ribs, measure and mark them at even intervals all the way around rim line; baskets may have as few as two ribs or many ribs, depending on the look desired.

> 1¹/₄ pounds bittersweet (not unsweetened) or semisweet chocolate
> 2 tablespoons solid white vegetable shortening (no substitutes)

Set foil-covered form in refrigerator until well chilled, at least 20 minutes. Meanwhile, ready some piping cones (see page 267), at least 4 for each basket made. Quick-temper chocolate following Master Recipe on page 220. To hold chocolate at proper temperature, place a heating pad (inserted in a heavy plastic bag to protect it from drips) under bowl of tempered chocolate. Turn pad to lowest setting, Lay a kitchen towel over plastic bag and, as you work, adjust the thickness of the towel as needed to keep bottom of bowl just barely warm. Stir chocolate every three or four minutes, watching temper carefully as chocolate must be kept tempered throughout piping.

Spoon tempered chocolate into piping cone. Slip inverted form over fingertips and begin piping chocolate over bottom of form, working from perimeter to center in neat, tightly spaced concentric circles. If adding ribs, pipe vertically from bottom to rib placement mark on rim line, repeating until each rib is piped; ribs should extend to but not beyond rim line. Retrace each rib, piping three or four more lines over first to build up and thicken each rib. Carefully transfer form, still inverted, to refrigerator and allow chocolate lines to set, about five minutes. Remove from refrigerator.

Slip inverted form over fingertips. Rotating form as you work, pipe a thick line over rim line. Go over line about four times to thicken rim and strengthen basket. Continuing to rotate form, pipe (crossing over ribs) horizontally around basket, spacing piped lines close together. (Piping should be neat but does not have to be perfect as mistakes will look like natural irregularities in the weave.) After piping for about two minutes, transfer form, right side up, to refrigerator to allow chocolate to set, about five minutes.

Then remove from refrigerator and continue piping around sides until bottom of basket is reached. Pipe three or four lines around basket bottom to reinforce edge. Invert and refrigerate for about five minutes, until chocolate sets; remove from refrigerator.

Carefully reinforce basket by piping additional horizontal lines around sides wherever piping seems thin; continue reinforcing until absolutely no foil shows through. Reinforce bottom by adding to concentric circles as needed.

Refrigerate inverted form and chocolate basket for at least 15 minutes, until chocolate sets completely. Then let stand at room temperature for about 10 minutes so chocolate will be less brittle.

Working carefully and holding form upright, pour a little warm water into it; do not splash on chocolate. Wait about 10 seconds until chocolate warms slightly (but *does not melt*), then loosen tape and slide foil and attached chocolate basket off form. Gently peel chocolate basket from foil; it's usually easiest to loosen foil around rim first and work inward. (If basket begins to break, immediately stop and patch breaks by piping additional chocolate lines over breaks. Then return to refrigerator and chill until chocolate sets before continuing.) As the foil is loosened, compress it into a small ball so it can be easily lifted from basket. When foil is removed, return basket to refrigerator for about five minutes to firm up; then let stand at room temperature again.

Store basket, covered and in a cool place, for up to 3 months.

Makes 2 to 4 baskets, depending on size

MODELING CHOCOLATE

Modeling chocolate (also called plastic chocolate), is a remarkable corn syrup–chocolate mixture that does not require tempering and that can be rolled, bent, and shaped in ways ordinary chocolate can not. It is especially handy for making chocolate decorations, such as the ribbons, bows, and roses on the Chocolate Box (see photo, page 238) and the ribbons and ruffled bows on the Fruit and Nut Christmas confection (see photo, page 211). Though very flexible during the modeling process, it gradually firms up and holds its shape. ❖ Modeling chocolate is chewy and chocolatey, but less tasty than regular chocolate. It is used mainly when a very malleable material is essential.

In top of a double boiler over about 1 inch of hot but not simmering water, slowly melt chocolate, stirring occasionally. (If preparing white chocolate, heat over very low heat and stir often or chocolate may lump). Do not allow any water into chocolate and be sure chocolate is completely melted and smooth. Remove double boiler from heat. In a small saucepan, heat corn syrup until just warm but not hot to touch; it should be the same temperature as chocolate. (Alternatively, spoon corn syrup into microwave-safe container and heat for 3 to 5 seconds in a microwave oven set at 50-percent power.) If tinting entire batch of chocolate, stir color into corn syrup until well blended. Very slowly stir warm corn syrup into chocolate, until incorporated. Mixture will stiffen and may look separated and oily; if separation occurs, stir to recombine several times during cooling. Spoon mixture into a shallow bowl lined with heavy-duty plastic wrap. Lay plastic wrap on surface of chocolate. Insert bowl in airtight plastic bag. Let stand at room temperature at least eight hours and preferably overnight before using. (Mixture may also be stored, refrigerated, for up to two weeks; allow to come to room temperature before using.)

> 5 ounces semisweet chocolate or white chocolate, coarsely chopped
> 3 tablespoons light corn syrup
> Food color (preferably paste type), optional

Unwrap mixture and rewrap in aluminum foil. In an oven that has been turned on to warm for two minutes and then turned off, heat mixture for about 10 minutes, until malleable and just slightly soft but not warm. (Or wrap in plastic wrap and microwave a few seconds on 50-percent power until slightly malleable.) Knead mixture until malleable and completely smooth. To keep kneaded portions from drying out as you work, rewrap in plastic wrap and unwrap only as needed. Shape modeling chocolate into ribbons (page 259), roses (page 257), carved pine cones (page 265), or other shapes following specific directions for these items. *Makes about 6 ounces modeling chocolate*

CHOCOLATE RUFFLES

For most people (including professionals), learning to produce delicate, gracefully shaped chocolate ruffles from tempered chocolate requires patience and practice. It requires some testing to recognize when the chocolate has set up just enough to be successfully scraped into ruffles. And it takes experimentation to discover just the right twist of the wrist and blade angle required. ❖ *The reward for this patience and practice is the ability to create some of the most arresting, artful, and downright beautiful decorative effects—from a flirtatious chocolate flounce around a dessert edge to a multi-tiered and frilled chocolate "petticoat" covering an entire cake top (see Chocolate Mousse Cake, page 11).*

❖ *Though the natural brittleness of tempered and set chocolate normally makes coaxing it into ruffles difficult, the following recipe overcomes this obstacle: Both the solid vegetable shortening and the quick-tempering process keep the chocolate from initially setting up too hard, which makes it easier to ruffle and less likely to break.* ❖ *Since making ruffles involves tempering chocolate, work in a cool kitchen on a cool day.*

Set out two 12-by-15-inch (or similar) sturdy baking sheets with bottoms clean and smooth enough to use as a work surface. Also set out a wax paper–lined tray for holding finished ruffles and an offset spatula, wide-bladed plastic snow scraper, or pastry scraper for forming ruffles. (Although it is a little more difficult to manipulate, I prefer a plastic scraper as there is less likelihood of inadvertently scraping up metal shards from the baking sheet.)

Quick-temper chocolate following Master Recipe on page 220. Immediately pour half of chocolate onto one inverted baking sheet and begin spreading over entire pan bottom using a long-bladed spatula or palette knife. Continue spreading into a smooth, scant ⅛-inch layer of even thickness, *stopping immediately if the surface shows any signs of setting on edges* (looks dull and starts to stiffen). Transfer pan, chocolate side up, to refrigerator for two to four minutes, until surface looks set and chocolate feels slightly firm when tested with a finger pressed into center of pan. Meanwhile, repeat process with remaining half of chocolate and second pan.

> *10 ounces bittersweet (not unsweetened) or semisweet chocolate, or white chocolate, coarsely chopped or broken into pieces*
> *1½ tablespoons solid white vegetable shortening*

As soon as entire surface of chocolate appears set, remove pan from refrigerator and let stand at room temperature for several minutes, until chocolate firms just slightly more. Begin testing consistency for forming ruffles as follows: Brace far side of pan against back of counter or other object and near side of pan against your body. Holding handle of offset spatula (or right side of scraper) in right hand (if you are right-handed), and left tip of spatula blade (or left side of scraper) with left hand, position blade almost flat (at about a 15-degree angle) against chocolate. (Start working around edges of pan as chocolate will set up here first.) Continuing to hold blade almost flat against chocolate surface and using a smooth, sweeping motion, draw blade toward you, pulling harder against left side of blade so it rotates counter-clockwise about 50 to 60 degrees at the same time the right side of the blade scrapes across the surface about ½ inch toward you. (When the rotating and scraping action is performed correctly, the area that is scraped free of chocolate will resemble a fan, as shown in the illustration on page 268.) If the chocolate is too soft and builds up on the blade, wait several minutes and try again. When it has firmed to the right consistency, the rotating and scraping action will cause chocolate to peel off pan in a thin, fan-shaped segment that is tightly pleated on the right side and gently ruffled on the left. The segment should measure about 1½ inches long on ruffled side and ½ inch on gathered side. (Don't worry if ruffles are imperfect; they will still look attractive when arranged on a dessert.)

Using a spatula, gently transfer ruffle to wax paper–lined tray. If necessary, while chocolate is still slightly flexible and soft, trim sides and base of ruffle segment with a sharp knife so ruffle sides and bottom are even; work carefully and handle only on the edges as ruffles are fragile and will show fingerprints if smooth surfaces are touched. (Don't wait to trim ruffles until all are made; they will have become too firm and brittle and will break.) Position blade over another area of pan and repeat rotating-scraping procedure, lifting off and trimming ruffle segments as they are formed, and working around outside of pan toward center, until the entire surface has been used. Repeat procedure with second pan of chocolate. With practice, ruffled segments of varying widths can be produced by shortening the distance between the left side of the blade, which is rotated, and the right side, which is drawn toward you ½ inch at a time. If chocolate begins to splinter or break as you are working, it has become too cool and no further ruffles can be made. (The sheet can be returned to a barely warm oven for a *few seconds* to warm the chocolate enough to continue, if desired.)

Let ruffles stand on tray for at least 30 minutes and preferably one hour, until firm. Often, the undersides are smoother and glossier than the tops, so determine the best side of each before arranging on dessert. Also, partially broken and imperfect ruffles can be used by intermixing and partially covering them with perfect ones.

To arrange on top of a cake or other dessert as shown on page 11, begin by placing the widest ruffle segments in an overlapping, unbroken circle around the outside of the dessert. Then add several narrower, slightly overlapping rows, working inward until the center is reached. The ruffle segments may be laid flat on icing (or whipped cream) surface, but are more dramatic when bases are anchored in icing and segments are positioned so the ruffles flare upward slightly.

Makes enough ruffle segments to cover one 8-inch cake top

CHOCOLATE WATER-LILY BLOSSOMS
OR CABBAGE ROSES

The same technique of coating real leaves with chocolate that is used to produce beautifully detailed chocolate leaves can be modified slightly to produce pretty water-lily blossoms (or cabbage roses; see Note). In this case, the forms for the blossom petals are brussels-sprout leaves, which yield graceful, curved chocolate "petals" that can be easily clustered together to form cup-shaped blooms.
❖ *The petals and finished blossoms are stored in the freezer, so no tempering of the chocolate is required (see Note).*

To form petals: Set within reach a small pastry brush, artist's brush, or very small paint brush or, if preferred, substitute a table knife. Cut bottoms from about 12 brussels sprouts. Carefully pull off outer, less crinkled leaves and reserve; discard interior portions (or reserve for cooking!). Wipe reserved leaves clean and dry with paper towels. To dry the leaves further, let them stand on a wax paper–lined tray or baking sheet for a few minutes; then refrigerate while chocolate is prepared. Place in the freezer a second wax paper-lined tray for holding finished leaves.

On stovetop, in a medium-sized, shallow, heat-proof bowl set over a small saucepan of very warm but not hot water, *slowly melt* white chocolate and shortening, stirring occasion-ally, until mixture is completely smooth. (Do not overheat or chocolate will lump.) *Being careful not to drip any water in chocolate*, remove bowl from saucepan. Wipe any water from exterior of bowl.

12 brussels sprouts
4 ounces white chocolate (or dark chocolate, if chocolate-colored blossoms are desired), broken into large chunks
1 teaspoon solid white vegetable shortening (no substitutes)
1 to 2 teaspoons dark chocolate shards (or white chocolate, if chocolate-colored blossoms are prepared) to serve as flower stamens (optional)

One at a time, prepare leaves by coating the *inside* of each with a generous ⅛-inch-thick layer of chocolate; make layer at base of leaf a little thicker and be careful not to drip chocolate onto other side. As leaves are prepared, immediately transfer to tray in freezer, coated side up, slightly separated. (If brush needs to be cleaned, wipe off with paper towel. Do not rinse with water as chocolate will seize.)

Allow leaves to chill for 10 minutes, or until chocolate is completely set and hardened. Working with one leaf at a time, and holding it with paper towels (to prevent the heat of your hands from melting the chocolate), begin loosening and peeling away leaf. Continue peeling away until leaf is removed, handling chocolate petal as little as possible and only on the edges. Return petals to freezer until frozen again, 3 or 4 minutes. Set leftover melted white chocolate aside in a warm place.

To prepare blossoms: Set out some mini-size paper drinking cups, 1¼-inch tartlet pans, mini-muffin paper baking cups (with three or four still stuck together for sturdiness), or other small cups that can be used to hold blossoms together while they set.

Select seven or eight petals of graduated sizes (leave remainder frozen) and lay on work surface. Generously dip base of two petals to be used in blossom center in remaining chocolate. Fit petals together attractively and set in muffin cup to hold them together while chocolate sets. If desired, dip one end of several dark chocolate shards in white chocolate and insert, upright, between petals, to suggest stamens. Continue adding petals, dipping into white chocolate and then arranging and adjusting angle around interior petals, until blossom is complete. With blossom still in cup, transfer to freezer. Allow to freeze completely before using, at least 10 minutes longer. Repeat procedure until all blossoms are prepared.

Store blossoms, preferably still in cups, in an airtight container in freezer, for up to three months. Blossoms may be removed from cups and placed, still frozen, on chilled desserts in advance and then held in refrigerator, but cannot be added to room temperature desserts until just before serving.   *Makes 4 to 6 1½- to 2-inch water-lily blossoms*

Note: Cabbage roses can be made by bending the top edge of some of the brussels-sprout leaves back so they furl attractively. Coat leaves with chocolate as for water-lily blossoms, except brush a little extra chocolate over the edge where the leaf bends to reinforce petal slightly. When assembling cabbage roses, place some of the furled petals around the outside of the bloom as shown on White Chocolate Grand Marnier Cheesecake, page 98.

For blossoms that do not require refrigeration, plain melted chocolate can be replaced with tempered chocolate (see page 220 for tempering instructions). In this case, transfer chocolate-coated leaves to refrigerator, not freezer, and let chill for 10 to 15 minutes until chocolate sets. After blossoms are assembled from petals, return to refrigerator for 10 minutes longer. Remove from refrigerator and store, airtight, in a cool place.

CHOCOLATE TULIP CUPS
OR TARTLET SHELLS

Serving a dessert in a chocolate cup or chocolate tartlet shell is a wonderful way to add drama and appeal. Tulip cups (see page 62) are perfect for presenting mousses, ice creams, fools, and similar desserts, and shallow cups make beautiful "pastry" shells for assorted fresh fruit tartlets. (The White Chocolate-Strawberry Tart filling, page 113, makes an excellent all-purpose base for such tartlets; simply top filling with fruit of your choosing, and glaze fruit with a little melted jelly or seived preserves.) ❖ *Although melted chocolate is normally tempered to ensure that it sets up hard and smooth, tempering is not required in this recipe. Instead, the chocolate cups are firmed up in the freezer and then kept chilled until needed. Because the untempered chocolate is merely frozen and not set, the cups never harden fully, and quickly soften and melt in the mouth—which makes them very easy to cut into and eat.* ❖ *The only drawbacks of untempered cups are that they are fragile and a bit tricky to unmold, and they must be stored in the freezer or refrigerator until serving time. If left at room temperature for more than about 15 minutes they will melt and lose their shape. (For chocolate cups or shells that unmold more easily and that can be held at room temperature, see Note at the end of recipe.)*

Set out some 6- or 7-ounce paper or plastic drinking cups to serve as molds for chocolate cups. Also cut apart seams of some 11½ by 12½-inch (or similar-size) plastic storage bags to yield flat sheets of plastic that are large enough to wrap around cup bottoms, completely cover sides, and extend about 1 inch above rims. Plan to prepare more chocolate cups (and sheets of plastic) than will be needed, as some will break during unmolding; for example, if you need eight, make at least three or four extra. Center each cup on a square of plastic. Gather the plastic at the ends and tuck inside each cup. Arrange plastic carefully so it forms evenly spaced pleats; don't allow it to bunch up in one spot or the chocolate may catch in the creases and break during unmolding.

> 12 ounces bittersweet (not unsweetened) or semisweet chocolate
>
> 1 teaspoon solid white vegetable shortening (no substitutes)

In the top of a double boiler, over about 1 inch hot but not simmering water, heat chocolate and shortening, stirring occasionally, until completely melted and smooth. Remove from heat, carefully wiping any moisture from bottom of pan. Pour chocolate mixture into a 2-cup measure or a deep bowl and stir a minute or two to cool slightly.

Grasping a cup by the rim and holding the plastic so it stays in place but is not pulled tight against the cup bottom and sides, dip bottom of cup into the chocolate; tip cup from side to side to yield an uneven, ruffled edge. Dip cup into chocolate ½ to 1 inch deep for tartlet shells and 1 to 2½ inches deep for tulip cups (shallower cups are easier to unmold). Still holding plastic in place fairly firmly but not tightly, lift cup from chocolate and invert it. (Don't scrape or shake off excess chocolate first or chocolate layer may be too thin and fragile.) Gently shake inverted cup back and forth several times so excess chocolate on bottom flows smoothly over bottom and sides. Carefully place cup, still inverted, on a tray in freezer. Loosen plastic *slightly* so the pleats flare away from cup sides. Repeat process with remaining cups, until all are prepared. Freeze cups for at least 45 minutes, until completely frozen. Gently slip each chocolate cup and attached plastic from paper cup; place chocolate cups in airtight container and return to freezer for up to a month, or remove plastic from cups and use immediately.

To remove plastic: Working with one cup at a time and keeping remainder frozen, grasp the chocolate through a sheet of plastic (touching chocolate directly leaves fingerprints and causes melting), and gently but firmly peel wrap from surface of cup. If plastic sticks, tug firmly. Don't expect all the cups to unmold without cracking; some breakage is normal. (Chocolate from broken cups can be melted and used again, if desired.) If chocolate begins to soften and melt during unmolding, immediately return to freezer to firm up before continuing. Return to freezer as soon as plastic is removed. Repeat process with remaining cups.

Store cups in freezer until ready to fill with mousse, ice cream, or other filling. Fill cup with *thoroughly chilled mixture*, then immediately return to freezer or to refrigerator until serving time. Chocolate cups will soften if allowed to stand at room temperature longer than about 15 minutes.

Makes about 9 to 12 chocolate cups or shells
(depending on size and depth), plus some extras discarded due to breakage

Note: To make Chocolate Tulip Cups and Tartlet Shells that can be held at room temperature, temper 12 ounces chocolate along with 1 tablespoon corn oil or safflower oil (the oil helps keep cups from becoming hard and brittle when they set) according to Master Recipe on page 220. Proceed with directions for dipping cups as described above, except transfer cups to freezer for 10 minutes only. Remove cups from freezer and let stand one hour in a cool place. Peel plastic wrap from chocolate cups; cups will be sturdier and easier to unmold than those prepared with untempered chocolate. Store cups, covered, in a cool place, but not refrigerated, for up to a month.

CHOCOLATE BAND

A chocolate band lends a professional finish to a dessert, yet when prepared by the following method requires no special equipment or skills. Melted chocolate is simply spread on a wax-paper band, chilled until partially set, and wrapped around the dessert. Then the wax paper is peeled away.

❖ *Bands are most often used on cakes (see Black Forest Cherry Cake, page 39), but they are also appealing on cheesecakes, mousse cakes, and molded mousses. Since this method calls for untempered chocolate, bands must be kept chilled, and thus are best suited for cold desserts (or ones that can be held in the refrigerator for at least 30 minutes once the band is added).* ❖ *Bands may be the same height or taller than the dessert, depending on the look desired. Always measure the circumference and height of the dessert before you begin. For a particularly decorative, romantic finish, I like to gently scallop the upper edge of the wax-paper strip with scissors and let the scalloped edge of chocolate extend slightly above the edge of the dessert. For a dramatic modern look, I prepare an extra-wide wax-paper band, and cut away the upper edge in a wavy "free-form" line.*

❖ *You will note that this recipe calls for a small amount of vegetable oil. Don't omit it or make substitutions as the oil softens the chocolate slightly so the band is less likely to shatter when you cut into your desert. To further ensure that the chocolate band stays intact when slicing, make cuts with a sharp knife that has been dipped in hot water and wiped dry.*

To prepare wax-paper band, tear off a sheet of wax paper long enough to encircle and overlap sides of dessert by about an inch. Fold over paper several times to form a sturdy strip that measures the width you desire; bands normally range from 25 to 27 inches in length and up to about 3½ inches in width. (For bands wider than 3½ inches make a recipe and a half of chocolate-oil mixture.) Lay band flat on a work surface. Place several baking sheets in freezer until very cold, at least 20 minutes. Have the dessert well chilled and on serving plate ready for the band.

In the top of a double boiler, over about 1 inch hot but not simmering water, heat chocolate and vegetable oil (add smaller amounts of chocolate and oil specified if making a band narrower than 1½ inches and larger amounts

> 4 to 5 ounces bittersweet (not unsweetened) or semisweet chocolate
> 2½ to 3 teaspoons corn oil, safflower oil, or other flavorless vegetable oil

if making a band that measures 1½ to 3 inches wide). Stir mixture occasionally, until completely melted and smooth. Remove from heat, carefully wiping any moisture from bottom of pan. Stir several minutes to cool chocolate slightly. Pour a line of chocolate mixture evenly along length of band; if band is very narrow you won't need all the chocolate. Using a long-bladed spatula, offset spatula, or knife, smoothly and evenly spread chocolate over strip in a scant ⅛-inch thick layer; spread to within ¼ inch of ends, leaving the uncoated paper at ends to serve as handles.

Remove baking sheets from freezer. Arrange inverted sheets in a row on counter so they form an unbroken cooling surface for band. Carefully lift band at ends and lay, chocolate-side up, on baking sheets. Let stand for about five to seven minutes, until chocolate partially firms up but is still somewhat flexible. Carefully stand band up on one baking sheet, gently bending inward into a circle as though readying chocolate side to fit against dessert. Transfer baking sheet to refrigerator and allow band to chill several minutes longer, until sturdier but *still flexible.* Wrap band around dessert, adjusting from wax paper–covered side so band bottom edge is flush with bottom of dessert plate and smoothing so band fits snugly against dessert side. At point where ends of band overlap, peel back wax paper slightly. Using a sharp knife that has been dipped in hot water and thoroughly dried, evenly trim off excess chocolate so ends just barely overlap. Leave wax paper in place around band. Transfer banded dessert to refrigerator and let chill at least 30 minutes, and up to 48 hours, if preferred. Gently peel wax paper from chocolate band just before serving.

When serving dessert, cut through chocolate band using a knife dipped in hot water and wiped clean between each cut. *Makes 1 band large enough for a 9-by-3½-inch dessert*

CHOCOLATE CURLS, CIGARETTES, FURLED STRIPS, AND SHARDS

Depending on the type of tool used, the temperature of the chocolate, and the specific scraping technique, it is possible to produce several different impressive-looking and appealing curled and furled chocolate decorations. Turning out long, tightly rolled "cigarettes" takes practice and requires a scraping utensil with at least a 3-inch blade (a wide pancake turner, pastry scraper, or windshield scraper, for example). However, pretty furled strips, shards, scrolls, and curls can be produced on the first try using only a pancake turner with a 2-inch blade or a cheese plane. I particularly like the less formal, random shapes of furled strips and rough scrolls because they look decorative, yet unfussy. ❖ For this recipe, it's best to have several 10-by-14-inch or larger smooth, portable Plexiglas or ceramic work surfaces, such as Plexiglas cutting boards or ceramic counter savers. Metal baking sheets may be substituted, but are less desirable because care must be taken not to inadvertently scrape up metal particles along with the chocolate. (If using metal baking sheets, select a plastic scraper such as a pancake turner or windshield scraper to avoid scratching metal from the sheets.) ❖ Wait to prepare this recipe in a cool kitchen on a cool day.

Set out several 10-by-14-inch (or similar) Plexiglas cutting boards or ceramic counter savers (or underside of baking sheets). Line a tray or large pan with wax paper; set aside.

Quick-temper chocolate following Master Recipe on page 220. Immediately pour half of chocolate onto one work surface and begin spreading out into a thin layer using a long-bladed spatula. Continue spreading into a smooth, scant ⅛-inch layer of even thickness, *stopping immediately if chocolate shows any signs of setting on edges* (looks dull and starts to stiffen). Repeat procedure using remaining chocolate and a second work surface. Transfer sheets of chocolate to refrigerator for two to four minutes, chilling only until chocolate appears set all over. Immediately remove from refrigerator. Test surface for proper consistency by holding scraper blade at about a 45-degree angle to chocolate surface, then pushing outward against chocolate. (If using a cheese plane, draw it toward you.) If chocolate builds up on blade instead of rolling into a scroll or curl, return chocolate to refrigerator for about one minute and then test again. When it can be pushed off in a thin strip that curls or rolls up as it forms, it is the proper consistency. Brace pan against counter so it doesn't slip as you work. If chocolate breaks and splinters, it is too cold. To warm it, turn on oven for 1 minute, then turn off. Place chocolate in oven for a *few seconds only* to warm it just slightly; be careful not to overwarm.

8 ounces bittersweet (not unsweetened) or semisweet chocolate, or white chocolate, coarsely chopped or broken into pieces
2 teaspoons solid white vegetable shortening (no substitutes)

By varying the pressure, blade angle, and the distance the blade is pushed away, you can produce large curls (which can be gently curled even further with the fingertips), compact cigarette-like rolls, or irregular furled strips and scrolls. For curls push out blade with steady pressure; for cigarettes use a very wide blade and push out further, harder, and at a slight angle; for rough furled strips and shards exert less pressure and lift blade sooner. (A cheese plane will yield very round, even curls the width of the plane blade.) Pick decorations up only at the ends (to avoid fingerprints) or use a spoon or the scraper to transfer to a wax paper-lined tray. Refrigerate decorations for 10 minutes.

Remove decorations from refrigerator and let stand until chocolate completely sets. Store decorations airtight and in a cool place, but not refrigerated, for up to three months.

Makes enough curls, furls, cigarettes or shards to decorate one large cake generously.

SHORTCUT CHOCOLATE CURLS
AND SHAVINGS

The traditional method of preparing chocolate curls calls for completely melting and then tempering chocolate, but there is an easier approach that works well. This involves simply warming and softening a chocolate block a bit, and then scraping curls and shavings from the surface using a vegetable peeler. If a microwave oven is available to warm the chocolate block, a quantity of curls can be turned out in just two or three minutes. (Curls can be prepared without a microwave, but warming the chocolate will take a little longer.) Shortcut curls are usually not quite as glossy or as perfectly shaped as ones made of tempered chocolate, but they are still pretty and appetizing and make a nice finishing touch.

When preparing shortcut curls, it's best to work with at least a 5- or 6-ounce piece of chocolate. (Individual 1-ounce blocks are more difficult to handle and yield only shavings and small, less attractive curls, but can be used if necessary.)

To warm the chocolate in a microwave oven, set a 5- or 6-ounce chunk (or small blocks) on a microwave-safe plate. Microwave on lowest power for 10 seconds. Let stand a few seconds and then test for proper temperature by scraping along chocolate surface with a vegetable peeler (or a cheese plane). If the chocolate scrapes away easily in a shaving or curl, the piece is at the right temperature. However, if the chocolate is hard to scrape off and small shards break away instead of curling, rotate plate 90 degrees and microwave for another 10 seconds on lowest power. Continue to microwave and test with a vegetable peeler until correct temperature is reached. (Alternatively, to warm chocolate without a microwave, let the piece stand on a plate in a warm spot, such as on the stove *near* a warm burner, in a sunny window, in a barely warm oven, or over a gas-range pilot light. Test the chocolate every few minutes by scraping with vegetable peeler. If chocolate shows any signs of surface melting, immediately transfer to a cool plate and remove from warm area before proceeding.)

To form shavings and curls, hold piece of chocolate over a sheet of foil or wax paper. Using a vegetable peeler (or cheese plane if preferred), scrape along chocolate surface. The pressure exerted and the angle will determine whether the chocolate rolls into a curl or curves slightly to form a shaving. As curls and shavings form, let them drop onto foil or gently lift from vegetable peeler touching only the ends or edges. (Smooth surfaces will show fingerprints if touched.) If the chocolate block hardens as you work and chocolate is difficult to scrape off, return the chunk to microwave oven and microwave on lowest power for 3 or 4 seconds to reheat.

Transfer finished curls to refrigerator for 5 minutes to firm chocolate slightly. Let stand at room temperature a few minutes longer until completely cooled. Use curls immediately or store in an airtight container in a cool place (but not refrigerated) for up to a month.

CHOCOLATE LEAVES

Chocolate leaves make a pretty garnish for all kinds of tortes, cheesecakes, and cakes. Although some methods call for tempering the chocolate, that procedure is not required here. Instead, the finished leaves are stored in the freezer, which ensures that the cocoa butter cannot rise to the surface and produce the whitish residue called bloom. See Note.

❖ *The type of real leaves used as a base when preparing chocolate leaves is important, since some can be peeled away from the hardened chocolate layer much more easily than others. For best results, select stiff, shiny leaves, such as gardenias, citrus and fig. While not stiff, rose leaves also work well. Avoid thin, irregularly shaped leaves like maple and oak, which are fragile and tend to break, or fuzzy ones like geranium, as they usually stick.* ❖ *Keep in mind that very aromatic leaves, particularly citrus and mint, will impart taste to the chocolate. In fact, mint actually yields chocolate-mint leaves (which, of course, make a wonderful garnish for mint-flavored desserts!)*

Set within reach a small pastry brush, artist's brush, or very small paint brush (or, if necessary, substitute a table knife) and a selection of whole, unblemished leaves. Wipe leaves clean and dry with paper towels. To dry further, let leaves stand on a wax paper-lined tray or baking sheet for a few minutes; then refrigerate while chocolate is prepared. Place in the freezer a second wax paper-lined tray for holding finished leaves.

In a medium-sized, shallow, heat-proof bowl set over a small saucepan of *hot but not simmering* water, heat chocolate and shortening, stirring occasionally, until mixture is completely melted, smooth, and just slightly hot to the touch (115° to 120°F.). *Being careful not to drip any water in chocolate,* remove bowl from saucepan. Wipe any water from exterior of bowl.

> *6 ounces bittersweet (not unsweetened) or semisweet chocolate, or white chocolate, or a combination of the two (see Note), broken into large chunks*
>
> *2 teaspoons solid white vegetable shortening (no substitutes)*

One at a time, prepare leaves by coating the *veined underside* with a generous ⅛-inch-thick layer of chocolate; make layer a little thicker at stem end and do not allow chocolate to drip onto top side of leaf. As leaves are prepared, immediately transfer to tray in freezer, chocolate side up, slightly separated. (If brush needs to be cleaned, wipe off with paper towel. Do not rinse with water as chocolate will seize.)

Allow leaves to chill at least 30 minutes and preferably an hour or more. Working with one leaf at a time, and holding leaf with paper towels or tweezers (to prevent heat of hands from melting chocolate), begin loosening and peeling away leaf at stem end. Continue peeling away leaf, handling chocolate as little as possible and only on the edges.

Store chocolate leaves in freezer, airtight, and preferably in a flat container with wax paper between the layers, for up to 3 months. Leaves may be placed, still frozen, on chilled desserts in advance and then held in refrigerator, but cannot be added to room temperature desserts until just before serving.   *Makes 20 to 40 1- to 3-inch chocolate leaves*

Note: For leaves that do not require refrigeration, plain melted chocolate can be replaced with tempered chocolate (see page 220 for tempering instructions). In this case, transfer chocolate-coated leaves to refrigerator, not freezer, and let chill for 10 to 15 minutes until chocolate sets. After leaves are peeled off, return chocolate leaves to refrigerator for 5 minutes longer. Then store, airtight, in a cool place.

Chocolate leaves in shades ranging from straw through mocha to medium-brown can be produced by stirring a few drops of dark chocolate into melted white chocolate until the desired color is obtained.

CHOCOLATE ROSES

Roses are among the prettiest decorations that can be made from modeling chocolate (see the roses on top of the chocolate box, page 238). When artfully shaped and tinted, white chocolate blooms, in particular, look not only attractive, but quite real. (Dark chocolate roses look especially dramatic and pretty on light-colored desserts.) ❖ I've found that one of the easiest ways to make modeled roses look truly lifelike is to create subtle color variations and mottling in the petals. I do this by adding a tiny amount of food color to my fingertips as I position the petals on each rose. The color then rubs off unevenly, flecking some petals and deepening the hue of others, to effectively suggest the natural shadings found in living roses. ❖ Modeling chocolate is quite malleable and easy to work with, so creating attractive roses is simply a matter of practice.

Knead the modeling chocolate until malleable and then rewrap in plastic wrap. (If it is very stiff, warm it for *a few seconds* in a microwave oven, or wrap in foil and place in an oven that has been turned on for two minutes and then turned off again.) If vividly colored roses are desired, knead some paste food color into the white modeling chocolate until distributed throughout, but plan to intensify the shade by adding more color to individual petals later. For each rose, pinch off about nine to twelve small balls from mixture, making some portions slightly larger than others; size of balls can vary from ¼ inch for tiny roses to ½ inch or larger for actual rose-sized blooms.

Choose largest ball and roll between palms until completely smooth and round. Taper and smooth one end of ball to shape it into a

One batch dark or white modeling chocolate (see recipe on page 245)
Paste or liquid food color, if white chocolate roses are prepared (optional)

cone; this will be the base for the petals. Working with one ball at a time and selecting the smaller portions first, roll between palms until very smooth and round. Lay ball between two sheets of plastic wrap and flatten with thumb into a petal shape. Then press out one side further, so it is very thin (almost as thin as the upper edge of a real rose petal but not so thin that it tears). Carefully peel petal from plastic wrap. (If modeling chocolate becomes soft during handling, set aside for a few minutes until it firms up again.)

As petals are formed, begin wrapping them around cone, arranging the first two, thin edge up, on each side of the cone and fitting them closely so that they cover all but its tip. As you "build" a white chocolate rose, occasionally brush a little food color on your fingertips so some will be randomly transferred to the petals. Using three slightly larger petals, add another row, thin edge up, arranging so petals offset one another; position so the petals stand up and away from the center core slightly. Randomly curl back the edges of some of the petals to suggest the natural furling of rose blooms. Continue shaping rose by adding three or four more petals in a third row; offset them and position so they flare away from the center core a bit further. Randomly furl petal edges. For a very full rose, add one more row of petals. If desired, open up the rose more by pinching the base of the cone. Trim off any excess modeling chocolate that has built up at the bottom of the rose. Place rose upright and let stand, uncovered and in a cool place, for at least 24 hours or until set. Repeat process for each rose made. (Roses can be used to decorate refrigerated or unrefrigerated desserts.)

Roses can be packed airtight and stored in the refrigerator for up to two months or in the freezer for up to a year. *About 4 to 6 large, full roses or 10 to 20 small roses*

CHOCOLATE RIBBONS

Chocolate ribbons, particularly contrasting dark-and-white-chocolate striped ribbons like the ones on the Chocolate Box, page 238, never fail to impress, yet they are fairly easy to prepare. The keys to creating realistic ribbons and bows are to roll out the modeling chocolate until it is very thin, and to carefully arrange the ribbon strips to suggest the graceful flow and draping characteristics of real ribbons. ❖ For subtle effects, single-color ribbons, such as the ribbons crisscrossing the Panforte, page 211, are attractive, but for a dramatic, showstopping appearance, prepare two-toned ribbons as directed. Especially attractive pairings include dark- and white-chocolate, dark chocolate and tan-colored white chocolate (it's tinted with a little dark chocolate), or white chocolate and pastel-tinted white chocolate. (In this latter case, prepare two batches of white modeling chocolate and then tint one with food color.) Both wide and narrow striped ribbons look appealing. ❖ Pastry chefs often roll out modeling chocolate for ribbons using a pasta machine, but for the small quantities required at home, it is just as easy to roll the mixture by hand, the method used here.

Knead each batch of modeling chocolate until malleable and then shape into a 9- or 10-inch rope and rewrap in plastic wrap. (If batches are stiff, soften slightly by placing for about 10 minutes in a microwave oven on 50-percent power for several seconds or by wrapping in foil and placing for about 10 minutes in an oven that has been turned on for a minute or two and then turned off again. The modeling chocolate should be slightly soft and just barely warm, but not at all melted.)

Lay one rope between 18-inch or longer sheets of wax paper. Using a rolling pin, roll out rope into a long rectangular strip about ⅛ inch thick, making sure layer is evenly thick all over. (If strip seems stiff and difficult to roll, place it, still between wax paper sheets, on a barely warm baking sheet for several seconds, then turn over and warm the second side for several seconds.) Check for creases on underside of paper and smooth out as necessary. With paper still in place, set layer aside on a flat surface. Repeat procedure with second rope. As you work, always replace top sheet of paper over layers to prevent them from drying out during standing.

One batch dark chocolate modeling chocolate (see recipe on page 245)
One batch white modeling chocolate

Gently peel off top sheet of wax paper from first layer and replace it. Turn over layer and gently peel off second sheet of paper. Using a long sharp knife and measuring and marking cutting lines in advance, cut layer lengthwise into long, thin strips that are all the same width; select a width from about ⅛ to ¼ inch depending on how wide the finished ribbons will be and how many stripes each will have. Repeat the cutting procedure with the second layer of modeling chocolate.

For each ribbon, gently transfer several thin strips to a clean sheet of wax paper, alternating colors and laying them absolutely straight and parallel; edges should be touching and fitted together snugly. The number of strips fitted together can vary, but keep in mind that the final ribbon will widen considerably as the strips are rolled out and flattened further. Cover the ribbon with another sheet of wax paper and roll out until $\frac{1}{16}$ inch thick all over. Using a long sharp knife, trim the sides to straighten the ribbon and to make it the width desired. Peel away and discard trimmings. Re-cover ribbon with wax paper. Repeat process for each ribbon desired. Ribbons can be allowed to stand a few minutes, but are easier to bend and arrange attractively if applied or formed into bows right away.

To arrange finished ribbons and construct bows: Neatly cut ties, bow loops, and ribbon ends to the desired lengths. Pieces used for loops of bows will need to be from 5 to 8 inches long, depending on the overall size of bow to be made. Gently curve loop pieces and pinch together at the ends. If ribbons are used to "tie up" the dessert, lay these in position first. Position bow loops and ribbon ends in a cluster as desired and "glue" together into a free-standing bow or attach them to a dessert or display piece with either a small amount of chocolate that is stirred until cool and starting to set, or with tempered chocolate. To keep bow loops from drooping and closing while the modeling chocolate firms, insert small pieces or rolls of aluminum foil inside loops or around loops to prop them up. Let stand, uncovered, for at least one hour, or until chocolate firms, before removing aluminum foil. Modeling chocolate will become very firm and sturdy if allowed to stand for 48 hours. (Bows can be used on refrigerated or unrefrigerated desserts.) Fully constructed bows can be stored, airtight and refrigerated, for two months, or frozen for up to a year.

Makes enough ribbon to produce a large, full bow and "tie up" a tall, 9 inch cake

CHOCOLATE WRITING AND OTHER PIPED DECORATIONS

One of the great advantages of chocolate writing and other piped chocolate decorations is that they can be prepared on a sheet of wax paper and then transferred to a dessert when they have set. This eliminates the chance of spoiling the appearance of a dessert with a piping error, and makes it possible to practice the desired writing, curlicue, or other design element until a perfect decoration is produced. (Your piping skills will improve dramatically with just a little practice.) ❖ Either tempered or untempered chocolate may be used for chocolate writing and piped decorations, although tempered chocolate decorations are sturdier, do not have to be stored in the refrigerator, and can be used on any dessert, candy, or chocolate display piece. Untempered decorations break more easily and must be kept chilled or they will eventually become tacky and soft and may discolor. ❖ Piped chocolate elements can be very simple, such as the small white chocolate hearts tucked among the ribbons on the Chocolate Box, page 238. But the same method can be used to produce elaborate inscriptions and components of border designs for adorning cake tops, or fanciful curlicues, butterflies, or other decorations for tucking into a serving of ice cream or mousse. (Texts on pastry and cake decorating often include many pages of piped designs, so consult these if you want more specific ideas.)

Set out several wax paper–lined baking sheets to serve as the piping surface. If you wish, slide a piping guide (a drawing or other design) under the wax paper. Prepare some paper piping cones following instructions on page 267. Temper or melt chocolate until smooth. If chocolate is not tempered, stir it a minute or two until it thickens slightly (this makes it easier to pipe smoothly). Fill and close a cone. Cut away the tip; for chocolate decorations the piped lines must be at least $\frac{1}{16}$ inch thick or the decorations will be too fragile.

Holding the top of the cone tightly closed between the thumb and fingers, apply enough pressure to squeeze out a steady line of chocolate; cut tip opening slightly larger if a thicker line is desired. (Always start with a few practice lines before attempting the actual design.) When ready to begin, position the cone vertically and touch the tip to the starting point of your design. If desired, steady the hand you are piping with by gently bracing the index finger of the other hand against it. With the chocolate flowing evenly, lift tip straight up from paper about an inch and allow chocolate to fall into the line formed by your hand motion. At the end of the design element, touch the tip to the surface and stop squeezing the cone at the same time. Repeat the process several times to produce extra decorations (in case of breakage) or to practice and improve your piping skills.

> *2 to 3 ounces bittersweet (not unsweetened) or semisweet chocolate, or white chocolate, melted and (if desired) tempered, or leftover tempered chocolate*

If piping *tempered* chocolate, immediately transfer baking sheet with piped decorations to refrigerator for about five minutes, until the chocolate appears set. Then let stand at room temperature for at least 15 minutes longer, until chocolate completely sets. Gently lift piped chocolate from paper using a small spatula or knife. Place decoration on dessert or store, covered and in a cool place, for up to three months.

If piping *untempered* chocolate, immediately transfer baking sheet to freezer for at least 15 minutes, until chocolate decorations are cold and hard. Carefully lift *completely frozen* decorations from wax paper–lined baking sheet with a small spatula or knife (decorations that are not frozen will be soft and too susceptible to breakage). Immediately transfer to a wax paper–lined airtight storage container. Cover and return to freezer. Arrange on a dessert shortly before serving time. Decorations will keep, frozen, for up to three months.

CHOCOLATE BIRD'S NEST

For sheer whimsy, nothing can quite match an Easter display or springtime centerpiece featuring dark chocolate bird's nests and white chocolate eggs (for egg recipe, see page 264). Tucked along the branches of blossoming bushes or fruit trees, and accented with ferns and wildflowers, chocolate nests look not only captivating, but also quite real. I have had guests ask (somewhat disapprovingly) why I gathered nests that still contained eggs!

❖ The following recipe takes a bit of patience and time, but requires only rudimentary piping skills. The technique involves piping a sturdy basket-shaped framework of chocolate lines over the foil-covered bottom of a small drinking glass or jar. Once this framework sets, it is carefully peeled from the foil and more piping is added to build up the nest. ❖   Chocolate nests are created with tempered chocolate, so work on a cool day or in a well air-conditioned room. Also, since it is difficult to maintain the proper temper of a small quantity of chocolate, the recipe calls for the same amount regardless of whether one nest or several will be made. (Any leftover chocolate can be allowed to set again and then reused in baking.)

Assemble supplies as follows: Select a jar or drinking glass with a rounded bottom the same diameter as the nest to be made. (Nests in the 2- to 3-inch range usually look best.) Cut a square of heavy-duty aluminum foil large enough to cover the jar bottom and to extend at least 2½ inches up its sides. Invert jar; smooth foil over bottom and down sides. Slip foil off jar, then replace it to ensure it will slip off easily once chocolate has been piped. Using several small pieces of masking tape at edge, fix foil in place. Set foil-covered jar in refrigerator until well chilled, at least 20 minutes.

Meanwhile, ready some piping cones (see page 267), at least 2 or 3 for each nest made. Quick-temper chocolate following directions on page 220. Set on heating pad as directed

> 1¼ pounds bittersweet (not unsweetened) or semisweet chocolate
> 2 tablespoons solid white vegetable shortening (no substitutes)

in tempering instructions to keep chocolate at proper temperature. Stir chocolate every 3 or 4 minutes, watching carefully and adjusting heat as necessary to prevent either excess warming or cooling; the chocolate must be kept tempered throughout piping.

To prepare nest frame: Put tempered chocolate into piping cone. For very small nests, cut piping cone tip off with a sharp knife to yield ⅛-inch-thick lines; for larger nests, lines can be a little larger. Begin piping chocolate over bottom of jar, working as though winding a vine or string around bottom and sides in rough, imperfect concentric circles, and extending lines about 1 to 1½ inches down sides of jar (depending on depth of the nest desired). For a natural, "bird's nest" appearance, keep "weave" irregular and random-looking rather than orderly. Work as quickly as possible, stopping after 3 or 4 minutes. Carefully transfer jar, bottom side still up, to refrigerator and allow chocolate lines to set (about 5 to 8 minutes). Then remove from the refrigerator and continue piping, refilling cone or using a new one as needed. When a *sturdy,* almost solid framework of lines is completed, refrigerate jar and chocolate frame and chill at least 15 minutes until chocolate sets completely. Then let stand at room temperature for about 10 minutes so chocolate will be less brittle.

Working carefully and holding jar upright, pour a little warm water into it; do not splash on chocolate. Wait about 10 seconds until chocolate warms slightly (but *does not melt*), then loosen tape and slide foil and attached chocolate frame off jar. Gently peel chocolate frame from foil. (If frame begins to break, stop and patch breaks by piping additional chocolate lines over breaks. Before continuing, return nest to refrigerator and chill until chocolate sets.)

With inside of nest facing up, pipe rough concentric circles into bottom and sides until nest looks filled out. Return to refrigerator until chocolate completely sets, about 10 minutes. Turn over nest and pipe rough concentric circles until bottom and outsides are built up. Refrigerate until chocolate sets completely. If desired, pipe a few chocolate lines to suggest loose "twigs" onto a sheet of wax paper. Refrigerate until chocolate sets. Lift from paper with point of paring knife. Arrange twigs in nest as desired.

Store nest(s), covered and in a cool place, for up to 2 months.

Makes 4 to 6 nests (or more, if very small, compact nests are made)

WHITE CHOCOLATE BIRD EGGS

The trompe l'oeil effect of a dark chocolate bird's nest is heightened further by a clutch of tiny eggs. Although it is difficult to buy egg-shaped molds that are small enough to create the right look, it is easy to hand-shape white chocolate eggs to whatever size you need.

With the addition of a little coffee powder or food color, it is even possible to imitate the look of a particular species—the speckled, cream-colored eggs of sparrows, or the blue eggs of robins, for example.

In top of a double boiler over about 1 inch of hot but not simmering water, *very slowly* melt white chocolate, stirring frequently, being careful not to overheat or allow any water into it. Remove double boiler from heat. If colored eggs are desired, stir a very small amount of food color into corn syrup until well blended. Very slowly stir warm clarified butter and corn syrup into chocolate until incorporated. Mixture will stiffen somewhat and may look separated and oily (if separation occurs, stir to recombine several times during cooling). Spoon mixture into a small airtight container. Cover and let stand at room temperature until mixture firms up, at least 3 hours. (Mixture may be stored, refrigerated, for up to 2 weeks; allow to come to room temperature before using.) Divide mixture into 15 to 20 equal portions (or more, if very small eggs are needed). One at a time, shape into balls between palms. Don't worry too much about tapering the balls at one end into a perfect egg shape if this seems difficult; bird eggs are often more rounded than hen eggs and the shape will not be noticeable once a clutch is in a nest. Lay eggs, slightly separated, on a wax paper-lined plate or tray. Refrigerate for at least 10 minutes, until firmed up, before using. If speckled eggs are desired, press a very small amount of instant coffee powder or crushed granules into a fingertip. Then, at random intervals, press granules into surface of chilled eggs.

Eggs may be stored, airtight and refrigerated, for up to 3 weeks. Bring to room temperature several hours before using. Eggs may stand at room temperature for several days.

Makes 15 to 20 bird eggs (or more very small eggs)

> *2 ounces good-quality white chocolate, coarsely chopped*
> *Paste or liquid food color (optional)*
> *1 tablespoon light corn syrup*
> *2 teaspoons clarified unsalted butter (see Note)*
> *Instant coffee powder or crushed granules (optional)*

Note: To clarify butter, bring 1½ tablespoons unsalted butter to simmer in a small saucepan. Simmer for about 3 minutes or until foaming subsides and solids drop to bottom and begin to turn pale brown. Immediately strain mixture through a fine sieve into a cup. Let stand until any remaining solids drop to cup bottom. Measure out 2 teaspoons clarified butter from top; discard remainder or use for another purpose.

CARVED CHOCOLATE PINE CONES

I find creating little pine cones from modeling chocolate particularly gratifying since the shaping and carving is easy and the cones look quite real. In addition, they make appealing garnishes for all sorts of holiday desserts, and can also be used along with peppermint-striped white chocolate ribbons to give chocolate boxes a festive appearance. (Directions for an edible chocolate box are on page 239.)

Prepare a batch of modeling chocolate according to directions on page 245.

Assemble supplies: Set out some toothpicks. Make a stand to hold pine cones upright on toothpicks during drying, as follows: Set a lightweight shoe-box bottom or similar box upside down on work surface. Using a metal skewer or very thin, sharp knife point, poke small holes in box, spacing them at least 1 inch apart. (Holes should be small enough for toothpicks to fit snugly when inserted.)

By hand, knead modeling chocolate until pliable and smooth. (If it is very stiff, soften first by microwaving on 50-percent power for two or three seconds, or by wrapping in foil and letting stand for about five minutes in an oven that has been turned on low for two minutes and immediately turned off again; mixture should not feel more than barely warm to the touch.) Shape mixture into a 12-inch-long log of even thickness. Measure, mark, and then cut log crosswise into equal portions: for 1½-inch pine cones, cut log into about 12 portions; for 1-inch mini-cones, cut into about 24 portions. Roll each portion between palms into a very smooth ball. Then roll between palms until ball elongates and tapers at one end into a pine cone shape. Insert a toothpick into bottom of each cone. Using toothpicks, place cones upright in cardboard stand. Refrigerate cones for at least 1½ hours and up to eight hours, until well chilled and very firm.

Working with one cone at a time (leave remainder refrigerated), begin carving petal-like scales as follows: Holding a cone by its toothpick and working around its top with a small paring knife, begin cutting into surface at a 75-degree angle to create a series of ⅛-inch-wide petal-shaped grooves, or scales. Bend back scales with blade a little as you cut so that they stand away from cone slightly. For clean cuts, frequently wipe off knife blade with a damp paper towel. Continue until a row of scales has been carved all the way around cone. Spacing so as to offset scales in first row, carve a second row of scales about ⅛ inch below first. Continue adding rows, each offsetting the preceding row, at about ⅛-inch intervals, until bottom of cone is reached.

Allow cones to dry for one or two days at room temperature, until chocolate firms up. Slide cones off toothpicks. Pack airtight and store in a cool place for up to a month.

Makes about 16 cones or 24 mini-cones

RUFFLED CHOCOLATE BOWS
AND MODELING CHOCOLATE RUFFLES

If you are entranced by the look of ruffled chocolate decorations, but do not wish to spend the time mastering the techniques for making tempered-chocolate ruffles, the ruffled bows and ruffle segments presented here on the perfect solution. Created from either striped or solid ribbons of modeling chocolate, they require attention to detail but no special skills. (A microwave oven is recommended for preparing these ruffles, but they can be produced without one.) ❖ *The same basic approach is used to produce a small ruffled bow, very full ruffled bow (see the Panforte, page 211), or quick bow tie–shaped decoration. While wonderful accents, modeling chocolate ruffles and bows should not be used to blanket a dessert; unlike tempered chocolate ruffles, they are too heavy and dense to eat in large quantities.*

Begin by preparing striped or solid ribbons as described in the recipe for Chocolate Ribbons, page 259. If striped ribbons are used, take care to assure that the stripes are firmly and smoothly pressed against one another during the rolling out process. (This will help keep the stripes from separating as the ribbons are pinch-pleated into ruffles.)

As soon as all ribbons are formed, cut them crosswise into segments of equal length; length selected can range from about 2½ inches for very narrow ribbons to 3½ inches for wide ribbons. Lay one segment at a time on a small sheet of wax paper. Transfer to a microwave oven and microwave on low-power for several seconds, until segment is just soft and malleable enough to pinch-pleat or loosely gather one side into a ruffle without cracking, but is not at all melted (see illustration). (Exact microwaving time needed will vary from oven to oven, so try a sample segment and adjust procedure as necessary.) Depending on the tightness and shape of ruffle desired, gently pinch the center section of segment together, or pinch in several places along segment side to yield a segment about 2 inches wide on ruffled side and ¾-inch wide on pleated side. Stop shaping as soon as the segment begins to firm, as any further manipulation will cause it to look cracked and leathery. Gently set aside on a wax paper–lined tray. Continue forming ruffles from segments using same procedure.

(Alternatively, if microwave is unavailable, lay each segment on a sheet of wax paper and warm the chocolate by blowing it with a hair dryer until just soft enough to pinch-pleat. Hold onto the wax paper so it isn't moved by the blowing air.)

Let ruffle segments stand for at least one hour and preferably several hours, until firm and sturdy enough to handle. To create a bow (as shown on page 211), cluster three or four segments in a single, close ring, "gluing" together or onto a dessert with a small amount of chocolate that is stirred until cool and about to set, or with tempered chocolate. If desired, add a second (or even a third) radiating ring of segments to fashion a larger, fuller ruffled bow, as shown. Two segments can also be used to create a bow tie for a dessert.

Ruffle segments or bows can be kept, airtight and refrigerated, for 2 months, or frozen for up to a year.

Makes 20 to 40 ruffle segments, depending on their width and length

PREPARING AND FILLING
A PAPER PIPING CONE

Paper piping cones are useful for all sorts of decorating tasks. One reason is that, unlike pastry bags fitted with metal writing tips, piping cones can be placed in a microwave oven and heated for a second or two to warm up chocolate that has begun to set. Moreover, once chocolate sets in a pastry bag it must be removed (not a simple matter) before the bag or tip can be used again. In contrast, when chocolate sets in a piping cone, the cone can be discarded, or, better yet, refrigerated until the chocolate hardens. Then the cone can be torn open and the chocolate neatly removed and saved for another use. ❖ For tasks requiring a lot of detailed piping, prepare your cones using baking parchment. While not as sturdy, wax paper can be successfully substituted for small jobs or when piping does not have to be too fine or exact. ❖ Since melted chocolate is often very fluid, it's important to carefully close piping cones to prevent seepage. Also take care not to overfill them.

Cut a triangle out of baking parchment, similar to the one shown in Step 1, page 268; size can range from 10 to 12 inches (on long side, Side C), depending on whether a small- or medium-sized cone is needed. (If substituting wax paper, cut out an *exactly square* sheet of paper; then fold square in half to form a triangle, neatly creasing paper along fold.)

To construct cone, grasp edge of Side A and roll around fingers inward to *center point* of Side C, as shown in Step 2; be sure roll forms a *tightly closed point* at center point.

Holding rolled portion in place with right hand (if you are right-handed), grasp edge of Side B with left hand. Snugly wrap Side B portion of triangle around previously rolled portion with left hand, until a tight cone is formed and edge of Side B overlaps Point D, as shown in Step 3; when edge of Side B is aligned as shown, hold edge firmly in place with right thumb. Hold cone tightly rolled with right hand and thumb and, with left hand, carefully crease and fold top edge of cone inward several times to keep cone from unrolling. Finished cone, with top edge neatly folded to the inside, is shown in Step 4.

Fill cone no more than a scant two-thirds full with chocolate as shown by dotted line in Step 5. Join top edges and fold once to close, as shown in Step 6. Then fold each corner toward center to keep chocolate from seeping out cone sides, as shown in Step 7. Tightly fold over top once more, as shown in Step 8. Always hold fold tightly in place while piping. Before piping, neatly snip off cone tip with sharp scissors; it's best to cut off only a small amount and then cut more if a larger piping hole is needed.

Making a Piping Cone

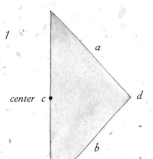

1 center *c* *a* *d* *b*

2 *c* *d* *b*

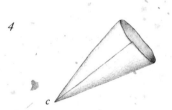

3 *d* *b* *c* fold line

4 *c*

Closing a Filled Cone

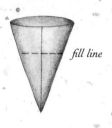

5 fill line

6

7

8

Making a Tempered Chocolate Ruffle

area scraped clear

Modeling Chocolate Ruffle Segment

ruffle segment

SWISS CHOCOLATE CHÂLET
Hexehüsli

The custom of making little cookie houses is popular in a number of central European countries, but Zurich—a city at the heart of the Swiss chocolate industry—takes the idea one delicious step further. During the Christmas season, several of the well-known cafés in town, notably Sprüngli am Paradeplatz and Café Schober, display and sell gaily decorated chocolate châlets. Typically, these depict the Hansel and Gretel fairy tale and include miniature figures of a boy, a girl, and an old witch along with the chocolate cottage. The houses are bedecked with colorful candies, glacéed fruits, royal-icing flowers, hearts and birds, small cookies, and nuts, and are accented along the eaves and roof peak with royal-icing "snow."

❖ *Creating the chocolate châlet presented here takes a bit of time, but is a fun family project and can be done in several stages. The plans yield a finished house about eight inches high, which is perfect for a holiday decoration, table centerpiece, or special child's gift.*

PREPARING THE CHOCOLATE

The châlet is prepared from a modeling chocolate mixture, which is rolled out and cut into pattern pieces. These are then set aside for several days until the chocolate firms up and holds its shape again. Prepare modeling chocolate as follows:

Place chocolate in a large microwave-safe bowl in microwave oven. Microwave on 50-percent power for three minutes, stopping and rotating bowl ¼ turn at one minute intervals and stirring chocolate until well blended. If necessary, microwave for two to three minutes longer, checking chocolate and stirring every 30 seconds until it is *completely melted and smooth.* Set aside. Place corn syrup in a microwave-safe bowl or cup in microwave oven. Microwave on 50-percent power for 10 seconds. Stir syrup. Touch syrup; if it does not feel just slightly warm, microwave a few seconds longer, but be careful not to overwarm it.

(Alternatively, to prepare chocolate on stove top, put chocolate in large bowl, preferably metal. Set bowl over pan of hot but not sim-mering water. Heat, stirring frequently, until chocolate completely melts and is very warm to the touch; *do not allow any water into chocolate.* Set aside. Heat corn syrup in a small saucepan over medium heat until barely warm. Remove pan from burner.)

Using a large wooden spoon, very slowly stir warm corn syrup into warm chocolate; be sure to scrape out cup so all syrup is incorporated. Continue gently stirring until mixture is very well blended and smooth; it may stiffen slightly. Line two pie plates or similar pans with plastic wrap, allowing wrap to overhang all around. Pour half of

> **Modeling Chocolate (for house pieces)**
> *1¾ pounds coarsely chopped or broken bittersweet or semisweet chocolate*
> *¾ cup plus 2 tablespoons light corn syrup*

chocolate mixture into each plate. Lay plastic wrap over each plate directly on chocolate surface to cover completely. Cover top tightly with foil. Let plates stand at room temperature for at least eight hours and up to 24 hours.

MAKING THE PATTERN PIECES

Refer to pattern illustration on page 275. Prepare pattern pieces as indicated using sturdy paper (a manila folder is a good weight). Cut out and label *the following pieces:*

❖ *One 7-inch-by-5¾-inch rectangle (for 2 roof pieces) labeled so 5¾-inch*
   dimension is across the top
❖ *One 2-inch-by-4¼-inch rectangle (for 2 house sides)*
❖ *One 5-inch-by-7½-inch rectangle (for house front and back pieces)*
❖ *One 1¾-inch-by-3¼-inch rectangle (for stovepipe chimney)*

To form the peaked shape of house front and back, measure and mark the center point of a 5-inch side; this will be center top (peak) of roof. Then mark 2 inches up from the bottom on each 7½-inch side (see pattern illustration). Using a ruler, draw lines from center top to the 2-inch high points to determine roof angle. Cut away excess paper following lines drawn. Measure and mark placement of a 1½-inch-wide and 2¼-inch-high front door opening in the center front of front/back pattern piece. Cut away paper for door opening.

CUTTING OUT HOUSE PIECES

Assemble the following:

❖ *One batch of modeling chocolate (see recipe on page 269), at room temperature*
❖ *About ¼ cup unsweetened cocoa powder, for dusting work surface*

Warm portions of modeling chocolate slightly by placing in a microwave oven and microwaving for about 10 seconds on 50-percent power. Rotate portions ½ turn and microwave a few seconds longer, checking every three seconds, until chocolate is just slightly soft, but only barely warm. (Alternatively, wrap portions in aluminum foil. Turn oven on to warm for three minutes; turn off and place chocolate in oven. Let stand 10 to 15 minutes, until chocolate is softened slightly but only barely warm.) Break off handfuls of chocolate and knead until flexible and smooth. Handfuls may also be "kneaded" in a heavy-duty mixer (with paddle) on low speed. Wrap kneaded chocolate tightly in plastic wrap to prevent it from drying out as you work. Repeat with second portion.

Working with half of kneaded chocolate, roll out into a scant ¼-inch-thick rectangle on cocoa powder-dusted surface. (Make sure layer is evenly thick.) Dust rolling pin with cocoa powder as needed to prevent sticking. Lift chocolate and lightly dust work surface with cocoa again. Using pattern pieces, cut out a roof piece, a side piece, house front and a rectangle for stovepipe chimney using a sharp knife. Following pattern,

cut away front door opening on house front using paring knife. Cut out round upper front window opening using a 1-inch (or similar) round cutter or drinking glass (see photo for window placement). Working from a longer side, roll chimney rectangle into a cylinder, pressing seam firmly to hold in place. Stand cylinder up on wax paper. Lay other pieces flat on wax paper–lined trays or pans. Brush or wipe all excess cocoa from pieces.

Wrap scraps in plastic wrap and set aside. Repeat rolling and cutting-out procedure with second chocolate portion, cutting out a roof piece, side piece, and house back (cut out a back window, if desired). If desired, using aspic or mini-cutters (or patterns), cut out an assortment of small hearts, stars, rounds, or other decorative shapes from any unused areas of chocolate (to use as roof decorations, as shown in photo). Working horizontally or vertically, lightly score one side of roof pieces with tines of fork to produce wood-grain look.

Knead all chocolate scraps together (warm up just slightly first, if necessary). To form chocolate foundation for house, roll leftover portion into a square, rectangle or irregularly shaped slab at least ¼ inch thick and at least 7 inches on all sides.

Let all pieces except cylinder for chimney dry for at least 48 hours. After about four hours, cut off one end of chimney cylinder at an angle so it will match the pitch of the finished roof (see photo). Let chimney dry along with other pieces.

Carefully turn over pieces and let dry at least 48 hours longer, or until fairly firm and sturdy (they may still be slightly flexible if bent, however). Pieces may be stored up for up to two weeks, lightly covered with wax paper.

CONSTRUCTING THE CHALET

Once the house pieces have firmed up, they are joined together with melted, cooled chocolate that serves as glue.

To prepare chocolate "glue": Heat chocolate in top of a double boiler over about 1 inch of hot but not simmering water, stirring until melted and smooth; *do not allow any water into chocolate.* Remove double boiler top from bottom; wipe exterior of pan dry. Stir chocolate until it is just barely warm and still fluid, but is on the verge of setting and is able to bond the house pieces together. If chocolate sets completely, double boiler top must be placed over hot water again and chocolate melted slightly and stirred well before "gluing" can proceed. (As you put house together, it may be necessary to warm and cool chocolate several times.)

To construct house frame: Stand up house front on a baking sheet lined with wax paper. Match up edges of house sides with lower

> Chocolate Glue
> *6 ounces semisweet chocolate, coarsely chopped*

section of front and back. Pipe or spread a line of chocolate along matched up edges. Fit front and side edges together, pressing into place until chocolate sets slightly. Match up edges of house back with sides. Fit pieces together, adjusting so house frame is square and stands up straight. Using a finger, smooth out chocolate at side seams of unit. Check and, if necessary, press together seams so pieces fit together tightly while chocolate sets. Add a thick, reinforcing line of chocolate along each inside seam; don't worry if it drips onto wax paper as it will not stick to paper. Let stand for at least 30 minutes, and preferably an hour, until structure is set enough to support roof.

To attach roof to frame: Match up two 5¾-inch-long sides of roof pieces to form roof peak. Pipe or spread line of chocolate along matched-up edges. Also put line of chocolate along eave lines of house front and back. Fit roof pieces onto house frame, adjusting pitch and centering pieces so they fit together neatly along peak and overhang an equal amount in front and back. Pinch together roof pieces along peak and add a heavy reinforcing line of chocolate. Carefully place props (such as small measuring cups, children's blocks, or boxes of gelatin) under lower edges of roof on each side to prevent pieces from sliding out of position before they set. Check that the house looks square and roof is straight and adjust if necessary. Gently press roof down against eave edges and frame to secure. Let stand for at least 30 minutes.

To reinforce house and attach chimney: Gently turn house upside down and add heavy line of chocolate to all interior seams. Turn upright again. Temporarily position chimney on roof; if necessary, trim away chimney bottom further so angle matches pitch of roof and chimney stands up straight. Spread chocolate on chimney bottom. Center chimney on one side of roof, placing as shown in photograph. Neatly pipe or spoon a little more chocolate around chimney to secure further. Hold chimney in place or prop up until chocolate sets. Let house stand for at least one hour, and preferably overnight, until completely set.

DECORATING THE CHÂLET

Swiss chocolate houses are usually abundantly adorned with decorations, including small frosted cookies, chocolate bonbons, hard candy drops, dried fruits, nuts, and piped royal-icing flowers and birds. While any of these may be used, it's easiest to decorate roof surfaces with flat-sided, lightweight items, such as candied cherry and nut halves, iced vanilla wafers, or chocolate cut-outs (such as those on châlet in photograph), as they stick more readily than round, heavy pieces. For an authentic Swiss look, avoid using peppermint canes and red-and-white pinwheel mints. Although these are typical American Christmas sweets, they are not traditional or readily available in central Europe.

Assemble the following decorating materials:

❖ *About 50 to 60 mixed decorating pieces, for adorning house front, back, roof eaves, and roof peak*

❖ *One batch of royal icing (recipe follows)*

To prepare royal icing: In a grease-free large mixer bowl with mixer on low speed, beat egg whites until very frothy. Add lemon juice and salt. If desired, add a drop of blue food color for an icy look. Raise speed to medium and gradually beat in powdered sugar. Beat on high speed until mixture is shiny and stands in firm but not dry peaks; it should be smooth and spreadable but not too soft. If mixture seems soft, beat in a bit more powdered sugar; if dry, add a few drops of water. Cover bowl with damp tea towel to prevent icing from drying out as you work. (If it does begin to stiffen, stir in a few drops of water.)

Decorate previously prepared chocolate cut-outs (or substitute vanilla wafers or other small cookies, if desired) as follows: Remove small amount of royal icing to several small bowls. Using food color, tint portions different colors as desired. If necessary, thin icing portions with a few drops of water until spreadable. Ice one side of cut-outs (or tops of cookies) using table knife or artist's brush. Decorate with colored sprinkles or nonpareils, if desired. Let cut-outs stand until icing sets, about one hour.

> ### Royal Icing
> 3 large egg whites, completely free of yolk
> 1/2 teaspoon lemon juice
> 1/8 teaspoon salt
> 1 drop blue food color (optional)
> 2 1/2 to 3 1/2 cups powdered sugar, sifted if lumpy
> Assorted food colors, liquid or paste

Decorate house front and back (and add optional piping around house front door and windows, if desired) as shown in photograph as follows: Gently tip over house so it rests on its back and front faces up. Place chocolate cut-outs, candies, glacéed fruit, or other decorations on house front as desired, gluing into place with royal icing. For piping, place small amount of white royal icing in a piping cone or small pastry bag fitted with fine writing tip. Pipe decorative straight or curlicued accent lines around front door and window. Let stand until icing sets, at least 30 minutes and preferably longer. Turn over house so back faces up and decorate house back as desired. Let stand until icing sets.

Glue prepared cut-out decorations onto house roof as follows: Stand house upright. Using photograph as a guide or following your own design, glue pieces to roof with dabs of royal icing, allowing it to become tacky before placing items on house or they may slide off.

Complete snow capping and icicle decorations as follows: Stir royal icing until smooth and well blended. Using a pastry bag fitted with a medium-sized plain tip or working with a spoon, decorate top of chimney with dollop of royal icing, allowing it to drip attractively down side. Decorate roof peak by generously piping or dropping the icing in icicle shapes along peak length. Add icicles along all eaves of house. If desired, before icing sets up, press some small candies into icicles on eaves and roof peak (see photograph). Let house stand until icing sets completely, at least six hours.

To attach house to chocolate slab foundation: Pipe or spread heavy line of melted and cooled chocolate "glue" along bottom edge of house all the way around. Place house on foundation slab, pressing down slightly all the way around. Add a line of chocolate all around outside base of house, smoothing against house with a finger. Let set at least one hour to secure. Always lift house by grasping slab, not house itself.

The châlet and decorations are edible for several weeks and can be kept for display purposes almost indefinitely. Store in a cool place loosely covered with cloth or plastic.

*S*wiss *C*hocolate *C*halet *P*attern *P*ieces

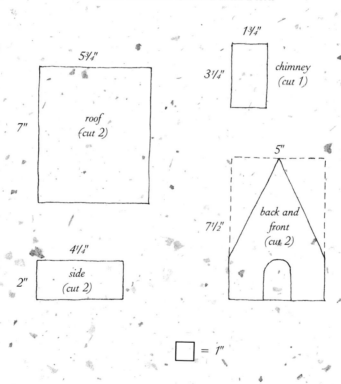

APPENDIX

PROP CREDITS

Front jacket: Plate courtesy of Frank McIntosh at Henri Bendel, New York City
Page 7: Plate courtesy of Annieglass Studio, Santa Cruz, California
Page 27: Fernand Toussaint's Lady in Pink *courtesy of Berko Fine Paintings, New York City*
Page 59: Plate courtesy of Solanée, New York City
Page 75: Plate courtesy of Frank McIntosh at Henri Bendel, New York City
Page 95: Lace pillows courtesy of Edward Boutross, New York City
Page 98: Plate courtesy of Frank McIntosh at Henri Bendel, New York City
Page 99: Plate courtesy of Annieglass Studio, Santa Cruz, California
Page 118: Plate courtesy of Contemporary Porcelain, New York City
Page 150: Painted surface by Joy Nagy, New York City
Page 186: Bowl courtesy of Adrien Linford, New York City
Page 211: Plate and napkin courtesy of Frank McIntosh at Henri Bendel, New York City
Page 222: Fondue pot and platter courtesy of WMF Hutschenreuther, New York City

CHOCOLATE RESOURCE LIST

Following are some mail-order firms that offer chocolate and related candy-making and baking supplies. No recommendations are implied. Call or write for complete product, price, and shipping information. Note that some of these companies do not ship chocolate during warm months. Chocolate brands are identified by (i) for imported or (d) for domestic.

Some wholesalers that sell to bakeries are also willing to sell bulk chocolate directly to consumers. Your local bakery may be able to help you locate firms in your area.

Assouline and Ting, Inc., *314 Brown Street, Philadelphia, PA 19123; Tel: 800-521-4491 or 215-627-3000. Chocolate, cocoa powder, baking and candy-making supplies. Cacao Barry (i), Belcolade (i), and Wilbur (d) chocolate (milk, semisweet, bittersweet, unsweetened, white, gianduia [hazelnut], mocha, and orange). Cacao Barry and Pleine Arôme (i) Dutch-process cocoa powder. Catalog/Mail Order.*

The Chef's Pantry, *P.O. Box 3, Post Mills, VT 05058; Tel: 800-666-9940 or 800-TRY-CHEF. Chocolate, Dutch-process cocoa powder. Callebaut (i) chocolate (milk, semisweet, bittersweet, unsweetened, white, gianduia [hazelnut], and mocha), Valrhona (i) by special order. Catalog/Mail Order.*

Confetti, *4 Embarcadero Center, San Francisco, CA 94111; Tel: 415-362-1706. Chocolate and cocoa powder.*

Callebaut (i), Ghirardelli (d), and Valrhona (i) chocolate (milk, semisweet, bittersweet, unsweetened, and white). Droste (i) and Ghirardelli cocoa powder. Price List/Mail Order.

❖

Ferncliff House, P.O. Box 177, Tremont, OH 45372; Tel: 513-390-6420. Chocolate and candy-making supplies. Merckens (d), Van Leer (d), Guittard (d), and Nestlé-Peter's (d) chocolate (milk, semisweet, bittersweet, and white). Catalog/Mail Order.

❖

Kitchen Krafts, P.O. Box 805, Mount Laurel, NJ 08054; Tel: 800-776-0575. Chocolate, baking and candy-making supplies. Nestlé-Peter's (d) and Merckens (d) chocolate (milk, semisweet, and white). Catalog/Mail Order.

❖

La Cuisine, 323 Cameron Street, Alexandria, VA 22314; Tel: 800-521-1176. Wide range of chocolate, cocoa powder, baking and candy-making supplies. Valrhona (i), Carma (d), and Lindt (i) chocolate (milk, semisweet, bittersweet, extra bittersweet, unsweetened, white, and gianduia [hazelnut]). Valrhona (i) and Cacao De Zaan (i) Dutch-process cocoa. Catalog and supplements for nominal fee/Mail Order.

❖

Maid of Scandinavia, 32-44 Raleigh Avenue, Minneapolis, MN 55416; Tel: 800-328-6722. Wide range of chocolate, baking and candy-making supplies. Lindt (i), Nestlé-Peter's (d), Callebaut (i), and Ambrosia (d) chocolate (milk, semisweet, bittersweet, unsweetened, and white). Catalog/Mail Order.

❖

Paradigm Chocolate Company, 5775 S.W. Jean Road, # 106A, Lake Oswego, OR 97035; Tel: 800-234-0250. Merckens (d), Guittard (d), Lindt (i), and Blommer (d) chocolate (milk, semisweet, bittersweet, unsweetened, and white). Guittard and Lindt cocoa powder. Catalog/Mail Order.

❖

G. B. Ratto & Company, 821 Washington Street, Oakland, CA 94607; Tel: 800-325-3483 or 800-228-3515. Chocolate, Dutch-process cocoa powder, pistoles. Callebaut (i) and Guittard (d) chocolate (milk, semisweet, bittersweet, extra bitter, white, gianduia [hazelnut], and mocha). Catalog/Mail Order.

❖

Albert Uster Imports, Inc., 9211 Gaither Road, Gaithersburg, MD 20877; Tel: 800-231-8154. Bulk chocolate, cocoa powder. Carma (d) chocolate (milk, semisweet, unsweetened and white). DeZaan (i) Dutch-process cocoa. $45 minimum order. Catalog/Mail Order.

❖

Williams-Sonoma, P.O. Box 7456, San Francisco, CA 94120; Tel: 415-421-4242. Chocolate, Dutch-process cocoa powder, baking and candy-making supplies. Valrhona (i), Callebaut (i), and Lindt (i) chocolate (milk, bittersweet, and white). Pernigotti (i) Dutch-process cocoa powder, under Williams-Sonoma brand. Stores Nationwide/Catalog/Mail Order.

CONVERSION CHART

American	British
light corn syrup	(no equivalent but can use golden syrup)
low-fat milk	semi-skimmed milk
muffin tin	deep bun tin
parchment paper	non-stick baking paper
semisweet chocolate	plain chocolate
unsweetened chocolate	bitter *chocolat pâtissier*
vanilla bean	vanilla pod
whole milk	homogenized milk

VOLUME EQUIVALENTS

These are not exact equivalents for the American cups and spoons, but have been rounded up or down slightly to make measuring easier.

American Measures	Metric	Imperial
¼ t	1.25 ml	
½ t	2.5 ml	
1 t	5 ml	
½ T (1½ t)	7.5 ml	
1 T (3 t)	15 ml	
¼ cup (4 T)	60 ml	2 fl oz
⅓ cup (5 T)	75 ml	2½ fl oz
½ cup (8 T)	125 ml	4 fl oz
⅔ cup (10 T)	150 ml	5 fl oz (¼ pint)
¾ cup (12 T)	175 ml	6 fl oz
1 cup (16 T)	250 ml	8 fl oz
1¼ cups	300 ml	10 fl oz (½ pint)
1½ cups	350 ml	12 fl oz
1 pint (2 cups)	500 ml	16 fl oz
1 quart (4 cups)	1 litre	1¾ pints

WEIGHT EQUIVALENTS

The metric weights given in this chart are not exact equivalents, but have been rounded up or down slightly to make measuring easier.

Avoirdupois	Metric
¼ oz	7 g
½ oz	15 g
1 oz	30 g
2 oz	60 g
3 oz	90 g
4 oz	115 g
5 oz	150 g
6 oz	175 g
7 oz	200 g
8 oz (½ lb)	225 g
9 oz	250 g
10 oz	300 g
11 oz	325 g
12 oz	350 g
13 oz	375 g
14 oz	400 g
15 oz	425 g
1 lb	450 g
1 lb 2 oz	500 g
1½ lb	750 g
2 lb	900 g
2¼ lb	1 kg
3 lb	1.4 kg
4 lb	1.8 kg
4½ lb	2 kg

OVEN TEMPERATURES

In the recipes in this book, only Fahrenheit temperatures have been given. Consult this chart for the Centigrade and gas mark equivalents.

Oven	°F	°C	Gas Mark
very cool	250–275	130–140	½–1
cool	300	150	2
warm	325	170	3
moderate	350	180	4
moderately hot	375	190	5
	400	200	6
hot	425	220	7
very hot	450	230	8
	475	250	9

BUTTER

Some confusion may arise over the measuring of butter and other hard fats. In the United States, butter is generally sold in one-pound packages, which contain four equal "sticks." The wrapper on each stick is marked to show tablespoons, so the cook can cut the stick according to the quantity required. The equivalent weights are:

    1 stick = 115 g/4 oz
    1 tablespoon = 15 g/½ oz

EGGS

Unless otherwise noted, all recipes in this book use American large-size eggs, which are equivalent to British standard-size eggs.

FLOUR

American all-purpose flour is milled from a mxiture of hard and soft wheats, whereas British plain flour is made mainly from soft wheat. To achieve a near equivalent to American all-purpose flour, use half British plain flour and half strong bread flour.

American cake flour is made from soft wheat and can be replaced by British plain flour alone.

SUGAR

American granulated sugar is finer than British granulated; in fact, it is closer to British caster sugar. British cooks should use caster sugar throughout.

YEAST AND GELATIN

Quantities of dried yeast (called active dry yeast in the United States) are usually given in numbers of packages. Each of these packages contains 7 g/¼ oz of yeast, which is equivalent to a scant tablespoon.

Quantities of unflavored powdered gelatin are usually given in envelopes, each of which contains 7 g/¼ oz (about 1 tablespoon).

INGREDIENTS AND EQUIPMENT GLOSSARY

Although the following ingredients have different names on opposite sides of the Atlantic, they are otherwise the same or interchangeable.

American	British
baking soda	bicarbonate of soda
cheesecloth	muslin
confectioners' sugar	icing sugar
cookie cutter	biscuit or pastry cutter
cookie sheet	baking sheet
cornstarch	cornflour
half-and-half	single cream
heavy cream	double cream
(37.6% fat)	(35–40% fat)
kitchen towel	tea towel

INDEX

Designed by Rita Marshall
Composed in Fournier Nicholas Cochin
by Dix Type Inc., Syracuse, NY
Printed and bound
by Toppan Printing Company
Tokyo, Japan